WOMEN
ON
THE
VERGE

WOMEN
ON
THE
VERGE

7 Avant-Garde American Plays

edited and with an introduction by
ROSETTE C. LAMONT

APPLAUSE
NEW YORK • LONDON

Library of Congress Cataloging-in-publication data:

Women on the verge: 7 avant-garde American plays/ edited by Rosette C. Lamont

    p. cm.

    Contents: Occupational hazard/ Rosalyn Drexler—Birth and after birth/ Tina Howe—Us/ Karen Malpede—What of the night?/ Maria Irene Fornes—The death of the last Black man in the whole entire world/ Suzan-Lori Parks—Letters to a student revolutionary/ Elizabeth Wong—The universal wolf/ Joan M. Schenkar.

    ISBN 1-55783-148-3 (paper): $14.95

    1. American drama—Women authors. 2. Experimental drama—Women authors. 3. Experimental drama—United States. 4. American drama—20th century. I. Lamont. Rosette C.

PS628.W6W664 1993
812'.540809287—dc20

                       93-11557
                       CIP

Applause Theatre Books, Inc.

211 West 71st Street	406 Vale Road
New York, NY 10023	Tonbridge KENT TN9 1XR
(212) 496-7511	Phone: 0732 357755
Fax (212) 721-2856	Fax: 0732 770219

First Applause Printing, 1993

CONTENTS

INTRODUCTION

One of the questions that often comes up in relation to contemporary theatre is whether Beckett and Ionesco have spawned a generation of young dramatists. In France, the name that surfaces in answer to this inquiry is that of the Spanish-born Parisian, Fernando Arrabal. In the United States, where audiences still expect realism on the stage, male writers have stayed away from poetic, philosophical theatre. With the exception of Albee's early *Zoo Story*, John Guare's *House of Blue Leaves*, Arthur Kopit's *Oh Dad, Poor Dad, Mamma's Hung You in the Closet and I'm Feeling so Sad*, and perhaps, at last, Tony Kushner's *Angels in America*, there are no politico-metaphysical farces, no absurdist tragi-comedies. Even Tennesse Williams' *Camino Real*, probably his greatest work, has not given rise to a refined, literary American theatre.

However, when we look for boldness, innovation, poetry on the American stage, we find all of these elements in the works of a number of women playwrights. Why should it be so? Perhaps because female artists have nothing to lose. In our society, they must make their way to high ground in order not to drown. The few who make it to Broadway have had to sell out, settling for the quick laugh of one-liners, and the easy tear of sentimentality. Yet, in the marginal spaces of Off-Broadway, a group of women writers have been working in the avant-garde idiom of the 20th-century. These women do not necessarily speak the same language, but all of them belong to a family of minds.

In *Women on the Verge*, we have assembled some striking examples of this aesthetic pursuit. These American women, from diverse social backgrounds and ethnicities, clearly transcend simple distinctions of class and race in their desire to give voice to deep, subtle feelings and thoughts. For the most part, they have shunned commercial success in favor of a noble commitment. Thanks to these courageous, creative women, America is becoming a world leader in truly contemporary dramaturgy.

The two first writers in this book, Rosalyn Drexler and Tina Howe, both hold up the Ionesco banner, both rally under it. For Ionesco, "everything is language," words, gestures, objects, action itself. The world of theatre does not mirror our own, it is parallel to it. As to words, they must be made more theatrical by being worked up "to such a pitch that they reveal the true temper of drama, which lies in frenzy." Language must be raised to another level; it should explode. "When I saw *Jack or the Submission*," Drexler exclaims, "I knew I had not only met an ancestor, but my own self."

On April 20, 1986, Tina Howe introduced from the stage of the New York City 92nd Street "Y" Eugene Ionesco, the speaker of the evening in the series Great Writers' Readings (from their works). Howe was audibly excited, having met her "idol" backstage. She said how, in 1960, when she spent a year in Paris after completing her B.A. at Sarah Lawrence, she wandered one evening into a tiny Left Bank theatre, La Huchette, where *The Bald Soprano* was being performed. "It was as if I had been struck by lightning," she said, "as the curtain went up and all hell broke loose. I had not seen such goings on since the Marx Brothers. The sheer outrageousness of Ionesco's dramatic sense and language, the way he turns things on their head. He is often referred to as an absurdist, but to me he is the supreme realist.

He shows us the laxness of reality, and what a pathetic time we have going through the day. It is kitchen sink drama and the formula comedies that are absurd because they present us with stereotypes, not the real world." Ionesco, who always says that writers must show the archetype not the stereotype, must have been delighted with this statement.

Both Drexler and Howe believe that today's playwrights have much to learn from Ionesco and his ancestors, Alfred Jarry and Tristan Tzara. A writer must aim at being larger than life, and show the grotesque side by side with the sublime. This was Victor Hugo's advice in his seminal preface to his play *Cromwell*. Today, however, it is the grotesque which is often sublime, as when Gogo and Didi discuss the misery of feet enclosed in tight boots, and Man's hopeless condition on this earth ("Nothing to be done"). Man is that creature suspended in the void, as.Pascal pointed out, and the abyss is as deep as hell, and as out of reach as heaven. A subtle reader of Pascal, Baudelaire stated that each one of us, at every instant of his existence, experiences the simultaneous pull upward and downward. In fact, the lower we fall, the greater our aspiration toward the empyrean heights. Such is the apprehension of both Beckett and Ionesco, and it is this view which informs the dramaturgy of their literary heirs.

Writer, painter, dramatist, novelist, song writer, singer, mud wrestler, and always poet, Rosalyn Drexler stresses the accidental. She is witty, gutsy, brave, and defiantly free, yet she never loses her American optimism and pragmatism. Her fundamental sense of life supports the structure of her plays which are collages, assemblages made up of bits and pieces of the real. In fact, if reality has been dynamited, blown apart, this is not Rosalyn's fault. She is there to pick up the pieces and rearrange them. The result is what I call her "semiotics of instability." In her lampoon plays, she destabilizes the accepted forms of discourse, and the dramatic genre as a whole. She deconstructs our fragile social architecture and refashions it into delirious castles in the air. The latter float up like kites, but like kites they always possess a strong string so they can be reined in, attached to our planet.

Some of Drexler's plays are *Home Movies* (1964), an Obie winner; *Hot Buttered Roll* (1966), *The Bed was Full* (1967), *The Line of Least Existence* (1969), *Starburn* (1983), *Dear* (1983), *The Mandrake* (1983), *Delicate Feelings* (1984), *Transients Welcome* (1985), *Pineapple Face* (1992).

Based on Kafka's fable, "A Hunger Artist," *Occupational Hazard* was first written in 1988. A new version of the play was completed in 1992. "It is a portrait of the artist as suicide," Drexler says with a smile at once tender and ironic. She adds: "It echoes one of the lines of my early novel, *I am the Beautiful Stranger*: "Tell me I'm good at dying and I'll do it."

In his introduction to *Selected Stories of Franz Kafka*, Philip Rahv makes the following statement: "Kafka is something more than a neurotic artist; he is also an artist of neurosis, that is to say, he succeeds in objectifying through imaginative means the states of mind typical of neurosis and hence in incorporating his private world into the public world we all live in." In "A Hunger Artist" Kafka makes bitter fun of himself as an artist who chose to live on the edge of the extreme, a solitary freak among the self-satisfied bourgeois who live to gorge themselves, and feed on the misery of others. Like the weird hero of his tale, Kafka found employment in an accident-insurance office. The work was hateful to him, mainly because it left no time or energy to do writing. The literary task had special significance for Kafka; he considered it a sacred duty, a transmutation of the religious experience. Although the act of writing gave him no joy, it would at times cause a trancelike state, bringing him to the outward boundary of the human condition.

This is the edge explored by the Hunger Artist. Like the

writer who exposes his pain when he allows his work to be published, Kafka's hero allows his state to become public. He has an impresario who monitors his spectacular bouts of fasting, not allowing them to go beyond forty days (a Bibilical number). The artist, however, resents breaking his fast when he has reached "his best fasting form." Although most onlookers do not believe that no food crosses his lips, he finds fasting easy, and would like to beat "his own record by a performance beyond human imagination." For a while, he lives "in visible glory, honored by the world," but with the passage of years and the vagaries of fashion there is less interest in his feats of asceticism. He then leaves his impresario and hires himself to a large circus where he will be one of the many freaks. Among them he is not the most popular. Thus, his straw-filled cage is placed near the animal compound where the public never fails to pass. Few stop to watch his subtle act, taken as they are by the energy of the wild animals. As he says: "Just try to explain to anyone the art of fasting! Anyone who has no feeling for it cannot be made to understand it." At the end of the fable, the vanishing hero dies almost unnoticed. He is removed like garbage, much like the bug in *Metamorphosis*. A young panther is placed in the empty cage, attracting attention with its vitality, hunger for meat, and "joy of life."

Turning Kafka's third person narration into a play, the dramatist introduces the social scene which forms the fable's fabric. However, in Kafka's spare text we only catch a glimpse of some of the subsidiary characters as they appear through the eyes of the speaker, and some of the Hunger Artist's reactions, as reported by the narrator. For example, Kafka tells us that there are observers of the man's fast, "casual onlookers" and also "permanent watchers selected by the public." The latter include "strangely enough...butchers" whose task it is to watch day and night, "three at a time." In Drexler's play we have, beside the

Impresario and the Circus Owner, a Butcher, a Baker, a Doctor, a woman who falls in love with the ascetic artist, much as Felice B. did with Kafka, her elusive, reluctant fiancé, and a number of circus animals and freaks. Since staging becomes a problem with such a heavy cast, Drexler suggests that actors might double roles, and that freaks and animals could be "animated soft sculptures." What she achieves, however, is changing an intimate portrait into a large, wide canvas, crowded with grotesque, grimacing types who want to act in some way upon the artist and his performance.

Occupational Hazard has a political dimension which is only hinted at in Kafka's fable. The Hunger Artist is being bullied, derided, insulted, tested, accused of cheating, and finally ignored. The basically indifferent, cruel crowd comments that starving oneself could hardly be considered a form of art. "Thinks he's better than we are," states the Baker whose craft has been rejected by the fasting man, as was also that of the Butcher. The latter takes the artist's project as a personal affront. He dangles a sausage in front of the performer's cage: "I raise the pig. Kill the pig. Grind the pig. Add the spices. And stuff the pretty little pockets of intestine with fragrant pig. Here it is. The very best." Given this description, it is no wonder that the Hunger Artist declares that he couldn't find any food to his liking. He adds: "If I had found it, believe me, I should have made no fuss and stuffed myself like anyone else." Here, Drexler simply reproduces the final statement of the dying man, as reported in Kafka's fable.

Both Kafka and Drexler suggest that artists are not average people. Not that they enjoy being "different," but that they cannot help being so. Nor are they able to safeguard their privacy, however fiercely they struggle against becoming reified, exposed and used as objects. To take a recent example, why did Harold Brodkey, one of the most secret of writers, come out with a statement about having contracted AIDS? Agents, the media, the masses who do not read writers but devour articles about them, expect to know everything. The greater the artist, the more he is turned into an industry. Thus, in Drexler's play, the Impresario capitalizes on his performer, making a mockery of his feat of endurance. He is peddling signed posters, T-shirts, tiny cages, skull rings, skeletons made of perfumed soap. Drexler's updated, American version of Kafka's text caricatures the public's endless capacity for vulgarization. The audience may not remember the performance, but it must walk away with a souvenir.

The 19th-century French poet, Charles Baudelaire, shocked his reader when he stated that every artist is indulging in prostitution since he offers himself to the masses. When the Hunger Artist leaves his impresario, signing up with a large circus, he bargains for "artistic control of (his) fasting." The circus owner makes some vague promise which he obviously will not be able to keep. All he wants is to present "a novelty." Adding insult to injury, he explains: "Every circus needs its Jew." Drexler reminds us that Kafka was isolated in Prague not only by his neurosis, but by the social malady of antisemitism. Like the Hunger Artist, Kafka felt that his metaphysical situation was that of an outsider, the eternal pariah. With the explosion of a materialist culture, the loss of any kind of idealism, artists today keenly experience this kind of estrangement. By raising the Kafka banner, Drexler spells out the nature of her own struggle, as well as that of all true artists who must try to survive "on the verge." And yet, staying on the cutting edge, however painful it is, is the only possible response to an unbearable, demeaning situation. So important is the statement made in this play that we have used it as the clarion call of our volume.

As a number of American artists, Tina Howe discovered herself in Paris. Her first contact with modernism came at Sarah Lawrence where the arts are still carefully nurtured. By a bizarre and fruitful twist of fate she was able to pursue her studies with Wilford Leach, her favorite teacher at Uni High (Urbana, Illinois). Leach had just been invited to join the faculty at Sarah Lawrence. Howe never forgot Leach's "graduate thesis," an original play performed at the University of Illinois. In her interview with Peter Ullian, she said: "It was filled with all sorts of hallucinatory scenes, modern dance and music, and profanity. It was like nothing I had ever seen before." The Sarah Lawrence classrooms opened upon the vast cultural spaces of New York City with its Museum of Modern Art, its theatres, galleries, and the never-ending street scene. When, after graduating, Howe arrived in France, a country in the throes of a powerful artistic renaissance following its recovery from World War II, the Nazi occupation, and the shameful Vichy regime it seemed to the budding writer that she had reached her spiritual home. Had she been British or French, she would have made an early mark as the natural heir of Beckett and Ionesco, a daring female voice speaking in the idiom of a new dramaturgic mode born ten years earlier with the first performance of *The Bald Soprano*: Metaphysical Farce. However, she resumed her life in the U.S., where she married a former acting student turned Ph.D. candidate. Shouldering many financial burdens, Howe put playwrighting on the back burner. When she turned to it at last, her first two works, *The Nest* and *Birth and After Birth*, were so wildly imaginative, so freely steeped in language games, that the New York critics, reared on Stanislavsky realism, did not know what to make of them. Her own agent "dismissed" her, as she says. Being female, at that time, was also a marked disadvantage. Howe realized that her career as a playwright might abort at that very instant.

Fortunately two off-Broadway directors with access to a mainstream audience lent her their full support. Joseph Papp put on *Museum* at the Public Theatre, a year after the play's huge success at the Los Angeles Theatre. He also invited A.J. Antoon to direct *The Art of Dining*. Next came Carole Rothman of Second Stage, who, as Howe still says, really understands her work and "makes it sing." With the support of these generous, perceptive artists, Howe was able to avoid the pitfalls of self-censorship. Eventually, she won over the establisment critic par excellence, Frank Rich of the *New York Times*.

Howe's precarious balancing act is the direct result of being a woman in the U.S. "Caryl Churchill nver had these problems," she says with a sigh of envy, "and that's because she's English. In America she's accepted as a daring European. She can get away with murder." Indeed, Americans have no tolerance for eccentricity unless it is imported. In the U.S. creative women over the age of forty had to learn to tread lightly, making their way along a fine, almost invisible line running through the minefield of gender-free territory, a no man's land which lies, alas, within the war zone.

To the majority of theatre-goers in the U.S., Tina Howe. is the author of *Painting Churches* (1983), a seemingly conventional play about an eccentric couple of aging Boston brahmins patterned on the writer's parents. Her father was Quincy Howe, a distinguished broadcaster of the 1940s and 1950s, married to a tall, highly dramatic Boston *grande dame* addicted to wearing extravagant hats. Her paternal grandfather was Mark Antony DeWolfe Howe, a poet and Pulitzer Prize-winning biographer. Both a brand of elegant eccentricity and a passion for words were passed on to Tina by her parents and relations.

Her first produced play, *The Nest*, was a roaring success in Provincetown but a disaster Off-Broadway despite the presence of young Jill Clayburgh in the cast. The piece was judged to be radically feminist although Howe was largely igonorant of feminist theory and ideology at that time.

No doubt that French feminists, such as Hélène Cixous and Julia Kristeva would have recognized Howe's "invaginated" (Jacques Derrida's term) discourse, however, in New York, even a thoroughly sophisticated journalist such as the british-born Clive Barnes found the play "repulsive." It closed the day following his scathing review.

In "The Mad, Mad World of Tina Howe," Ross Wetzsteon stresses that the dramatist became more determined with every reverse. He quotes Howe saying: "It's the New Englander in me: The more I get slapped down, the harder I work to show them they're wrong." After this rejection, she sat down to write the still unproduced *Birth and After Birth*, considered by a number of readers as her best play.

In the course of a recent conversation I had with Tina Howe (June 1992) in New York; she made the following statement: "These days most women write about issues. I prefer to explore the mystery of the hearth." In *Birth and After Birth* the hearth is the kitchen-playroom at the center of the Apple family home. The official head of the family is "the daddy," Bill Apple, an executive in his middle thirties whose job and social position may be threatened by his failure to close an account with a certain Fiedler. He is frightened at the prospect of becoming a non-person, so much so that he reverts to infantile behavior.

The real head of the family is "the mommy." Still on this side of middle age, Sandy feels menopausal and finds it hard to accept the fact that she might not be able to have another child. Her attention is focused on her "firsty," as her son calls himself. He is four years old, and is supposed to be played by an adult.

In Howe's grotesque stage cartoon of the loving American family, the roles are reversed: children are monstrously knowing and controlling, while grown-ups cultivate infantile behavior and use baby talk. Communication is achieved by game playing. One of these games is called "Babies," a poetic evocation of the state of pre-birth. Little Nicky does not wish to leave the womb, and daddy would like nothing more than to crawl back into it, safe from the brutal business world where he has to face professional death at every turn.

Since the Apples are celebrating their only child's birthday, they are visited by relatives, a childless couple. Mia and Jeffrey Freed (their family name is an indication of their life style), both anthropologists, have opted for a free existence, unencumbered by obligations other than the one to their profession. They wander all over the world, studying exotic mores. From their voyages they bring back a veritable treasure trove of wondrous tales. Howe lets her imagination soar as she invents primitive tribes and astonishing rituals. She erects a spiral of absurdisms worthy of the surrealist game, *le cadavre exquis*, or of Ionesco's dada fables with which the Fire Chief regales the Smiths and the Martins in *The Bald Soprano*.

When Tina Howe began to write her first metaphysical yet also highly physical farces, most theatre journalists believed she had conceived monsters. Looking back at these early works, it is quite clear that they were sired by the great European dramatists she discovered on the continent. Back in the U.S., she carried these amazing foetuses through a long gestation, much like the female of the elephant. When they saw the light, they resembled both their French father (Ionesco) and their American mother. Like her, they are full of bounce and optimism, of an antic self-derision coupled with womanly warmth and a healthy playfulness. The form, however, is derived from Dada/Surrealism, and its direct descendant, the metaphysical farce.

Tina Howe's latest play, *One Shoe Off*, was presented at the Public in April 1993. The reviewers did not quite know how to take this comedy of manners tinged with weirdness. In many ways it is closer to her early work than to *Coastal Disturbances* or even *Approaching Zanzibar*. Yet, like most of her work, it is a surrealist comedy of manners.

One Shoe Off centers on a couple, Leonard and Dinah, who still love one another after many years of marriage, and still believe in marital fidelity. However, something peculiar is going on in their house which is literally invaded by the outside vegetation. Ivy is creeping up the walls, trees have taken root in the living room floor, and huge, phallic-looking carrots, together with all manner of swelling squash and gourds have turned the stairs into a vegetable garden. Heidi Landesman's evocative set metaphorized perfectly the half-dormant passions of Dinah. They are in fact the objective correlative of secret erotic impulses. What Dinah will not speak, her disintegrting Greek revival farmhouse loudly whispers.

This time, the play's muse is the gently ironic Anton Chekhov. Starting with Act II, the guests have changed into "elegant 19th-century Chekhovian costumes." This is not difficult since Dinah is a theatre costume designer. She herself sits at the head of her table, dressed in Masha black, "mourning for (her) life." These are trappings of real woes since Leonard, Dinah's actor husband, who triumphed in the roles of Richard II and Cyrano (like him, losers) when he was directed by his friend Parker, has been unable to land a part for the past eleven years, ever since Parker turned big-shot Hollywood director of horror films. When Leonard imitates a famous actress playing Madame Ranevskaya, the lines he quotes reveal the depth of his despair: "I'm sinking to the bottom, but I love that stone and live without I cannot."

This is Howe's play about theatre as a passion. She suggests that our social selves are masks, our clothes costumes. What she loves most about the theatre is that for her it is "an arena of extravagance and catastrophe where we celebrate our darker moments." A violent, almost Artaudian scene catches the audience off-balance. It is when Dinah, the imperfect hostess, comes in tossing a huge salad in an immense plastic bowl. Suddenly she throws the contents of the bowl at Parker, who once tried to seduce her but is now attempting to bed the pretty and willing wife of one of the guests. Dinah's seemingly senseless gesture betrays her immense need to spill herself all over the man she still finds overwhelmingly attractive.

"I am a visual artist," Howe said to me in interview. "I often start with a set because I believe a play should astonish and amuse the audience. The public must be shown something totally familiar, like a suburban home, and yet detect in it an element of strangeness, something threatening." When Howe meditates upon what she is trying to achieve in her art, she believes that it is "to uncover pain." "I'm a scream writer," she says with a smile. A joke may uncover pain, and then pain gives way to bitter humor. For Howe this is the key to the aesthetic of our time.

Do women know something special about pain? Perhaps. Interviewed by Kathleen Betsko and Rachel Koenig, Howe issues a word of warning: "Wait until we yoke our delicate touch and way with words to the darker impulses of theatre. All I can say is when that moment comes...LOOK OUT BELOW."

A similar warning could be issued by Karen Malpede, a poet of the stage. Karen began by creating a mythical theatre in *A Monster Has Stolen the Sun*. Then, gradually, she went on exploring the poetics of the real, of the everyday. For her, poetry can never be divorced from politics, from her pacifist, anarchist, feminist pursuits. She is a disciple of her friend Judith Malina, who directed *Us*. Most recently she created a seamless amalgam between myth and her political concerns by translating to the stage Christa Wolf's sublime1983 novella, *Kassandra*.

On May 1st, 1993, a "Kassandra Symposium" took place at

the New York University Tisch School of the Arts as part of the play's performance. Some of the participants were Judith Malina, Grace Paley and the novelist Jane Lazarre. Speaking of her lifelong interest in the Cassandra myth, Judith Malina, the co-founder of the Living Theatre, posited a question raised by Malpede's dramatization: "Is there anything of Cassandra left in us?" She provided an immediate answer to her question: "We're all crying out like Cassandra, saying 'No' to the structure. We must save the city." Clearly Troy becomes an allegorical image for what Jane Lazarre called "moral memory."

Christa Wolf knew that it was essential to force the truth from experience, to create boldly, courageously. When she distanced herself from her erstwhile religion, Marxism, and the centrality of the class struggle, she set out walking a tightrope stretched out over an abyss. She remained a socialist in name, but preached a better kind of socialism, and the exploration of a third path. She developed what she calls her "poetics of subjective authenticity". These were impeccably served by Karen Malpede's poetic dramatization. Indeed, Malpede followed a similar path for over twenty years. For her, theatre is an act of witnessing, a place to learn and become wiser. Like her mentors, Judith Malina and Julian Beck, Karen believes that violence has reached an impasse, that political conflicts cannot be settled by violent means. The only possibility of reaching peace and understanding, between individuals and nations, is by the exercise of empathy.

The concept of empathy and community is also basic to Lydia Koniordou's directing technique. She calls it "breathing together," and it was developed in the form of breathing exercises with the New York University students who participated in the "Kassandra Project." Hearing the director's analysis of her work at the Symposium, one could not help but associate this process with natural childbirth. Lydia Koniordou, a member of the

Larissa Municipal Theatre where Greek tragedies are presented in a style melding dance, ritual and the classical tradition, has developed some important feminist approaches to her work. For her, rehearsal becomes the breathing of a collective, and it creates for all of us—participants and audience—the possibility to draw breath, to breathe more easily in a world where instinctive, natural functions are not always made easy.

This is also the message of Karen Malpede's *Us*, perhaps her most poetic and deepest play. It is the story of the sexual life of two sets of parents and of their children, who, as adults, are drawn into a wildly passionate, yet tortured love affair. Confessional in its language, the play reveals the inner landscape of six people's desires. There is also a political dimension in the cultural conflicts within the play between American Italian-Catholic and Jew, French and Arab Algerian. Inescapable erotic pulls keeps the two sets of parents fused and creates off-spring who are sexual time bombs, formed by childhood experiences of incest and violence.

Judith Malina directed the play at Theater for the New City which was presented in a multi-levelled set designed by the director. The play which ran from December 17 to January 10 was an event. It marked Judith Malina's return to directing since *The Brig* (1963). Crystal Field and George Bartenieff performed all six characters, two pairs of ethnically diverse parents and their adult children who become lovers.

Themes of sexual desire and social violence have long fascinated Judith Malina whose direction of Living Theatre productions has had seminal influence on the European and American avant-garde. She was drawn to Malpede's play because of its "hotness." She still believes that a good deal of experimental theatre in New York is cold. In contrast, *Us* is lush, beautiful, passionate. It tells us important things about our private lives and about the social world in which we conduct them. "Whether we wish to or not, we take to our beds whatever happens out there," Malina stated forcefully.

She knew she was taking a chance by staging Karen Malpede's provocative poetic drama, but then the Living Theatre had never lacked courage. In December 1987, when I interviewed her for the "Arts and Leisure" section of the *New York Times*, Malina traced the past and the possible future of the new Living Theatre, after her husband's death: "We are still exploring two fundamental principles: pacifism and anarchism, peace and freedom. Julian and I lived in a state of symbiosis ever since we met in our late teens, and he is still our guiding spirit. But we must try new approaches. Karen's play is the best work for the necessary step we must take in our historical development. It helps us understand our relationships to each other in a personal, sexual and epic sense, to sort out who we are, and how we got that way. Karen is a poet, and a politically committed person. She's not afraid to write the kind of words which are not usually heard on the stage, words most people dare not voice to themselves, not even on the psychiatrist's couch.

Judith Malina saw her work on *Us* as a natural extension of her production of Peter Hamel's antiwar opera, "Kassandra," which she directed the previous September at the Frankfurt Opera Festival. There is a strong continuity, according to Malina, between the epic spectacle, based on the Trojan War, and Malpede's chamber-music stage pieces. "Both plays are about the suffering endured by women at the hands of men," the director said. "On the one hand, there are the enslaved Trojan women, the spoils of war of Greek generals; on the other, we have Karen's violated, battered, insulted low-class European and American females. In both texts there exists, however, the possibility that women might be able to defuse, transform and eventually ennoble male hostility."

Both Malina and Malpede believe that the basic formula for a feminist theatre is based on seeing a woman's body not merely as a vessel for male pleasure and for procreation, but as a spiritual instrument. In *Us*, poetic theatre without being verse drama, echoes from "The Song of Songs" pervade what appears at times to be brutally realistic speech. Scene after scene issues from the raw material of dream. One of the taboos that pervade the text is incest: father and infant daughter, adolescent nephew and young aunt. The action takes place between 1945, "the birth of the bomb," and the present. Both the Algerian war and the threat of nuclear disaster are haunting presences in the characters' psyches.

There is a great deal of cross-dressing in the early scenes (a woman, dressed to look like her father, is hitting a dummy of her mother against the wall, acting out the violence she witnessed between her parents; a man, dressed as a larger-than-life female, strips to reveal his true gender, then, reversing the process, assumes once again the mask of his mistress). These disquieting scenes are designed to illuminate people's ambivalence about their social personae and their private selves. The gender ambiguity in *Us* can be traced directly to Jean Genet's influence on both women. "It is a woman's view of the same terrain," says Malpede. Judith Malina adds: "I enjoy the gender flip-flopping in Karen's plays. These scenes bring us into the psycho-sexual life of the characters. Even the set I designed for it, a bas-relief wall composed of the rooms of various houses, is a panorama of the mind."

One of the most beautiful scenes in the play shows an intensely erotic moment in a young couple's life. Hannah and Michel will be held in a kind of cocoon-hammock, and, as they speak to one another of the sexual bliss they attained together, they swing gently to and fro, sometimes drawing momentarily apart, often entagled together.

"The play is about all of us, hence the title," Judith Malina explained on the set. "It is an odyssey from the unknown to another unknown."

Us is the culmination of Karen Malpede's exploration of sexual myth and reality. In her 1984 verse play, *Sappho and Aphrodite*, which was premiered in London and then presented in New York, she drew a frank portrait of the great poet's lesbian lifestyle. Malpede may be a militant feminist, but gentleness is inscribed in her ideology and praxis.

Another gentle feminist with roots in avant-garde French drama is Maria Irene Fornes. Interviewed by Scott Cummings for *Theater* (Winter 1985), she admitted that her first exposure to drama before she started writing herself was when she saw Roger Blin's original production of *Waiting for Godot* in Paris. This is how she describes this experience: "I didn't know a word of French. I had not read the play in English. But what was happening in front of me had a profound impact without even understanding a word. Imagine a writer whose theatricality is so amazing and so important that you could see a play of his, not understand one word, and be shook up. When I left that theatre I felt that my life was changed, that I was seeing everything with a different clarity."

A major voice in American drama, the Havana-born New Yorker has been consistently active on the Off-Broadway scene for over thirty-five years. Her *oeuvre* is extremely varied, going from absurdist farces, to social and political drama. Her increasingly minimalist plays convey human isolation, and explore the position of women on the verge of self-definition. Indeed, Fornes is the quintessential woman playwright "on the verge."

Fornes started writing in the sixties. Some of the plays from that period are *The Window* (1961), *Tango Palace* (1963), *Promenade* (1965), *A Vietnamese Wedding* (1967), *Dr. Kheal* (1968),

Molly's Dream (1968). In all these plays Fornes was exploring the "condensation" of words, how they form and in turn shape thoughts. Her real breakthrough happened in 1977 with *Fefu and her Friends*. Not only did the eight female characters become three-dimensional, but the audience was invited to step into the play as it walked through three locations in the American Place Theatre, listening to three scenes performed simultaneously. Fornes says that she abandoned writing in a linear way, and that she wrote the play in the manner of exercises, putting the characters in situations and letting them find their own voices. Women, she feels, communicate through nuance, conveying by gestures, expressions, intonations something of what they feel deep within themselves. This form of drama is anti-Aristotelian, emphasizing changes in each person, constant shifts, rather than a single illumination or recognition. In her ground-breaking book, *Feminist Theatre*, Helene Keyssar suggests that with the alteration of social roles and traditional relationships, recognition scenes have been replaced by "repeated occurrences of transformation." The unveiling of identity, according to Keyssar, and the drama of individual crisis are not suited to the intent of changing society. This is particularly relevant to feminist dramaturgy since change for women means surpassing the confines of existing social order. In *Fefu*, for example, the character called Julia suffers the pain of a hunted-down deer. She becomes mysteriously impaired, physically and mentally, until Fefu shoots a rabbit whose blood appears on the sufferer's body. This ritual must be accomplished by the whole community of women (Fefu and her female friends), joining together to banish the victim from within themselves. A drama of transformation is inherently political, even though politics may never be discussed within the play. Keyssar's argument is that feminist theatre is an outgrowth of Marxist/Socialist drama. Although Bertolt Brecht was no feminist—in his personal life he exploited women who worked with him, turning them into servants—his politics of metamorphosis inform archetypal feminist theatre.

However, the sense of common purpose, of community, vanishes from Fornes' recent minimalist works. A darkness fills the stage, both visual and spiritual. It is briefly illumined by moments of vague recollection of another form of existence, or by human affection and the kind of love that transcends gender. Both memory and love are drowned in the unbearable brutality of the everyday, a bestial preying of the strong upon the weak.

What of the Night? (1989) is composed of four separate, yet connected playlets, spanning a historical period beginning before World War II and projected into the future: *Nadine—1938, Springtime—1958, Lust—1983, Hunger—A Time in the Future.* The work these four plays most resemble is Fornes' 1982 anti-nuclear weapons play, *The Danube*, also an assemblage of short vignettes. They are also permeated by the kind of physical violence the playwright exposed in *The Conduct of Life* (1985), in which she portrayed a Latin American colonel who tortured political prisoners. However, the language of *What of the Night?* is spare, as in *The Danube*. It re-establishes a connection between Fornes and Beckett.

Nadine takes place in an economically depressed community of the South West of the United States. The set is almost as bare as that of *Godot*: "An empty lot. In back a sunny sky with billowing clouds. Upstage, from right to left, is a sideboard, a bassinet, a rocking-chair and a tree..." The play begins with two men: Charlie, an innocent, gentle, yet street-wise 16 year old, and the stupid, mean, middle-aged Pete, a bully. Pete has been training the boy in picking up "stuff" he can sell, mostly old clothes. When Charlie does not produce what he requires he punches the boy and kicks him repeatedly, savagely. From what Charlie says, it is obvious that some of the better clothes were pulled off a man, a homeless bum. He did not have the heart to strip him totally. As he is being beaten by the older man, Charlie cries out: "He was naked! I didn't want to leave him naked! He was cold! I felt sorry for him! To be lying in the street cold and hurt! I wouldn't want it done to me! I wouldn't want it done to me ! I wouldn't want it done to me ! I wouldn't want it done to me!" The merciless kicking only stops when Nadine, Charlie's mother, comes in. Gradually we find out that she has had to survive by becoming a prostitute. She also has a sick child, Lucille, in need of medicine. The only way she is able to get some money from Pete is by arousing him sexually.

In the next scene we meet Nadine's friend Leah. Life left both women high and dry on some deserted shore. Unlike Leah, who never loved any of the men she slept with, Nadine had real feeling for Charlie's dad. "He got inside my heart." However, after "little Charlie's" birth, he went off with another woman, not even a pretty one. Nadine, who saw her once, describes her as "a dog. Worse." None of this makes sense or is supposed to. It is as arbitrary, as absurd as the process of living and dying. Nadine has three more children: Rainbow, a sensitive girl of nine, the sick Lucille, and, "before Rainbow," Ray, whom she had to give up for adoption. "I had no milk in my breasts." Ray will make a brief appearance in *Springtime* (the audience will not even know at that point who he is), and then reappear in *Lust* and *Hunger*.

Scene 3 starts with a conversation between the two young girls in the group: Rainbow and Birdie, an orphan of 14 who has already been arrested for petty thievery. In jail she was tortured by a brutal female guard: "She'd put our head in the water and hold it there till we started to drown...Someone said that Kitty was a dike and that she liked hurting us because she knew we wouldn't go for her." Nadine keeps on counting the silver in the sideboard and staring suspiciously at Birdie, the jail bird. There is more than a little resemblance between Birdie and young Jean Genet.

Charlie is in love with Birdie and wants to marry her, but he will not leave home. A kind boy, he realizes he must help his mother. Pete watches this scene from behind a tree. He hopes Birdie will go off with him.

Nadine is Fornes' *Lower Depths*, except that here women are at the forefront.

Fornes also shows us what Gorky did, namely that when people are "at the bottom" (the Russian title of Gorky's play) they can never hope to make it to the top, despite the American myth of the self-made man, and the U.S. as the land of opportunity. In *Springtime* a 29 year old Rainbow, "slim and spirited," will turn to a life of crime to purchase needed medicine for her German lover, Greta. She will eventually be jailed, just like her childhood friend Birdie. This outcome is suggested in the farewell note she leaves for Greta inside a book: "My beloved,—I'm sometimes obliged to do things that are dangerous,—and to do things that I hate." It is also suggested that once she has stolen a man's watch, she falls under his domination. He prostitutes her, and forces her to pose for obscene photographs. All of this is hinted at, never spelled out. However, what is spelled out is the powerful attachment between the two women. Fornes is in many ways true to her Latin-American upbringing; she is not afraid of showing romantic feelings. In the Scott Cummings interview mentioned earlier, she makes the following declaration: "I'm a romantic. I have a very feminine nature. I'm very tough in some ways but I have taste for the feminine. Lyricism is romantic. I remember having what became almost an argument with a friend of mine who is very political. It was about my play *Molly's Dream*. She said it was romantic and meant it as a criticism and I said, "yes, isn't it?" and meant it as a high compliment." For Fornes, it is important to experience heightened feelings, to see things at times "in a different light." "To respond to the beauty that's around you, there's no deception in that. That's why I like lyricism," she explains. In *What of the Night?* where so much is ugly, and where people are forced to lead brutalized lives, it is even more striking to find these tender emotions, particularly in the love relationship between two women. Rainbow gives her definition of love: "For me to love is adoring. And to be loved is to be adored. So I never felt I was loved before. Till I met you." Nor does Rainbow feel that she ought to pretend to be attracted by men. "If I don't like men why should I pretend that I do? Why should I try to love someone I don't love when I already love someone I love?" Never before did Fornes make such a clear declaration.

There is nothing approaching the purity of this emotion in the erotic scene between two men, Ray and Joseph, in *Lust's* opening scene. In fact, as the older man, Joseph, twists Ray's body to have his back to him, and pulls down his trousers, he continues to conduct a business conversation. When Ray questions: "Is this ordinary, is this the way you conduct business?" he answers in a cool voice: "Yes, frequently. This is frequently the way I conduct business. It doesn't interfere with business. Yes, we can continue our discussion as we do this."

In the last play, *Hunger*, Ray is a man of 67, in rags. His mate, Reba, is 50, and also ragged. Birdie is 74, reserved and still attractive, and Charlie is a man of 76. His suit is stained, and his memory is failing him. Reba makes the following statement: "We all have to forget where we came from. " Like Beckett's Hamm and Clov, or the aged parents in the garbage cans, they are all sinking into greater and greater poverty, into oblivion. An Angel walks among them, but he is not a gilded work of art. One of his wings is broken, and he carries a wooden box around his neck containing animal entrails. There is no hope coming from this apparition. There are only shards of memory, there is still tenderness and caring. But the end, death, is in sight.

In the *Village Voice* of September 19, 1989, Alisa Solomon

tells of her strange encounter with a girl on a bus after both of them came out of a performance at Franklin Furnace. The girl approached her with an unusual request: "I'm a playwright," she said "but I write in a non-traditional way. Would you know of anyone who might read my scripts?" Solomon gave her some names; the rest is history.

Suzan-Lori Parks, the astonishingly gifted young African-American dramatist, has made an indelible mark on American dramaturgy in the past three years. Directed by Liz Diamond, both her *Imperceptible Mutabilities in the Third Kingdom*, and *The Death of the Last Black Man in the Whole Entire World* were performed at the Brooklyn BACA Downtown. The second was also presented at Yale's Winterfest, along with plays by two other women, Maria Irene Fornes and Colette Brooks. Suzan-Lori Parks has completed a third play, *The America Play*, which Liz Diamond has directed at Dallas, and will bring to Yale in January. The play takes place "in the Great Hole of History," and is about a man who travels West impersonating Abraham Lincoln.

Most critics are so puzzled by Suzan-Lori Parks' exaltation of black English into a poetic code that they have no idea how to approach this non-narrative, absurdist work. They state that she writes with a late '80s edge, but this does not come close to grasping a phenomenal breakthrough. Alisa Solomon, an unusually intelligent, cultured critic explains that "she uses formal experimentation to explore the gaps between image and reality in African-American experience." Indeed, her plays testify to her profound interest in history and identity. However, from this base her imagination soars on the wings of a musical language compounded of the rhythm of her beloved grandmother's speech—she is reported to have said: "Granny, the way you talk is wonderful!"—and literary English. The juxtaposition creates a rich tension, but it also encapsulates the ambivalence of black Americans. There is none of this tortured feeling in the writer herself who states: "We are not Africans, but African-Americans. We have to make beauty out of what we're stuck with."

Reading her texts, one comes to realize that this highly original work is grounded in the equally original creations of a number of literary forebears: Maria Irene Fornes (by Parks' own admission), Zora Neale Hurston, Adrienne Kennedy, the first black American to have turned away from realism and used the avant-garde idiom, Gertrude Stein and Jean Genet. It was James Baldwin who steered her toward theatre when he was her teacher at Mount Holyoke. He praised her ear for dialogue in the short stories she brought to his class, and suggested that she try writing plays. Soon, she realized that speech implies action and began creating her dialogic poems. Devoid of stage directions, they are musical in essence, cantatas, verbal fugues, choral outbursts. The influence of jazz can also be detected in her verbal riffs. Although there is nothing didactic about these texts, this is clearly politically urgent work. *Imperceptible Mutabilities* takes place on a slave ship, and *The Death of the Last Black Man* compresses into a time capsule various forms of lynching. One feels the writer's deep compassion toward her characters yet her experimental probe of history can only be compared to the stage canvases painted by performance artists such as Laurie Anderson and Paula Vogel.

Perhaps one can explain Parks' attitude vis-à-vis language, her ability to stand away from it, observing it with curiosity and delight, by the fact that as a child she spent four years in Germany with her father, a military man. Without knowing a word of German, she was sent to school, and had to acquire a foreign tongue. There she experienced fully the disjunctions between sound and meaning, between the written and the spoken word.

The love of language, of languages, so natural to a bilingual dramatist such as Maria Irene Fornes, was forced upon the young girl's subconscious by the rich experience of estrangement. Like the people described by the character called Before Columbus, she realized the world is "roun." She was able to round out her own universe. Her plays teach us to "scurry out," to be unafraid, to face the dreadful past and issue "whole entire."

The feeling of estrangement can be equally strong when you visit the land of your ancestors, if the culture and the political situation have created a different environment. This was the case of Elizabeth Wong when she visited Communist China with her parents in 1983. There she met very briefly a girl her age. They became pen pals. Elizabeth kept all the letters in a box, and in September 1989, following the Tiananmen Square massacre of June 4, she took out this correspondence and re-read the old letters. In her program notes she writes: "As I reread her letters, her thin spidery hand-writing, I realized that no one, without exception, has written me with such volume and constancy. I must confess I never read those letters carefully until now. But looking at them in their entirety was like reading them for the first time. It occurred to me that I hadn't heard from her since spring. Her steady stream of correspondence had stopped. This play is my way of saying, "Karen, I haven't forgotten you.""

On May 7, 1991, Elizabeth Wong's first play, *Letters to a Student Revolutionary* opened at the New York Playhouse 46 at St. Clement's Church where it was staged by the Pan Asian Repertory Theatre in commemoration of the second anniversary of the Tiananmen Square rebellion. The production was a world premiere, and the first Western play written about this tragic political event.

The cultural differences between America and China are embodied by two young girls, in their early 20s. The set is divided into two separate areas, representing China and the United States. A central space is to be neutral territory, "wherein the rules of time and geography are broken." The two girls, Bibi and Karen, are embodiments of their letters to one another. They are able to speak to each other over ocean miles of space, and long stretches of intervening time, yet there is something intimate and immediate about their contact, as there is indeed when we receive the letter of a friend. Wong does not work in the medium of realism, as do almost all Asian-American playwrights, with the notable exception of Hwang; she uses an avant-garde idiom to convey the freshness of the two girls' communication. She also introduces a chorus made up of three men and one woman who play multiple small roles.

The cultural/political differences are so great it is not always easy for the girls to make themselves understood. Karen explains in a letter written in the summer of 1986 that she took her first trip to the mountains with her brother and a friend. They had to "get a permit for travel." We realize that something is brewing in these young people in the next scene, when Lu Yan suggests: "Ask Bibi to send us a copy of this Bill of Rights." Brother chimes in: "What is this pursuit of happiness"? Even if I were to have it, I would not know how to go about this "pursuit of happiness"

In May 1989, Karen sits in a tent in Tiananmen Square. She cannot write at the moment, but she speaks an imaginary letter, addressing the theatre audience: "I cannot begin to describe—there is this change in the air—to be here, surrounded by comrades—student activists and ordinary citizens—men and women, all patriots for a new China. I think this is what "pursuit of happiness" must be. Bibi, for the first time in my life, I believe I can be somebody, I believe my contribution will make a difference. I believe freedom will not grow out of theory but out of ourselves..." Bibi answers in May 1989, asking Karen to be careful. "I do believe change will come, but it must be at your own pace." The play culminates in the Chorus' report of the massacre. Sitting at her desk, Bibi writes in Spring 1990: "I want you to know I haven't forgotten you...Somehow let me know if you are all right."

This is war and world events seen through the eyes of two girls. The intimacy of the tone, the simple human emotions so well expressed lend great power to this text. Where a man would compose an epic song, a woman whispers in the ear of another, whispers it in the form of a letter, perhaps an even more direct mode of address than conversation.

We have saved for dessert in this book a work which the author herself calls "a confection." This deliciously intelligent post-modern tidbit, based partly on a cartoon version of Structuralism, caricatures and reconstructs (after destructuring it) a famous fairy tale, "Little Red Riding Hood." It is written in an invented, inventive form of *franglais*.

Joan M. Schenkar is a prolific writer of experimental plays. Some of the best known are *Cabin Fever, Signs of Life, Family Pride in the 50's, The Lodger, The Last of Hitler, Fulfilling Koch's Postulate, Between the Acts, Fire in the Future, Hunting Down the Sexes*, and *The Universal Wolf*. At the present time, Joan Schenkar is working on a screenplay, *Burning Desires*, which will show the rebirth of Joan of Arc in Seattle (Joan's hometown) where she cannot be burned since it rains all the time.

"*The Universal Wolf* is about appetite," Schenkar explains. "The really hungry, meat-loving character in the play is the hard-hearted hard-drinking Grandmother. She is also a 'professional woman,' as Little Red calls her, since she had a butcher shop in the Paris Bois de Boulogne. Little Red boasts that most of the tiny mammals in the Bois de Boulogne ended their lives on 'chère grandmère's' butcher block. The old woman is the triumphant heroic figure of a story from which the Woodsman has been excised. She will not merely survive, but will devour all the other characters, including her ninny of a granddaughter. In fact, she's the real Wolf of the tale, while Mr. Wolf is nothing but a patsy."

Schenkar derived the title of her play from a passage in Ulysses' speech in Shakespeare's *Troilus and Cressida*. Ulysses evokes a state of disarray, with planets wandering in disorder, raging seas, earth quakes, "And the rude son (striking) his father dead" (I.iii.115). These are unbridled times when all are ruled by their desires, their love of power, their appetites. The passage deserves to be quoted in full:

Then every thing include itself in power,
Power into will, will into appetite,
And appetite, an universal wolf
(So doubly seconded with will and power),
Must make perforce an universal prey,
And last eat himself up .... (I.iii. 119-124).

Schenkar's "confection" is not sugar and rose water; it is made of meat, blood, thick red wine and raucous laughter.

Where does this strange guffaw issue from? Once again, like so many of the women playwrights in this book, Schenkar raises the standard of Ionesco and Beckett. About Beckett in particular she says: "He returned my life to me in a form I recognized, which is the highest compliment we can pay to art. His costive manner of speaking ignited my imagination. Also, like Beckett, I was and am devoted to French culture. I am half French, half Russian, an explosive combination. My mother is French, and the first song I learned as a small child was the "Marseillaise." I still go to Paris every year, and I have had French lovers—the best way to learn a language."

A fascinating feature of *The Universal Wolf* lies in the appearance throughout the play of projected images of France's cultural icons: Claude Levi-Strauss, Roland Barthes, Alain Robbe-Grillet, Julia Kristeva, Gaston Bachelard, Pierre Louys.

We also get the ultimate feminist icon, Teresa de Lauretis, "in full doctoral costume, raising her right hand and declaring: 'The female sex is invisible in psychology and in semiology it does not exist at all.'"

In the play, however, the female sex is prominently featured, and is triumphant. Toward the end, when the Wolf appears at grandmother's house (after she has been forewarned by Little Red, now hiding in the armoire containing an axe), ridiculously costumed in a cerise tablecloth and a cottonwool bib, a disguise that "could fool no one," there is a telling exchange between the old woman and the would-be predator:

> **M. WOOLF:** I can only conclude, dear grandmozzer, zat in your armoire is concealed a dreadful, female imposter, 'oping to supplant me in your abundant affections.

> **GRANDMOTHER:** Could it be M. *Woolf*, Little Red? Could it actually be the *big*, *bad*, *wolf* and could that *wolf* be a *female*?!!

A leading question indeed for a feminist writer to ask. Why should only males have appetites, and assuage their desires? Why can't we deconstruct the old patriarchal fairy tales and turn them upside down, on their heads? This is certainly what Joan Schenkar has done with immense wit and a bit of appropriate cruelty. She also has something to say about women playwrights who choose to write in the experimental vein: "We are the forgotten sisters of the literary world. But we must form our own community, and feel free to be transgressive."

What does it mean to be an experimental writer? Rosalyn Drexler has an answer: "Life is experimental because it is changing from moment to moment, and you're never quite sure of the result, but you know something is happening and you are going in an organic direction. Only death is non-experimental. There's nothing more to work with."

Rosalyn Drexler

OCCUPATIONAL HAZARD

CHARACTERS:

The Impresario, *the Hunger Artist's manager*

The Hunger Artist, *a man whose act is fasting*

The Butcher, *an observer of the Hunger Artist*

The Accountant, *an observer of the Hunger Artist*

The Baker, *an observer of the Hunger Artist*

Rose, *a young woman in the crowd*

Emma, *a woman in love with the Hunger Artist, returns as circus performer*

Mrs. Grubba, *the butcher's wife*

The Official, *President of the Accident Insurance Institute*

Lazarus Bloch, *petitioner deceased; returns as circus performer*

Isidore Braun, *petitioner alive; returns as a circus performer*

Doctor, *the doctor who examines Hunger Artist*

Georg von Schonerer, *a circus owner*

Camille, *a slack wire artist*

The Great Jimmy, *an animal trainer clown*

The Dog, *a midget in a dog's costume*

The Overseer, *circus maintenance boss*

The Attendant, *Overseer's assistant*

Also: A small circus band: brass, woodwinds, cymbals, drum.

(Note: Many of the actors may double roles. Freaks and animals may be animated soft sculptures.)

Time: The 1900's.

Place: In or near Prague

ACT I

SCENE 1: *A cleared space outdoors. A small cage on wheels. The cage's floor is covered with straw. A scrim is drawn around the cage. A clock is hung on the cage. It strikes the hour. Close by is a large placard with a daily calendar upon which the* IMPRESARIO *keeps a record of how many days the* HUNGER ARTIST *has fasted. Not far from the cage, on a platform stands a table with a cash register and shelves containing souvenirs and* HUNGER ARTIST *posters, etc. The* IMPRESARIO *delivers his sales pitch while standing on this platform. He speaks through a megaphone at times when addressing the spectators.*

IMPRESARIO: Step right up folks. Don't be shy. The Hunger Artist is about to enter the thirtieth day of his fast. See a human being just like yourselves starve himself to death. Come on now, buy your tickets early and reserve a place up front. Enjoy the show from a vantage point. Friends, be the first in your neighborhood to observe the horrifying refinements of a master faster! Count his ribs, watch him disappear as he turns sideways. You won't be disappointed. The Hunger Artist is an artist's artist. Respected by all who come in contact with him. Revered universally for his sacrifice of comfort and nourishment, for art.

BAKER: [*Heckling.*] Since when is starving an art? If that's true then three quarters of the world's population are artists.

BUTCHER: When I'm hungry I don't make a spectacle of myself.

ACCOUNTANT: The bottom line is survival. Why should I be guilty because he won't eat? Why should he make me feel like a pig just because I put food into my mouth? I believe in satisfaction, and the sooner the better.

IMPRESARIO: There's truth in everything you say, gentlemen, but that shouldn't prevent you from buying a ticket. Think of the Hunger Artist as an opportunity to wile away a few hours in the company of an entertaining fellow; nothing more, nothing less.

BAKER: I read all about the Hunger Artist in the *Prague Tagblatt*. The critic described his act as a laugh a minute romp defining the human condition. I wouldn't miss it for the world.

IMPRESARIO: I'm proud to sell a ticket to a literate man such as yourself.

[BAKER *buys ticket. Others line up behind him to buy tickets. The ticket holders stand in groups around the cage.* IMPRESARIO *pulls the scrim aside revealing the* HUNGER ARTIST *asleep in his cage.*]

[*To the* HUNGER ARTIST.] Time to wake up, Sir. Time to refuse a good breakfast.

BAKER: I've brought a hot cross bun for you.

[*Thrusts the bun through the bars of the cage.*]

It's nice and fresh. How can you resist, Sir?

BUTCHER: Perhaps the Hunger Artist would care for a home made sausage? Quality controlled from beginning to end. I raise the pig. Kill the pig. Grind the pig. Add the spices. And stuff the pretty little pockets of intestine with fragrant pig. Here it is. The very best.

[*He dangles the sausage in front of the cage. The* HUNGER ARTIST *reacts with disgust to all that's offered.*]

BAKER: Thinks he's better than we are. Thinks he can live on air and sips of water like a hummingbird.

IMPRESARIO: Step right up, folks. Still plenty of room up front. Feel the arms, the legs, the ribs poking through paper-thin skin. Receive proof positive that the Hunger Artist is wasting away. Not a crumb of food has passed his lips for thirty days.

He's going for the record, folks.

ROSE: I'm scared.

IMPRESARIO: Nothing to be frightened of, young lady; Sir is in a cage yet he is not an animal, he's a human being.

ROSE: Then why is he in a cage?

IMPRESARIO: Your enquiry is a serious one, dear child, therefor I will answer you in kind: the Hunger Artist requires the protection of a cage since the curious and over-eager populace is liable to pull him apart. He is a celebrity...of sorts. And to further answer your question of why this arbitrary separation of man from man, I reply, it has always been so. The Hunger Artist welcomes what most of us fear, the realization of a dream, the exposure of a soul in flux. If the Hunger Artist were a healthy, happy person such as yourself, what kind of a tourist attraction would he be? Who would pay to see him? So you see, my child...what is your name?

ROSE: Rose.

IMPRESARIO: So you see, Rose, the cage is not only a shelter, but the outward manifestation of a severe inner state. And what is more, if I've learned anything in this world, it is that nothing sells tickets faster than misery!

HUNGER ARTIST: But I'm happy.

BUTCHER: What'd he say?

HUNGER ARTIST: I'm happy!

BUTCHER: If you say so.

IMPRESARIO: [To spectators.] Perhaps our living skeleton would care for a sip of water. [To HUNGER ARTIST.] Would you care for some water, Sir?

[The HUNGER ARTIST nods "yes." IMPRESARIO pours some water from a pitcher into a small glass. He gives the HUNGER ARTIST a *drink.*]

Ladies and gentlemen, the Hunger Artist has deigned to take a drink of water, but do not be deceived; to him this water is more delicious than wine or beer. It has the power to create a heady delirium in the poor fellow and to sustain what little life is left in him.

ROSE: [*Approaches cage. To* HUNGER ARTIST.] What are you doing?

HUNGER ARTIST: I'm having a drink of water.

ROSE: Is it good?

HUNGER ARTIST: There's a piece of straw in it, but I don't mind. I can spit it out.

MRS. GRUBBA: [*Comes closer to cage. Holds her nose.*] There's a nasty sulpherous smell around here. You'd think someone would dunk the man in a soapy tub before allowing him to perform. He's a star after all.

EMMA: He doesn't have the strength to do it himself.

MRS. GRUBBA: Mr. Impresario, you could clean him up, but no, you're all for authenticity: the odor of turds and piss. If God had meant for us to endure this smell he would not have put our noses at such a great distance from it. Indeed, we'd still be crawling about on all fours like the beasts.

IMPRESARIO: I'm sure, madam, that Sir appreciates your concern over this matter of his personal hygiene, but be assured, he wants it this way. Appearing in his natural state is the Hunger Artist's unique approach to being perceived as a human being.

BAKER: Sitting there half-naked and filthy is no way to be perceived as a human being.

[*He struts about.*]

Am I any the less human because my clothing is laundered, my body splashed with cologne? My nails manicured? My hair barbered in the latest fashion? Is it a sin to wipe one's behind properly front to back and to wash one's hands afterwards?

[*Crowd responds.*]

No!

IMPRESARIO: Oh? Would you have our Hunger Artist be an arbiter of fashion? Dressed to kill?

BUTCHER: He IS dressed to kill, himself!

HUNGER ARTIST: More water, please. Just a drop or two to moisten my lips.

IMPRESARIO: [*Gives the* HUNGER ARTIST *a sip of water.*] Slowly now. Don't choke yourself, dear Sir.

HUNGER ARTIST: Thank you.

IMPRESARIO: Dear people...you who have been so kind as to attend our little show...You may now ask the Hunger Artist or myself any questions that come to mind. We will try to answer them as honestly as we can. Don't be shy. Speak up. [*He acknowledges the* ACCOUNTANT *who is waving his hand in the air.*] Yes? You, the gentleman with the pen in his pocket.

ACCOUNTANT: Standing here, observing the audacity of a man who will obviously do anything to hog the limelight, I pose my question to that man, the Hunger Artist...Dear Sir, what was your life like before you embarked on this unusual career?

HUNGER ARTIST: Where shall I begin?

IMPRESARIO: Somewhere in the middle, Sir.

HUNGER ARTIST: Not at the beginning?

IMPRESARIO: We don't have all day...Start with the story of your last employment, that should satisfy the question.

HUNGER ARTIST: Alright then, before I embarked on my present vocation, the career of Hunger Artist, I was a public servant.

An ineffective administrator who passed every document he received on to the next administrator as quickly as possible. But that didn't put an end to it for me. I'd follow the document in my thoughts from one department to another, from desk to desk, through the chain of hands it passed through before reaching its final destination. My imagination was always breaking out of the four walls of my office. Yet my horizons did not broaden. For what was I? I was just a bit of waste matter, a mere nothing in the glutinous bureaucracy of the Accident Insurance Institution.

ACCOUNTANT: In short, dear Sir, you realized as many of us do, that an office life is a dog's life?

HUNGER ARTIST: Yes. Yet I didn't bark at anyone. I didn't bite. As a former vegetarian I lived only on my own flesh. I was well liked by my superiors and could have retained my position...when suddenly it all changed...the straw that broke the camel's back so to speak brought me to my knees.

SCENE 2: *Office of the Bureau of Accident Claims. The* HUNGER ARTIST *is wearing a tie and a jacket. Shielding his eyes is a transparent green visor. He writes in a pad. The* ADMINISTRATOR *is seated behind a desk piled high with folders and papers. Those making claims are seated in banked chairs, as at a stadium. The* HUNGER ARTIST *is seated somewhere in between at a small table of his own, like a court stenographer.*

HUNGER ARTIST: I bring to your attention, Mr. Official, the case of petitioner Lazarus Bloch.

OFFICIAL: Case number, please.

HUNGER ARTIST: Number 650237D.

OFFICIAL: One moment please. [*He searches through the pile of folders on his desk. He finds folder he is looking for.*] You may continue.

HUNGER ARTIST: Case number 650237D is deceased. His family makes claim for insurance benefits due them in the event of said case's demise...which has occurred. Case number 650237D, as duly recorded on the forms filed with our office, met his end as the result of an unfortunate accident on the job.

OFFICIAL: [*Irritated.*] Case number 650237D, also known as the worker Bloch, has not come forth on his own behalf. He is suspected of taking an unauthorized sabbatical without pay.

HUNGER ARTIST: The worker Bloch, due to his fatal condition, is unable to appear on his own behalf. Exhumation at this time would further complicate the situation.

OFFICIAL: What proof is there that he is dead? We have examined his locker at the factory and found that it still contains his coffee cup, a pair of protective goggles, and his apron. Obviously he is coming back to claim them.

HUNGER ARTIST: If you will, Sir Mr. Official, turn to page two of the request for funds, you will notice that the apron is described as being blood stained, and the goggles as broken beyond repair.

OFFICIAL: But I don't see the doctor's certificate of death. Has it been filed with our office?

HUNGER ARTIST: I don't understand. It was sent weeks ago and should be in worker Bloch's file.

OFFICIAL: Should be? Should be is not the same as is! Neither worker Bloch nor his death certificate are here.

HUNGER ARTIST: I will begin a search immediately, Sir...but meanwhile may I present the facts in this case?

OFFICIAL: I venture you know the difference between a fact and a fiction?

HUNGER ARTIST: As I understand it, Sir Official, for every fact there must be proof, but for every fiction there must be a continuous invention of things as if they were facts.

OFFICIAL: Well then let's get on with it. There are other cases to dispose of.

HUNGER ARTIST: Simply put, worker Bloch worked in a lumber factory at a machine that had no safety precautions. The piece of wood that he was cutting had a knurl in it that caused the machine to jam. When worker Bloch sought to clear the cutting wheel his hand got caught and was cut clean off. Subsequently he bled to death. His family is asking compensation for his loss as a wage earner.

OFFICIAL: Denied.

HUNGER ARTIST: Denied?

OFFICIAL: Denied.

HUNGER ARTIST: But why? You have in front of you, Sir Mr. Official, the signed statements of two witnesses and the plant foreman attesting to the justification of this claim. The machine was poorly designed. It must be removed before others are maimed or killed.

OFFICIAL: With regard to your sentimental bias, dear colleague, the government cannot be so softhearted. Worker Bloch is well known as a grouser who wanted to leave his job. Thought that he was made for better things. Well, wouldn't you say that he has achieved his fondest wish? Hasn't he managed to retire without warning? We do not distribute government funds for acts of insubordination.

HUNGER ARTIST: But his family...they have no means of support.

OFFICIAL: They may reapply after the proper amount of time. More facts are needed. Your evidence is unconvincing. What if every malcontent decided to kill himself on company time? Think! Think, my dear colleague! We would not be able to pay our own employees, men such as yourself who are so diligent and faithful. Next!

[*The* HUNGER ARTIST *continues to make notes. He stamps the file and places it at the bottom of the pile of files.* BRAUN *enters and sits before the* OFFICIAL.]

OFFICIAL: Case number?

HUNGER ARTIST: 333A. Also known as three-hundred and thirty-three Alive.

BRAUN: My name is Isidore Braun. I suffer from terrible headaches and my right hand shakes something awful. It all began when I fell off a ladder and broke my skull.

OFFICIAL: Why were you on a ladder?

BRAUN: I was ordered by my superior to change a light bulb. The ladder, Mr. Official, had one short leg and wobbled. It was due to be replaced, God knows when. My hard luck, yes? Now I'm good for nothing but kicking the dog.

OFFICIAL: Your head looks okay to me.

BRAUN: Oh the surgeons did the best they could. Replaced the top of my head with a fine piece of metal. Listen to this. [*He bops his head smartly. A resounding note rings out.*] The best protection a brain can have if one has lost his own top...but I still have these headaches. The pain is so great I cannot see. All I'm able to do is cry out and frighten my wife. She has threatened to leave me. I can't stand it.

OFFICIAL: As I see it, worker Braun, you are fully capable of supporting yourself. You are a very musical fellow. That head of yours is a blessing in disguise.

BRAUN: I? Musical? What do you mean, Sir Mr. Official? I don't sing or play an instrument. Can't read a note of music. Even my wife's voice, melodious as it is, drives me mad.

OFFICIAL: [*Rises and clops* BRAUN *on his head. A note rings out true and clear.*] The sound emanating from your head is self-explanatory, worker Braun. It is a note true enough for an entire orchestra to tune up with. You may not be musical, but your marvelous head, sheltered by its resounding metal carapace, is certainly musical. In fact it has perfect pitch.

BRAUN: But my headaches...I suffer...My hand has difficulty carrying a toothbrush to my mouth. Please help me. Before my accident I worked for fifteen years without a mishap. Never absent. Never late. I deserve compensation.

HUNGER ARTIST: He does deserve compensation.

OFFICIAL: I think not, worker Braun. For it is you who were at fault. You lost concentration. Perhaps you were dreaming of a steaming plate of Weiner Schnitzel as you went up the ladder step by step, step by step. Or perhaps you were thinking of your wife at home, waiting for you in a seductive chemise.

BRAUN: [*Sighs.*] Yes, waiting for me. Waiting to give me a tender embrace.

OFFICIAL: And so you lost concentration, didn't you. [*Louder.*] Safety first, worker Braun! If you had been more careful there would not have been a misstep and a fall! Petition denied. Next!

[BRAUN *exits.* EMMA *enters. She is limping prettily.*]

EMMA: Excuse me, is this the office of the Review Board of the Accident Compensation Authority?

OFFICIAL: [*Impatiently.*] Yes, yes, yes. It's printed on the door.

EMMA: It must be in very small print then.

OFFICIAL: It's as large as it has to be.

EMMA: No it's not, or I would have seen it.

OFFICIAL: Perhaps you need glasses, madam. Now if you don't mind, state your business.

EMMA: I've been down one corridor and up the next. Directed here. Directed there. Been at it every day of the week. Are you quite sure this is where the review board meets? My tootsies are killing me.

HUNGER ARTIST: [*Pulls a chair in her direction.*] Please, have a seat, madam.

OFFICIAL: Now that you are settled, would you mind telling us your case number?

EMMA: I've forgotten it. Besides, I don't like being a number. Why haven't you people alphabetized your files? Other departments do. I haven't forgotten my name though; shall I give it to you?

OFFICIAL: Alright, what is your name?

EMMA: Emma Licht. The last name means light. The first is just a name.

HUNGER ARTIST: What a hopeful name. Licht! Emma Licht.

OFFICIAL: [*Gives the* HUNGER ARTIST *a dirty look. He searches through the pile of files and finds* EMMA*'s.*] Here it is...Emma Licht.

EMMA: Oh goody.

OFFICIAL: You express yourself very sincerely, worker Licht. If you continue in that manner I think we will be able to come to an understanding.

EMMA: Understanding? About what? You haven't even examined my claim, Sir?

OFFICIAL: [*Gazing at her amorously.*] I have, I have. Yes, your claim is worthy not only of examination, but perusal. I am at this moment perusing it. [*He opens her file.*] Hummmm. Aha....hummmm.

EMMA: Repetition has ruined my life.

OFFICIAL: Worker Licht, this is no time for revelations of that sort.

EMMA: But...

OFFICIAL: One more insurrection and out you go.

HUNGER ARTIST: Behave yourself, worker Licht. He means what he says.

EMMA: Oh okay.

OFFICIAL: So you were hired by the Baby Bunting Doll Manufacturing Company to work on the assembly line. Is that true?

EMMA: It was one screw after another, Sir: first the arms went into the sockets, then the legs were set in, and lastly the heads. After two years of assembling those cute little Baby Buntings I found that I had terrible pains in my arms. The pain went up and down, up and down. It has never left me. Every night I wake up crying out in pain: OH, oh, oh! The doctor says that my condition is chronic. Oh dear, Mr. Official, I'm much too young to be chronic.

HUNGER ARTIST: [*Romantically.*] What is chronic to one, may be tonic to another.

OFFICIAL: [*Gives the* HUNGER ARTIST *a dirty look.*] I sympathize with you, worker Licht. Someone of your tender age and sensibilities should not have to endure pain. However, I will have to test the validity of your claim, after which the amount of your compensation will be decided.

EMMA: Okay.

OFFICIAL: Please clear the room. You there clerk...go, go. I'll let you know when to return.

[*The* HUNGER ARTIST *and others leave the room.*]

[*To* EMMA.] Come here my pretty little Emma. Let's check the strength and usefulness of those darling plump pink hands. Being the humane and sensitive creature that I am, my heart goes out to you. [*He takes* EMMA's *hands and kisses them. He goes from her wrists to her shoulders.*]

EMMA: [*With a quick movement she pushes him to the floor.*] Oh I'm

so sorry, Mr. Official. These spastic seizures come upon me
so suddenly, that I'm liable to do anything. I virtually turn
into a raging maniac. I hope I haven't hurt you.

OFFICIAL: [*He remains on the floor looking up* EMMA's *skirt.*] No
harm done.

EMMA: Thank God!

OFFICIAL: Thank your legs.

EMMA: My legs?

OFFICIAL: Thank those expressive appendages you are standing
upon, Emma. Your legs are your fortune. They can dance
you anywhere you want to go. Royalty will be at your beck
and call. I kid you not. [*He thrusts his head between her legs.*]
Give me a squeeze, dear girl, and I promise you'll get your
workman's compensation plus a nice bonus...Oh what joy!
Make me faint with delight. Immediately!

EMMA: [*She squeezes too hard. He lies there choking.*] There's those
seizures again. Oh what shall I ever do. And you being so
generous and kind to me.

OFFICIAL: [*Recovering.*] Your seizures are heaven sent, Miss Licht.
Never have I been held in such tender bondage; pain and
pleasure battling for ascendancy within my tormented flesh;
pleasure winning out as I yield to you. Oh what a feeling. I
thought I had lost it. Thank you, darling mistress. Your wish
is my command. Your command is my order. Speak, oh
goddess. What is your request?

EMMA: This is so sudden.

OFFICIAL: I implore you most humbly to give me a task. Don't
hesitate to make it a difficult one. The harder the better.

EMMA: Something's going on here that I don't understand.

OFFICIAL: Yes! Some things are beyond understanding. Just go
with it.

EMMA: Well okay then. How about a lifetime pension, a pair of red satin shoes, and a season pass to the opera?

OFFICIAL: And if I'm a naughty boy, what will you do to me?

EMMA: You know what naughty boys get.

OFFICIAL: What? What?

EMMA: Kept in after school.

OFFICIAL: No! No! Try again.

EMMA: A good thrashing?

OFFICIAL: You're close. Think back to a few delightful moments ago...

EMMA: Naughty...boys...get...their...necks...squeezed...so hard they lose consciousness and see stars!

OFFICIAL: Yes! Oh yes! That's what I deserve. [*He takes some money out of his pocket and forces her to take it.*] Consider this a small down payment for your services. And remember, mum's the word. Your future depends on it.

EMMA: [*Takes the money.*] Thank you. I won't breath a word to a soul.

OFFICIAL: [*Goes to door and calls the petitioners and the* HUNGER ARTIST *back in.*] Halloo! The Review Board is ready to continue. Hurry up, please, we don't have all day.

[*The people return. The* HUNGER ARTIST *takes his seat again.*]

HUNGER ARTIST: [*Whispers to* EMMA.] How'd it go? Are you alright?

EMMA: [*To* HUNGER ARTIST.] Would have gone better if it had been you. I like you.

HUNGER ARTIST: Oh, Emma, you mustn't say such things. You don't know me.

EMMA: All I know is that I've been struck by lightening.

OFFICIAL: Please, there is to be no speaking or whispering in the room while serious business is being conducted...Good. Now I, the President and Treasurer of the Accident Insurance Compensation Board, have decided, after much consideration and discussion with myself, to award a goodly sum of money to worker Emma Licht. This money is to be used in part for her training as a cabaret dancer. It is my habit to follow the well-known maxim: Give a man a fish and he has enough for his dinner, but teach a man to fish and he'll never go hungry. Next!

[As EMMA *exits she throws a longing glance at the* HUNGER ARTIST, *who shyly looks away à la Chaplin.*]

Next!

HUNGER ARTIST: [*Approaches the* OFFICIAL.] It is I.

OFFICIAL: It is you?

HUNGER ARTIST: I am ill.

OFFICIAL: No you're not.

HUNGER ARTIST: Yes I am.

OFFICIAL: You're not. You're in excellent health.

HUNGER ARTIST: My soul has been seriously compromised. I cannot go on.

OFFICIAL: You must.

HUNGER ARTIST: I won't. I quit.

OFFICIAL: If you quit we will have to withhold your pension. Then what will you do, dear colleague?

HUNGER ARTIST: I don't know.

OFFICIAL: This is out of character for you. What has happened?

HUNGER ARTIST: Something.

OFFICIAL: Something? How will you live?

HUNGER ARTIST: Somehow.

OFFICIAL: Somehow? Where will you go?

HUNGER ARTIST: To Prague.

OFFICIAL: To Prague?

HUNGER ARTIST: To Prague.

SCENE 3: *Early evening. It is not yet dark. The* IMPRESARIO *is walking backwards around the cage. The* HUNGER ARTIST *is walking forward, but in the same direction as the* IMPRESARIO.

IMPRESARIO: Exercise is good for you, Sir. Just one more turn around the cage and we're done.

HUNGER ARTIST: But I'm out of breath and my bones ache.

IMPRESARIO: You lay around too much. Step up the pace, will you!

HUNGER ARTIST: I don't like to walk unless I'm going somewhere.

IMPRESARIO: Think of our walks together as practice for a trip in the future. Should you have to go somewhere you'll be in shape for it.

[*He stops walking.* HUNGER *artist also stops.*]

However, we've done enough for today.

HUNGER ARTIST: I'm in perfect condition for where I'm going.

IMPRESARIO: I try to cheer you up, Sir, but you remain morbid. Anyone ever accuse you of being stubborn? Just because you're starving doesn't mean you can't be cheerful. We're in this together you know.

HUNGER ARTIST: It's not the same.

IMPRESARIO: You're right. I can walk out on you, find another more profitable act to manage. I can leave and never look back. But you, you're stuck with yourself. You're an artist! And a mighty unpleasant one. You know, Sir, there are times I wish you'd die. Much as I love and respect you I wish you'd die...and the reason is I can't stand your act. You disobey me.

You won't break your fast. You want to go on, and on, and on until...Forget it, here come some customers...Quick! Back into your cage. [*To the spectators.*] Welcome, dear friends. Welcome. Once again it gives me great pleasure to greet those of you who believe, and those of you who are still Doubting Thomases. The Hunger Artist and myself, in order to prove that never, not even under forcible compulsion, will he swallow the smallest morsel of food, invite you to stay the night observing him. Do you suppose that our Hunger Artist would sully the honor of his profession by cheating?

[*Mixed reactions from the spectators.*]

Do you think that he keeps a private hoard of refreshments hidden beneath the boards of his cage? Find out for yourself. Stay the night and receive proof positive. We will present you with a tasty breakfast come morning. Any volunteers? Chairs and blankets provided. Flashlight available.

BUTCHER: I'll have a go at it.

BAKER: Me too. How about you, Mr. Accountant?

ACCOUNTANT: Count me in.

IMPRESARIO: Thank you. Thank you, gentlemen. [*To spectators.*] We now have three honorable men whom you all know would not bear false witness.

HUNGER ARTIST: No matter the conclusion they come to, it is I who am bound to be the sole, completely satisfied spectator at my own fast.

[*He rests upon the straw. The* IMPRESARIO *decorously draws the scrim around the cage. The spectators shake the hands of the witnesses and wish them luck.*]

IMPRESARIO: [*In a more intimate tone.*] I draw the curtains to give an illusion of privacy. The Hunger Artist cannot see us, but we see him. With this gesture we show compassion, for who among us would not go mad if he or she were not granted a moment's privacy? As you can see, our Hunger Artist is conserving what little strength he has. One wonders what dreams are left to him. Does he dream about food? Does he dream that he eats it? Only he knows the answer, my friends. However, his dreams do not concern us; his waking hours do. Not that we are indifferent to the dream, rather we are partisans of the palpable. And so without further ado I am prepared to offer, at bargain prices, these souvenirs commemorating the historic, non-caloric visit of the Hunger Artist to your fair city.

[IMPRESARIO *takes his place behind the cash register. Spectators step up to examine the merchandise: posters, T-shirts, tiny cages, skull keychains, shopping bags, postcards.*]

No pushing, please, everyone will be taken care of. [*Holds up a jointed* HUNGER ARTIST *doll; demonstrates the doll.*] Yes, madam, there's a one year warranty on all moving parts, something your husband didn't get when he married you. Just a joke, folks. I'm a great kidder. Honestly. [*Holding up a poster.*] Handsome poster, don't you think? An exact likeness of the Hunger Artist. Every poster signed personally by himself. Every poster an authentic collector's item. [*Holding up a T-shirt.*]. This T-shirt will not shrink; it is 100% cotton and pre-shrunk. I offer it to you at bargain prices. Take it away, folks. One size fits all. We have key chains, skull rings, skeletons made of perfumed soap, tiny bags of straw tied nicely with satin ribbons, and real live field mice to take home as pets for the children. Hurry, hurry, hurry. This offer will not be repeated. One for the price of two. Two for the price of three. [*He winks.*] Make your purchases now; we can't guarantee a full selection tomorrow. Don't lose out because of timidity, folks. We, the citizens of Prague, are noted for our willingness to act. Be brave. Dip into your pocketbooks and buy yourself a gift. You'll be the envy of everyone who lives on your strasse. I'm not closing up till every item is gone. Why thank you, madam. Thank you, sir.

[*Lights dim.*]

SCENE 4: *Nighttime. A card table is set up near the cage. A flashlight is set on the table. The* BUTCHER, BAKER, *and the* ACCOUNTANT *play cards: perhaps Poker. Card game ends.*

BUTCHER: The Hunger Artist hasn't made a sound all night. Let's see what he's up to.

[*He aims flashlight at the sleeping* HUNGER ARTIST. HUNGER ARTIST *wakes.*]

[*To* HUNGER ARTIST.] What a silly profession you've chosen, Sir. Pretty soon no one will be able to look at you. Come on, you can confide in me, wouldn't you like a nice warm bed and someone to share it with?

HUNGER ARTIST: In spite of everything, it isn't bad you know, to lie against a pile of fresh straw and bury your face in it.

BAKER: I suppose you think you're a hero, loving hardship the way you do; but to me you're a coward. Why don't you just end it all now? I'll supply the gun and bullets. [*He pulls a gun from his belt. He starts to load the gun.*]

HUNGER ARTIST: I'm neither a coward nor a hero. I'm an artist. I do what I do.

ACCOUNTANT: Then tell me, Sir Do-Do, what have you been taking juicy little bites of while we were playing cards? What syrupy liquids have you wiped from your mouth with that skinny arm? Was it a ripe cherry?

HUNGER ARTIST: Only blood from a scratch.

BUTCHER: And what are you putting into your mouth now?

HUNGER ARTIST: Words.

BAKER: Not much nourishment there. Even lice are better for you.

HUNGER ARTIST: [*Sings.*]

La la la lice spice nice
La la la mice rice ice
La la la lice spice nice
La la la mice rice ice

[*Continues singing but very softly.*]

BUTCHER: Why is he singing? There's nothing to sing about.

BAKER: He's a clever fellow. Wants us to believe that since he's singing, he's not eating. Let's pretend to ignore him. We'll catch him at it, believe you me.

BUTCHER: [*Gives the* BAKER *a knowing wink. He speaks a bit louder, making sure the* HUNGER ARTIST *hears.*] So I say to her, chopped meat has an icebox life of two to three days. If you keep it longer don't complain to me. Don't expect me to refund your money. Then she accuses me of hiding old meat in the middle of the beef patties. If you don't like it, I say, shop for your meat elsewhere, I don't force you to come here.

BAKER: You told her off.

BUTCHER: Oh she left in a hurry she did, but with a parting shot like all women: I wouldn't feed that meat to a dog, she says. The bitch!

BAKER: When you deal with the public anything can happen. A case in point: my day old bread provides as much nourishment as the fresh and it's a lot cheaper, yet I still get complaints; call that a day old? It's hard as a rock. Belongs in a slingshot, not in someone's stomach. Put it in the oven, I say; use your ingenuity. Stale bread makes excellent bread crumbs. Use it for stuffing the goose. If they want fresh bread let 'em pay the price.

[*They take surreptitious glances at the* HUNGER ARTIST. HUNGER ARTIST *resumes singing softly.*]

ACCOUNTANT: I'm glad that I'm an accountant. Not many understand numbers. Doesn't stop 'em from complaining though. Are you sure my taxes can't be lowered just a little? Surely you can juggle the columns. Who'd know? Use your eraser, Mr. Accountant, that's what it's for. I'm trapped in a dishonest world, gentlemen. Sometimes I'm ashamed to hold my head up high. The universe is entirely mathematical, but I swear I've lost the key. God in his heaven keeps himself busy changing the equations. Take the seashell...

BUTCHER: The seashell?

ACCOUNTANT: A perfectly constructed piece of work. Beautiful to look at and entirely functional. An example, my friends, of what life could be if it were a seashell.

BAKER: Yes, life is certainly not a seashell. A pebble perhaps but never a seashell.

BUTCHER: [*Indicating* HUNGER ARTIST.] He gives me the creeps. Can't even sing a decent tune.

BAKER: Have they examined his straw? Could be food hidden in it.

BUTCHER: Sure! Dead rats with their heads bitten off.

ACCOUNTANT: Kept me alive in the army. Are you a veteran, Mr. Baker?

BAKER: Proud of it. Learned how to take care of myself in the army: how to recognize the sweetness of victory, avoid the bitterness of defeat. Ech! Nothing but blood pudding in the end, salted with a tear.

BUTCHER: Pure poetry, Mr. Baker.

HUNGER ARTIST: I know a poem too.

BAKER: Do you? Then let's hear it, Sir. It'll be better than that racket you've been making. That la la la is driving me kookoo.

HUNGER ARTIST:
>If the noodles
>Had not been so soft
>I couldn't have eaten
>Them at all
>And move the lilacs
>Into the sun

ACCOUNTANT: He's hallucinating. That isn't a poem.

HUNGER ARTIST:
>See the lilacs
>Fresher than morning
>Yesterday evening
>A late bee drank the
>White lilac dry
>Where is the eternal spring?

BUTCHER: It's a secret code, composed to confuse us. But who cares? He can't get my goat.

ACCOUNTANT: How about another hand since we're here to stay the night.

BUTCHER: I'm game. [*Turns flashlight toward the table.*] Let's cut for dealer.

[*They cut the cards. High card deals.*]

BAKER: Guess it's me again.

[*He deals the hand. They play cards silently. We hear the shuffle and slap of the cards on the table.* HUNGER ARTIST *starts to sob quietly.*]

ACCOUNTANT: Is someone weeping?

BUTCHER: I don't hear anyone.

ACCOUNTANT: Are you sure?

BUTCHER: Does a bear shit in the woods? I'll take three cards, Mr. Baker.

BAKER: [*Dealing off the top of deck.*] Three cards crisp as toast for the butcher.

[HUNGER ARTIST *continues sobbing softly.*]

It's the Hunger Artist. [*To* HUNGER ARTIST.] Are you crying, Sir?

HUNGER ARTIST: Yes, I am.

BAKER: But why?

HUNGER ARTIST: Out of pity.

ACCOUNTANT: For who?

HUNGER ARTIST: For anyone who needs it.

BUTCHER: Must be feeling sorry for yourself.

HUNGER ARTIST: For me, or for you.

BUTCHER: Say, don't take things so hard. Do you like us? Or do you hate us after all?

HUNGER ARTIST: I'll give it some thought.

BUTCHER: Yes, you do that. And whatever you decide, don't be ashamed of it. Shame can throttle you as easily as I can. Believe me, I know.

HUNGER ARTIST: You know shame? A man such as yourself?

BUTCHER: A butcher's life is not all hearts and flowers. A butcher's face can be as red as his hands. Dear Sir, do you have a soft spot in your heart for animals? For fluffy little rabbits? For the pig with his elegant, delicately stepping feet and noble snout? For trustful lambs with their soulful gaze?

HUNGER ARTIST: Yes I do.

BUTCHER: Me too. Once I kept pets for love, not murder. Once I was a lonely child with no friends…

HUNGER ARTIST: How sad. No friends.

BUTCHER: [*Recovering himself.*] Forget it. I don't need your pity, thank you. [*Sneakily.*] But now that we're on more intimate terms, now that we're friends, tell me...How did you manage to steal a few bites of food while we were watching?

[*Light dims on card players. A piece of scrim is drawn across the cage. The* HUNGER ARTIST *makes animal shadow figures that move on the scrim: a swan, a rabbit, a fish, etc. (Note: it would be swell to have larger duplicates of the animals, created by laser beam within the stage area.) Music to close of scene.*]

SCENE 5: *Outdoors. Sunrise. The thirty-fifth day of the fast.* HUNGER ARTIST *resting in cage.* EMMA *sneaks up to cage.*

EMMA: Sir, are you awake?

HUNGER ARTIST: Who's there?

EMMA: Emma Licht. We met at the Insurance Compensation Board. I've been following your career. I haven't missed a day of your fast.

HUNGER ARTIST: I thought I saw you but I wasn't sure.

EMMA: I've been worrying about you.

HUNGER ARTIST: You musn't do that.

EMMA: I'm so fond of you. Give me your hand.

HUNGER ARTIST: [*Puts his hand through the bars.*] Do you want to count the bones? Do you doubt that this is the thirty-fifth day of my fast?

EMMA: Oh no, Sir! I believe you. I just wanted to... [*She kisses his hand.*] Oh my sweet man...Can't you see that I'm a lonely woman. These trips to see you fill my life with joy. Why don't you break your fast and come home with me. I'll take care of you; nurse you back to health. I earn a good living now. I'm a featured dancer at the cabaret: EMMA "LEGS" LICHT. Wanna see my legs? [*She lifts her skirt to the knee.*]

HUNGER ARTIST: It's too late for love, Emma. I'm no longer capable of it. The question of permanence grips me with terror. I tremble whenever I hear those bourgeois drums beating a path to my door. Makes me want to run and hide. Nothing delights me: not even the sight of a rosy female behind. I prefer the mice who share my cage with me.

EMMA: You haven't been offered any rosy behinds lately have you? So why act as if there's a choice to be made? Listen to me, I can take you away from all this. Planned the whole thing. The train to Wran leaves at 6:05. At 7:45 we shall walk the first step towards Davle where we shall eat breakfast at Lederer's. I know the owner.

HUNGER ARTIST: I can't.

EMMA: But darling, we'll be treated like royalty. Real royalty...Oh, and at twelve o'clock we'll lunch at Stechowitz and enjoy some lively conversation as we look out at the garden from the patio.

HUNGER ARTIST: I really can't.

EMMA: No such thing as can't. Here's something you won't be able to resist...Something I know you've been training for with the Impresario: a hike through the woods! We shall walk along a trail till we come to the rapids above which we shall row about. You may recline. I shall handle the oars. By then it will be a quarter to four, with the whole evening ahead of us.

HUNGER ARTIST: Emma, you are demented.

EMMA: Demented? You bet I am. Simply mad for you, Sir. Please, just one day out of your schedule, dearest! I promise that by seven o'clock I'll have you safely on the steamer to Prague...Alright, we can skip the breakfast at Lederer's if you wish. Say yes. Come with me.

HUNGER ARTIST: Emma do you think I've never traveled?

EMMA: The first time I saw you, you were imprisoned in an office. The second time in a cage.

HUNGER ARTIST: But I go out. I come in and I go out. In the past that was my way. Why, once I saw the aeroplanes at Brescia. On each hanger the names of the aviators: Cobia, Cagno, Rougier, Moucher, Anzani, and Bleriot. That Bleriot! His engine was intractable. Had six assistants working on it. Then with a turn of the screw the engine roared into life. [*He stares transfixed, reliving the incident.*]

EMMA: Sir, you musn't exert yourself. You must save your strength for our excursion.

HUNGER ARTIST: The plane is in the air...Go on, Bleriot, climb, climb!...Look above us. There's a man twenty meters above the earth imprisoned in a wooden box. He is pitting his strength against an invisible danger...OH! There he goes towards the woods. He's disappeared. Gone from sight, dear Emma. Now his course will have to be determined by the stars...No! There he is again still climbing. Up! Up! Continue, Bleriot! [*Panting. Exhausted.*] But I...I must go deeper into the heart of darkness alone.

EMMA: What a time to speak of darkness, the sun is out. Do you mind if I take a drink from your glass?

[HUNGER ARTIST *pours some water from a small pitcher into his glass. He extends the glass to* EMMA.]

HUNGER ARTIST: Wipe the rim of the glass before you drink. Wouldn't want you to catch what I have.

EMMA: And what is that?

HUNGER ARTIST: It has no name.

EMMA: Your mysterious disease doesn't frighten me. [*She drinks from the glass without wiping the rim.*] But I shouldn't have bothered you. Please forgive me for trying to tempt you back into the real world, my darling, my love.

HUNGER ARTIST: No, no. I thank you for thinking it possible.

EMMA: But why isn't it possible? Why?

HUNGER ARTIST: Emma, the world is a perfect place, which is why I am a stranger in it.

EMMA: Darling, you sound so weak. How will you ever last till the fortieth day of your fast.

HUNGER ARTIST: Forty days is nothing. I could go beyond forty days, but the Impresario won't let me. He says that people lose interest after that amount of time. That I'd be starving to an empty house.

EMMA: I'll be around, Sir.

HUNGER ARTIST: You, only you.

EMMA: One witness is all you need.

HUNGER ARTIST: Just six days and I'll be forced to begin again. How I hate beginnings. I want to finish! Some day the Impresario and I shall part and I will be on my own, free to test the limits of my art.

EMMA: Yes.

HUNGER ARTIST: Timing is everything, Emma. Timing can make or break a career.

SCENE 6: *The fortieth day of the fast. A band is playing. The cage is tied with ribbons and flowers. Spectators eagerly wait. A* DOCTOR *is in attendance.* ROSE *and* EMMA *assist prettily in the style of magician's assistants. The* IMPRESARIO *on his platform addresses the audience.*

IMPRESARIO: Ladies and gentlemen, it is with great pleasure that I speak to you today on the occasion of the fortieth day of the fast. I invite you all to observe the thoroughly scientific examination of the Hunger Artist conducted by our good doctor Klopstock, M.D., PHD, and Honorary Diplomat of the order of M.A.D. Doctor, if you please.

[*The* DOCTOR *takes a bow.* IMPRESARIO *unlocks the cage.* ROSE *and* EMMA *help the* HUNGER ARTIST *out of the cage. They seat him on a chair.*]

DOCTOR: [*Examining the eyes.*] There is a minor irritation. Redness due to strain. Perhaps the Hunger Artist has been trying to see something that does not exist. I recommend washing the eyes in a warm solution of boric acid. And at least eight hours of sleep every night. Take this pill prescription, Sir. These will help you sleep should you suffer from insomnia. [*Examining mouth and neck.*] No enlargement of lymph glands. Good. Open your mouth, please. Wider. Yes, membranes clean. No suspect white spots. Lesions absent. Gums smooth and pink. [*Inserts tongue depressor into* HUNGER ARTIST'*s mouth.*] Bite down on this my friend. Aha! I detect some weakness of the mandible. You must strengthen your mandible by chewing, Sir, even if it's only on a piece of wood, otherwise weakness will be followed by inertia, and inertia by despondency. You must guard yourself from despondency, Sir, for it is more harmful than sin. Do you hear me? I say, DO YOU HEAR ME?

HUNGER ARTIST: Yes…and no.

DOCTOR: Yes and no? I see, you are deaf in only one ear. [*He writes something on a pad.*] Now, dear Sir, would you please put your good ear to the ground. Our lovely assistants Rose and Emma will help you. That's it. Easy does it. Tell me what you hear?

HUNGER ARTIST: I hear the alarm trumpets of nothingness.

DOCTOR: An aural hallucination. A unicorn of sound. Only a miracle can cure you of this misapprehension. However, since much of medicine is predicated upon the body's healing of itself, you might one day hear the alarm trumpets of somethingness again. Don't give up hope, Sir.

IMPRESARIO: Oh wonderful, eminent, professor of medicine! Oh doctor supreme! What do you suggest we do in the meantime while waiting for a miracle?

DOCTOR: We shall take a conservative approach since the Hunger Artist is in a fragile state: first one must dip a tiny ball of cotton into hot linseed oil, then insert it into the ailing ear. This must be done every night before bedtime until there is some improvement.

IMPRESARIO: What about his heart? Is it holding up?

DOCTOR: [*Listening to the heart.*] Lovely. Lovely. The heart keeps a steady cadence. Beat by beat it follows the mysterious laws of involuntary pulsation.

IMPRESARIO: But is his heart healthy?

DOCTOR: How healthy can it be, Mr. Impresario? The heart has been eating itself. The Hunger Artist must find other nourishment or succumb.

BUTCHER: [*With derision and superiority.*] What about his sex? He's still a man, isn't he? Or has something been eating away down there too?

DOCTOR: [*With a magnifying glass. Examines* HUNGER ARTIST *then announces his findings to the crowd.*] THE MAN'S GENITALS EXIST!

[*Crowd applauds and otherwise demonstrates approval.*]

Yes, in spite of an inclination to hide, they exist. Here is truth and nothing but the truth. Here is an organ that pines away in lonely desperation, yet it is ready to establish, with a little kindness, the generosity of nature in simple things. [*To* HUNGER ARTIST.] Treat your privates well, Sir, and the good soldier will stand up to life again. [*To spectators.*] The Hunger Artist's capacity remains unimpaired.

IMPRESARIO: [*To band conductor.*] Music, maestro, if you please.

[*Band plays a lively tune.*]

The Hunger Artist is ready to partake of some food.

[ROSE *and* EMMA *help the* HUNGER ARTIST *to the banquet table.*]

[*To* HUNGER ARTIST.] Would you like to say a few words to your admirers, Sir?

HUNGER ARTIST: Yes. A few words. Dear admirers. The very thought of food makes me ill.

IMPRESARIO: He's only kidding, folks.

[*The* HUNGER ARTIST *is force-fed by the* IMPRESARIO. *The food dribbles out of his mouth.*]

Your favorite foods, Sir: mashed potatoes softened with milk and butter. Apple sauce. Some cabbage soup. Just what the doctor ordered. Some beer to wash it all down with. Soon you'll be strong enough to honor the ladies at the bordello again.

[*The* HUNGER ARTIST *whispers into the* IMPRESARIO'*s ear.*]

Good people of Prague, I've been asked by the Hunger Artist to drink a toast to you all. So here goes. [*He raises his glass in a toast. There is a musical flourish.*] Friends, may all your strivings come to joyous fruition, and your bellies remain forever full! [*He drains the glass of champagne.*]

[*Music and dancing.*]

ACT II

SCENE 1: *A year later. The* IMPRESARIO, *the* HUNGER ARTIST, *and* GEORG VON SCHONERER, *the owner of the Circus Teutonic, are present. Contracts are on a table. In the background we hear the stops and starts of a band rehearsing. The* HUNGER ARTIST *wears tights, a white shirt, jaunty bow tie with tiny flashing lights, and on his feet a pair of silver platform-soled shoes.*

IMPRESARIO: [*With a flourish.*] Here's the release, Sir. [*Hands the* HUNGER ARTIST *the release.*] Well then, this is the proverbial parting of the ways for us. I'll miss you, Sir. [*He embraces the* HUNGER ARTIST.] We've had a few laughs along the way, haven't we, dear. I wish you the best, old friend.

GEORG: [*Handing the* IMPRESARIO *a check.*] This should satisfy the terms of our agreement, Mr. Impresario.

IMPRESARIO: Pleasure doing business with you, Mr. Von Schonerer. The Hunger Artist is yours. Take good care of him. He blossoms when treated well. Change the straw in his cage at least once a week. Keep a pitcher of water handy at all times. Make sure that a faithful record of days fasted is kept where all can see it, and you've done your part. However, if interest falls off as it's liable to these days, he's learned a zippy new dance to attract the young crowd.

GEORG: Good. I'd like to see it. I really would. Oh would I ever like to see a zippy new dance! Zippy is the kind of dance I go for. Dance for me, dear Sir. I'm easy to please, but I warn you, I've seen everything.

[*Band music.* HUNGER ARTIST *does a dance with some comic elements, perhaps Chaplinesque. There are silly drum rolls when he falls or does not accomplish some trick. The* HUNGER ARTIST's *face remains sad throughout.*]

[*When dance is finished.*] What do you call it?

HUNGER ARTIST: I don't have to call it. It is already here.

GEORG: Yes, of course. [*Laughs at the joke. Stops.*] Now, dear Artist, since money has already changed hands, won't you sign on the dotted line? Just a formality. It's the standard contract approved by the Hunger Artist's Guild, amended by the Society of Circus Performers, and recently revised by the Committee for Fair Treatment of All, regardless of Race, Religion, or Color. Though as you must have heard, Religion *ist einerlei, Rasse ist die Schweinerei!*

HUNGER ARTIST: Please, Mr. Von Schonerer, what does that slogan mean?

GEORG: It means: whatever their religion, it's their race that makes them pigs!

HUNGER ARTIST: It's their race that makes them pigs?...And just who are you referring to, Mr. Von Schonerer?

GEORG: The Jews of course.

HUNGER ARTIST: But I am a...

[*The* IMPRESARIO *shushes him by placing a finger on his lips. The* HUNGER ARTIST *understands that he is to remain silent as to his religion.*]

But I am a...fraid that I'll have to read the contract first before I sign it.

GEORG: [*Impatiently.*] Well then read it, read it.

HUNGER ARTIST: On second thought, no, I won't. What if I don't agree to your terms, where else can I go? Can I enter another profession? Not at my age...and besides there have been no other offers. All I want to do is to be able to continue with my art.

IMPRESARIO: Excuse us for a few moments, Mr. Von Schonerer. My client and I have a few things to talk over. Best to nip unforeseen difficulties in the bud. [*He takes* HUNGER ARTIST *aside. Speaks to him in a confidential manner.*] Fasting has nothing to do with age, Sir. The older one becomes the easier it is to fast: no money for food, no strength to prepare it. One loses interest in life. I don't have to tell you that, you of all people. And you might as well read the contract, it's the sophisticated thing to do, make sure you're not being cheated...You might want to suggest some small change. It might even be honored. Changes are still possible. For example, what if your clock breaks down and no longer strikes the hour? Will it be replaced by management? If the bars of your cage rust, will they be repainted? And what if you are sued by some other hunger artist who accuses you of stealing his act? Who'll pay the lawyer's fees? You, my friend, if you're not careful.

HUNGER ARTIST: I appreciate your attitude, Mr. Impresario, but you've already read the contract. I trust your judgement.

IMPRESARIO: Tut tut tut, dear Sir. I see that you put yourself above such mundane things as contracts. That you care for only one thing, your art! An attitude such as yours is going out of fashion fast. You'll be left behind, believe you me!

GEORG: [*Approaches* IMPRESARIO *and* HUNGER *artist.*] I don't mean to rush you, gentlemen, but I have other business to attend to.

[*They all return to the table.*]

HUNGER ARTIST: [*Signing the contract.*] You may use my name in all advertisements and promotional campaigns. I am available for interviews to the press, and am free to travel having neither family nor friends who might suffer from my absence.

GEORG: [*Shakes the* HUNGER ARTIST'*s hand.*] Congratulations! You are now a member of the greatest circus on earth: the Circus Teutonic! Lights, color, music! The enchantment of female beauty, the dominance of male strength, the ferocity of lions, the hilarity of clowns, the shock of nature's fabulous grotesques! Can you stand it? Don't answer, nobody can. It's far too exciting. Now how do you sleep, Sir? Any problems there?

HUNGER ARTIST: I appear to sleep, but I'm not asleep. I'm ever vigilant. However, to be perfectly honest with you, there must be times that I do sleep, but I'm not aware of it. Mr. Von Schonerer there is one request I must make.

GEORG: Ask it.

HUNGER ARTIST: I would like to have artistic control of my fasting.

GEORG: Say no more. You are to be the sole arbiter of your act. How's that?

HUNGER ARTIST: You won't be sorry; for I will establish a record never before achieved.

GEORG: Forget it. Nobody cares about records. Public opinion has shifted. They want diversification, variety, new faces, new backsides to kick.

HUNGER ARTIST: Then why have you hired me?

GEORG: You're a novelty, Sir. A vintage curiosity. Someone to blame when things go wrong. An example to the youth of Czechoslovakia of where neo-romantic politics can lead one. Every circus needs its Jew, Sir. Who knows what will become trendy again. I won't even venture a guess: perhaps bigotry and prejudice can still pack 'em in. Maybe yes, maybe no. I'm taking a chance on you I admit, but that's the kind I am.

HUNGER ARTIST: When do I begin?

GEORG: As soon as your straw arrives from Prague.

HUNGER ARTIST: And my pay?

GEORG: A roof over your head as long as you live. Clothing fumigated monthly to control maggots and lice. Commodious porcelain chamber pot. Fresh straw as required. Pitcher of water...and as a show of good will, a chirping cricket in its own cage to keep you company. [*To the* IMPRESARIO.] Don't be a stranger, Mr. Impresario, come and visit us as a guest of the establishment. You're welcome anytime. [*To the* HUNGER ARTIST.] Come along now. I'll show you around. Introduce you to the personnel. Before long you'll come to regard us as family.

[*They bow to one another in solemn fashion.* GEORG VON SCHONERER *and the* HUNGER ARTIST *go off together. The* IMPRESARIO *exits in another direction.*]

SCENE 2: *Circus music. A scrim is hung above the stage, stage rear. This is the area where we see, as in a dream, the circus acts. e.g. the high wire artist, or the clown-dog act. The real scene goes on (simultaneously) on stage below. On platforms around the arena freaks are displayed: Half-man/Half-woman, the Fat Woman, the Giant, the Transparent Wonder, the Two-Headed Boy, the Wolf Boy. The* HUNGER ARTIST*'s cage is part of this display.* CAMILLE *the high-wire artist is visiting with the* HUNGER ARTIST.

HUNGER ARTIST: I have become an impediment on the the way to the big show.

CAMILLE: We can't all be the main attraction, Sir.

HUNGER ARTIST: Even the Wolf-Boy draws a bigger crowd than I do. He's sacrificed nothing to achieve his celebrity. I've worked at my act. I deserve more.

CAMILLE: Sir, the sight of the Wolf Boy chills one to the bone. He is a danger to all who observe him. They say that once he bit a child's hand off and wouldn't give it back. Can you top that?

HUNGER ARTIST: You're right, Miss Camille. I aim to amaze and delight, not to frighten anyone.

CAMILLE: Vitality, animal sexuality, the possibility of seeing someone change from animal to human is a thrill. Just yesterday the Wolf Boy ate with knife and fork, a linen napkin tucked under his chin. He is learning the alphabet and how to shoot a gun, yet one may see him in a natural state of degradation, doing in public what we civilized human beings do in private. He plays with himself. He makes strange sounds that pass for speech. He eats the fleas and lice that congregate upon him as if he were an ape. In short, he attracts the patrons because he displays the baser instincts that reside in us all. Have you caught my act?

HUNGER ARTIST: My apologies. Mr. Von Schonerer has given orders to keep me out of the big tent.

CAMILLE: I'm queen of the high-wire. One needs very sensitive feet. Yes, the feet must have eyes of their own.

HUNGER ARTIST: Have you ever fallen?

CAMILLE: Many times; into a net of course. The customers would prefer there was no net. Confidentially, Sir, my fans would like me a lot better if on occasion I broke a few bones, or worse. They're a cold blooded bunch all of 'em.

HUNGER ARTIST: Yet we keep on.

CAMILLE: Yes.

[*We hear over a loud speaker* GEORG VON SCHONERER *announce the high-wire act.*]

GEORG: [*Offstage.*] Ladies and gentlemen, the Circus Teutonic is proud to present to you at this time, the super-sensational Miss Camille in her artistically conceived, death defying performance upon the high-wire...Miss Camille, if you please!

HUNGER ARTIST: [*To* CAMILLE *as she rushes out.*] Good luck!

[*We see the act as a rear projection on the scrim, stage rear, above the stage.* EMMA *approaches the* HUNGER ARTIST.]

EMMA: Sir, Sir, it's me, Emma.

HUNGER ARTIST: Ah, the beautiful Emma.

EMMA: That's me alright.

HUNGER ARTIST: You came to see me again? All the way from Prague?

EMMA: I have good news.

HUNGER ARTIST: Is there such a thing?

EMMA: Yes, dear friend. First of all, do you remember the petitioner Lazarus Bloch deceased?

HUNGER ARTIST: I remember the case, yes, but I did not know the gentleman when he was alive.

EMMA: He has come back from the dead, Sir, and is presently employed by this very circus: billed as Lazarus a Modern Miracle. Concern for his family forced him to re-enter the world of the living. His salary, a pittance to be sure, has nevertheless eased the strain of poverty for them.

HUNGER ARTIST: I'm happy for him.

[*Over the loudspeaker we hear* GEORG VON SCHONERER *announce the next act.*]

GEORG: [*Offstage*] Friends, a serious moment if you please. The Circus Teutonic has spared no expense to bring you an act that is non-pareil and one of a kind. It is an act that has only biblical precedent. An act that could not have been repeated without holy intervention. I give you without further ado, the amazing Lazarus who will now dramatize his escape from eternity.

[*Lugubrious band music. On scrim, we observe a coffin. Coffin opens and Lazarus emerges. He gets in and gets out slowly but repeatedly, as scene on stage below continues.*]

HUNGER ARTIST: [*To* EMMA.] I wouldn't have believed it, but seeing is believing.

EMMA: True. Seeing is believing. And here is something else I wouldn't have believed if I hadn't seen it myself. Your Mr. Braun, formerly identified as case number three-hundred and thirty-three A for Alive, the gentleman with the metal plate in his skull, has also found his niche.

HUNGER ARTIST: He has? Where?

EMMA: Here.

[*We hear over the loudspeaker the resounding note* A. *As the note rings out Lazarus returns to his coffin. The coffin disappears.* MR. BRAUN *appears behind the scrim. He hits the top of his head with an implement (perhaps a large spoon). The note* A *rings out again. A clown holding a hoop appears behind the scrim. A midget in a dog's costume jumps through the hoop. Then the midget in dog's costume holds the hoop. The clown jumps through the hoop. This goes on during the scene on stage below.*]

HUNGER ARTIST: One would think the circus existed only as a haven for society's bitter rejects. Yet, because of its generosity to our Mr.Braun he has developed into a true genius of calamity; however I don't envy him his belated success.

EMMA: Nor I. I don't envy anyone. I'm the luckiest woman in the world.

HUNGER ARTIST: How wonderful, Emma.

EMMA: That is what I've really come to tell you; the reason I'm the luckiest woman in the world.

HUNGER ARTIST: Tell me then. Tell me, dearest Emma.

EMMA: I'm engaged to a man who is both sensitive and passionate. You know him very well.

HUNGER ARTIST: I do?

EMMA: Your former boss, Sir, Mr. Official, President and Treasurer of the Bureau of Accident Claims. He says that I am a great talent and has retired from his position at the bureau in order to manage me. The dear man loves to watch me practice, especially the splits and high kicks. He's an exacting critic if I do say so myself, and my dancing has improved oodles under his tutelage. By the way, my first professional engagement is with the Circus Teutonic. Doesn't fate work in strange ways?

HUNGER ARTIST: [*Dejected.*] It does.

EMMA: Give me your blessing, Sir. We're going to be married this week.

[*Tears roll down the* HUNGER ARTIST'*s cheeks. Soft, romantic waltz music underlines the action.*]

Why so sad, dear friend?

HUNGER ARTIST: [*Agitated.*] How did it happen? Tell me the details. Leave nothing out. Has he kissed you? How often? Where? Has he held you? Touched you? Seen your body?

EMMA: Except for the kissing nothing happened. I'm a respectable woman. What are you thinking of?

HUNGER ARTIST: What might have been.

EMMA: [*She opens her blouse revealing her breasts to the* HUNGER ARTIST.] This is all the Impresario has seen. Now you've seen it too.

[*She moves closer to the cage. The* HUNGER ARTIST *extends his hand. He caresses her breasts.*]

Ahhh. Ahhh, dear one. So lonely in your cage. If only you had come with me. If only you had chosen me above your art. I wanted you. I still do. I love you. Kiss my breasts. Kiss me, darling…Oh kiss me, my sweetheart, my own…Kiss me forever and forever and forever…AAAHHH.

[*The* HUNGER ARTIST *first leans his cheek through the bars of his cage to brush her breast with it. He then manages to put the nipple into his mouth, and suckles on it like a baby. Lights dim on the* HUNGER ARTIST *and* EMMA. *Music leading into next scene.*]

SCENE 3: *The* OVERSEER *of the circus and his assistant are doing maintenance work, sweeping, painting, etc. The* HUNGER ARTIST'S *cage has been moved to a less prominent position than it once had. It is now over a week since* EMMA'S *visit. It is early in the day. Circus folk straggle across the lot in morning disarray. Sound of an instrument tuning up. Sounds of animals: roar of a lion, an elephant call, dog barking. Human voices calling to one another.* OVERSEER *comes upon the* HUNGER ARTIST'S *cage.*

OVERSEER: [*To his* ASSISTANT.] Why is this perfectly good cage standing here empty, with nothing but dirty straw in it?

ASSISTANT: Don't have a clue…But hold on a minute, what's this say? [*He reads the barely legible notice board beside the cage.*] The Hunger Artist. Days fasted fifty-five. What a load of bull.

OVERSEER: [*He pokes at straw with a stick.*] Anyone home? I say, anyone at home?

HUNGER ARTIST: [*Weakly.*] It's me the Hunger Artist resting a bit in the straw.

OVERSEER: Are you still fasting? When on earth do you mean to stop?

HUNGER ARTIST: Forgive me, everybody, forgive me.

OVERSEER: [*Taps his temple to let his* ASSISTANT *know that the* HUNGER ARTIST *is nuts.*] We forgive you.

HUNGER ARTIST: I always wanted you to admire my fasting.

OVERSEER: We do admire it.

HUNGER ARTIST: But you shouldn't admire it.

OVERSEER: Well then we don't admire it. But why shouldn't we admire it?

HUNGER ARTIST: Because I have to fast, I can't help it.

OVERSEER: What a fellow you are. And why can't you help it?

HUNGER ARTIST: [*He speaks into the* OVERSEER'*s ear.*] Because I couldn't find the food I liked. If I had found it, believe me, I should have made no fuss and stuffed myself like you or anyone else. [*The* HUNGER ARTIST *reclines in the straw. He dies as softly as a whisper. Perhaps a last sigh escapes his lips.*]

OVERSEER: [*Pokes at straw to see whether the* HUNGER ARTIST *is dead. To* ASSISTANT.] Well, clear this out now. He's dead.

[*As they begin to put the straw into a wheelbarrow, lights dim and our focus of attention changes to the lit scrim above the stage. We see a close-up photo still of the* HUNGER ARTIST *suckling on* EMMA'*s breast. Words scroll on a loop across bottom of scrim as if on a movie screen. As we read the words there is one long drawn out note: the note A played (on various instruments: trumpet, etc.) till words finish.*]

[*Words:*] WAIT LIVE WAIT BORN WAIT EAT WAIT SHIT WAIT DRINK WAIT PISS WAIT SEE WAIT CRY WAIT CRAWL WAIT STAND WAIT WALK WAIT RUN WAIT TALK WAIT SING WAIT TOUCH WAIT HOLD WAIT THROW WAIT KISS WAIT LOVE WAIT HATE WAIT WORK WAIT REST WAIT STAY WAIT STAY WAIT WAIT WAIT WAIT WAIT DIE WAIT WAIT...

[*Go to black. The end.*]

Tina Howe

BIRTH AND AFTER BIRTH

CHARACTERS:

> **Sandy Apple,** *the mommy, in her early thirties*
>
> **Bill Apple,** *the daddy, in his middle thirties*
>
> **Nicky,** *their four-year-old son*
>
> **Mia Freed,** *an anthropologist without children, in her early thirties*
>
> **Jeffrey Freed,** *an anthropologist without children, in his forties*

The Apples' kitchen-playroom, the center of the house—a big, cheerful room with a few overstuffed chairs and all the usual kitchen appliances. A dining table and five chairs are in the center of the stage. There's also a closet in the room, and a large inherited mirror hanging on the wall.

ACT I

The curtain rises. Today is NICKY'*s fourth birthday. It's very early in the morning, the stage is in near darkness.* SANDY *and* BILL *are in their bathrobes getting everything ready before* NICKY *gets up.* BILL *shakes a tambourine.*

SANDY: [*Wrapping presents.*] Ssssssssssssshhhhhhhhh!

BILL: God, I love tambourines!

SANDY: [*Whispering.*] You'll wake him up.

BILL: What is it about tambourines?

SANDY: We'll never finish!

BILL: They kill me.

SANDY: Bill!

BILL: If I had my life to live over, I'd be a tambourine virtuoso.

SANDY: I haven't even started wrapping the masks yet.

BILL: Imagine being the...greatest tambourine virtuoso in the world...

SANDY: At least *you* got some sleep last night.

BILL: Concerts on every continent: Europe, Australia, South America... [*Plays with enthusiasm, doing a few flamenco steps.*]

SANDY: There's still the puzzles and coloring books.

NICKY: [*Bursting into the room in his pajamas.*] Where's my presents? Where's my presents?

SANDY: [*Dropping everything.*] Oh, Nicky, you *scared* me!

BILL: [*Snatching up a movie camera, starts filming* NICKY.] Don't do a thing 'til Daddy gets his new camera!

NICKY: [*Tearing through the darkness looking for his presents.*] Where's my presents? Where's my presents?

SANDY: Mommy and Daddy have been up all night getting everything ready for Nicky's party. Does Nicky want to see what they've done? One, two, three! [*She turns on the lights.*]

[*Crepe-paper streamers crisscross the ceiling, balloons hang in clusters, a huge* HAPPY BIRTHDAY *banner is stretched across the room. The table is set for five and seems to float under the weight of favors, candies, noisemakers, and hats. Everything stops; even* NICKY *is stunned.*]

BILL: [*On top of it all with his camera.*] I'll bet you never expected anything like this, old buddy, did you? Huh? You never dreamed it would be like this!

SANDY: [*Throwing her arms around* NICKY.] Just look at you! Mommy's great big four-year-old!

NICKY: Where's my presents? Where's my presents?

BILL: Daddy's present to Nicky is a whole movie of Nicky's party.

SANDY: Such a big boy...it seems like only yesterday I was bringing him home from the hospital.

BILL: Quik Foto has same-day service now, you know. Bring in the film at noon, pick up the printed reel at three.

NICKY: [*Finding his presents, shrieks, diving into them headfirst.*] Presents! Presents! Oooooooooooh, look at all my presents!

BILL: Keep it up, Nick, you're doing great, just beautiful... beautiful.

SANDY: Nicky, you're not supposed to open presents now. Presents after cards, you know that's the way we do it! [*Starts picking up the shredded wrapping.*]

[NICKY *ignoring her, tears open musical instruments, plays them.*]

BILL: [*Filming.*] Atta boy, Nick, show 'em how good you can play. Look at Daddy and play something. Over this way...look at Daddy!

SANDY: [*As manic in her cleaning as* NICKY *in his wrecking.*] Nicky, I asked you to wait. We do cards first. That way we avoid all of this mess at the beginning.

BILL: Oh, Nicholas, are we making one hell of a movie!

NICKY: A red wagon! [*Pulling it around the room in rapture.*]

BILL: Towards Daddy, honey, come towards Daddy. Oh, Christ, I don't believe this kid.

SANDY: [*With a broom.*] Nicky, how is Mommy going to clean all this up? Do you want to have your party inside a great big mess?

BILL: *Stop everything, Nick!* Daddy just got an idea! Let's get some footage of Nicky pulling Mommy in his new red wagon! [*Rushes to* SANDY *and forces her into the wagon.*] Come on, Mommy, Nicky's going to give you a ride.

SANDY: Hey, what are you doing? We have company coming tonight!

NICKY: [*Jumping up and down.*] Nicky's going to pull his big Mommy present. [*Starts pulling.*]

BILL: [*Filming.*] Too much...Oh, Jesus...Jesus...Too much!

SANDY: [*Dropping her head in her hands.*] Please, Bill, I'm a mess. I haven't even brushed my teeth yet.

NICKY: [*Pulling lickety-split.*] Look at Nicky go! Look at Nicky, Daddy. Nicky's pulling his big Mommy present!

SANDY: I've got to clean up.

BILL: Will you look at that kid go?! Don't tell me my son isn't football material!

[NICKY *pulls* SANDY *all around the room making hairpin turns. He suddenly sees an unopened present and runs off to it.*]

Hey, where are you going? You were doing great!

NICKY: More presents, more, more, *more!*

SANDY: [*In the wagon, depressed.*] My breath smells.

BILL: Hey, Nick, what the hell? You were pulling Mommy and doing great. Now come back here and pick up that wagon handle!

SANDY: Nobody cares about anything around here. [*Starts combing her hair in the wagon.*]

BILL: I've got an idea. Let's put in some of these presents *with* Mommy! [*Starts piling presents on top of* SANDY.]

SANDY: I haven't even had a chance to pee.

NICKY: [*Throwing his last opened present across the room.*] Nicky's presents are all gone! [*Starts to cry.*]

BILL: Daddy asked you to pick up wagon handle and pull!

NICKY: I wanted a bunny! And I wanted a puppy...and a pony. *Where's my pony?* You said I could get a pony for my birthday!

SANDY: [*Combing her hair.*] I stay up all night decorating the room, wrapping the presents, blowing up the balloons, making a really nice party, and what does he do? Just tears into everything. Rips it all up! Ruins everything. [*Gets out of the wagon and sits at the birthday table.*]

BILL: All the presents are in the wagon. So get over here, Nicholas, and pull! [*Films.*]

NICKY: [*Kicking the wagon, cries.*] You promised me a pony. *You promised!*

SANDY: And not one thank you. I never heard one thank you for anything.

BILL: I'm waiting!

SANDY: Do you know what my mother would have done if I ruined all my birthday presents and never said thank you?

BILL: [*Slamming down his camera.*] Thanks a lot, Nicky. Thanks for ruining a great movie!

SANDY: She'd flush them down the toilet, that's what she'd do!

[NICKY *gets into the wagon, lies down, sucks his thumb.* BILL *sits with* SANDY *at the birthday table.*]

BILL: Jesus Christ, Nicky.

[*Silence.*]

SANDY: He shouldn't be up this early.

BILL: He got up too early.

SANDY: [*To* NICKY.] I have a good mind to take you back up to your room!

BILL: If you ask me, he should be sent up to his room!

SANDY: Do you want Daddy to take you up to your room?

BILL: You'd better watch it, young man, or it's up to your room!

SANDY: How would you like to be sent up to your room on your birthday?

[*Silence.*]

BILL: He got up too early.

SANDY: Come on, Bill, take him on up.

[*Silence.*]

BILL: That kid gets away with murder.

[SANDY *sighs.*]

Absolute murder...

[SANDY *sighs. There is a moment of silence.* BILL *imitates* NICKY *sucking.* SANDY *sighs.*]

He sounds like some...sea animal...some squid or something. [*Imitates the sound.*]

SANDY: All children suck their thumb when they're upset.

BILL: [*To* NICKY.] You'll get warts on your tongue if you keep that up!

SANDY: I used to suck mine.

BILL: He'll push his teeth all out of shape.

SANDY: [*Popping her thumb into her mouth.*] This one.

BILL: Do you know how much fixing that boy's teeth is going to cost? About three thousand dollars, that's all!

SANDY: I sucked my thumb until I was twenty-two.

BILL: You'll have warts on your tongue and three-thousand-dollar braces on your teeth!

SANDY: I used to suck it during lunch hour when I worked at the insurance company. I'd go into the ladies' room, lock the door, sit on the toilet, and just...suck my thumb. [*Laughs.*] It sounds ridiculous, a grown woman sucking her thumb on a toilet in the ladies' room.

BILL: Aside from the warts and the three-thousand-dollar braces, it's just so goddamned disgusting! [*Imitates* NICKY *again.*]

SANDY: Come to think of it, I didn't really stop sucking it until Nicky was born.

BILL: ...in the same category as nose-picking.

SANDY: [*Scratching her head.*] It's funny how that sucking instinct gets passed on from the mother to her child.

[*Silence.*]

BILL: Four years old…Wow!

SANDY: [*Scratching.*] Ever since I woke up this morning, I've had this itching…

BILL: When a kid turns four, then it's time to buy a movie camera, right?

SANDY: It's strange, because I've never had dandruff…

BILL: Put away the Polaroid and bring out the Super 8.

SANDY: When I looked in the mirror this morning, I saw an old lady. Not *old* old, just used up. [*She scratches her head; a shower of sand falls out.*] It's the wierdest thing, it doesn't look like dandruff or eczema, but more like…I don't know, like my head is drying up and leaking…

BILL: You see, if Daddy didn't take pictures on your birthday, then none of us would remember what you looked like when you were little.

SANDY: My head is leaking…

BILL: [*Picking up his camera, starts shooting* NICKY *at close range.*] Time passes so fast, before you know it, you'll be an old man lying in a nursing home.

SANDY: [*Shaking out more sand.*] My brains are drying up…

BILL: Not a lonely old man, Nick, but one with movies of his youth: birthday parties, Christmases, visits to the zoo.

SANDY: [*Pulling out a fistful of hair.*] And now my hair is falling out by the roots.

BILL: Shit, you'll be the most popular guy in the nursing home. "Have you seen Mr. Apple's movies of his fourth birthday party?" the little old ladies will say.

SANDY: Poor Mommy's going bald.

BILL: From every floor the old people will crowd into your room, perch on the edge of your bed, block your door with their wheelchairs...

SANDY: [*Scratching and leaking more sand.*] When she looked in the mirror this morning, she saw an old lady.

BILL: All for that one backwards glance at the radiance of youth.

SANDY: Poor old feeble leaking Mommy...

BILL: Someday you'll thank me for this.

SANDY: Bald as an egg.

BILL: Come on, give Daddy a big smile now.

NICKY: [*Still in the wagon, sucking his thumb.*] I want to make my birthday wish.

BILL: [*Holding out a mask for* NICKY.] Hey, Nick, how about putting this mask on?

[SANDY *sighs.*]

Come on, give us a roar.

SANDY: Oh, put on the mask for Daddy!

NICKY: I want to blow out my candles and make my birthday wish.

SANDY: Oh, Nicky, *put it on!*

BILL: I tell you, when we show this movie to the Freeds tonight, they'll eat their hearts out!

SANDY: [*Putting the mask on* NICKY.] Look at Nicky!

BILL: Run around the room and pop out from behind the chairs.

NICKY: I don't have to if I don't want to.

BILL: Nicky, I said pop out from behind the chairs! Now, do it!

NICKY: I want raisins.

SANDY: Oooooh, my neck is stiff.

BILL: [*Pulling* NICKY *out of the wagon.*] *Move!*

NICKY: [*Lying on the floor.*] Raisins!

BILL: Will you *please* get him to run around the room and pop out from behind the chairs!

SANDY: Come on, Nicky.

NICKY: *Raisins!*

BILL: We're showing the movie to the Freeds tonight, so let's get going!

SANDY: That's right. Jeffrey and Mia are coming over to celebrate with us.

BILL: Jeff may take good slides, but I promise you he's never seen a movie like this!

SANDY: They're bringing you a special present and everything...

NICKY: Presents!

SANDY: And you know what great presents Jeffrey and Mia give!

BILL: Nobody gives presents like Jeffrey and Mia. So come on, Nick, pop out from behind the chairs.

SANDY: Remember the Imperial Chinese warrior doll they brought him last year?

NICKY: Presents, presents, presents...

SANDY: Jeffrey and Mia are first cousins, honey. Jeffrey and I have the same grandpa.

BILL: *Will you move, goddammit!*

SANDY: I've known Jeffrey ever since he was your age. We used to throw apples on sticks.

BILL: *Nickyyyyyy!*

SANDY: Mommy's planned such a wonderful party with our cousins.

[*Nothing happens.*]

BILL: [*Lunging at* NICKY.] I said...*move!*

[NICKY *runs around the room, popping up from behind the chairs, but all so fast that* BILL *can't keep up with him.*]

Will you slow down for Christsake?!

[SANDY *laughs.* NICKY *stops and falls down flat inside his wagon.*]

[*Slamming down his camera.*] Thanks a lot, Nicholas. I'll remember that! [*He sits down.*]

[*Long silence.*]

SANDY: My neck is so stiff I can hardly turn my head.

[*Silence.* BILL *pulls a letter out of his pocket and reads it, depressed.*]

Four years ago Nicky came out of my tummy and made me the happiest mommy in the world.

BILL: I wish you'd look at this letter sometime.

[SANDY *sighs.*]

It came through the office mail last week. I told you about it the other day, remember?

SANDY: I'm a mommy!

BILL: It's from Continental Allied.

SANDY: Who ever thought that I'd be a mommy?

BILL: [*Reading.*] "Dear Mr. Apple. It has come to the attention of the accounting department that certain papers in the Fiedler file are either missing or incomplete..."

SANDY: Hey, Nicky, I'm a mommy!

[NICKY *puts on one of his masks. It's the face of a baby.* SANDY *is enchanted.*]

Oh, Nickyyyyyyyyyyy.

BILL: "You assured us last month that the Fiedler account had been settled."

SANDY: Does Nicky want to play Babies?

BILL: "...or, indeed, you never did close the account with Mr. Fiedler as you indicated..."

SANDY: Nicky, we can't play now, Mommy has to get the party ready.

[NICKY *coos and gurgles inside his mask.*]

BILL: "...Mr. Brill has brought to our attention the outstanding work you did on the Yaddler account..."

SANDY: Look at all the mess, honey.

[NICKY *gurgles louder.*]

Don't you want to have a nice tidy birthday party with everything in its place?

[NICKY *crawls over to* SANDY, *gets in her lap, hands her a mask of a pop-eyed Cinderella.*]

Ohhhhhh, Nicky, not now...

BILL: "...rest assured, everyone here at Continental Allied knows what a delicate procedure that was..."

SANDY: [*Putting on her mask.*] Sweet baby.

[*The game of Babies starts.* NICKY *is inspired: going limp, gurgling, cooing, and laughing.*]

[*Rocking* NICKY.] Do you know what baby Nicky looked like when he was born, hmmm? [*Kissing him.*] A shiny blue fish! Mommy's little blue trout!

BILL: "...We are full of admiration for the good judgment you showed on that particular account..."

NICKY: I was blue?

SANDY: Of course you were blue. All babies are blue when they're inside their mommies' tummies. It's because there's no air inside the little plastic bag they live in.

NICKY: I want to be blue again. I want to be blue again!

SANDY: Once the baby pops out of the plastic bag inside his mommy's tummy, he breathes air for the first time. And do you know what happens to him then?

BILL: "...What puzzles us, Mr. Apple, is the professional inconsistency you exhibit in your work..."

SANDY: He turns bright pink! As pink as a seashell!

BILL: "Professional inconsistency."

SANDY: Actually, you were a little jaundiced at birth, so your skin was more golden than pink. Mommy's *gold fish!*

NICKY: I was gold?

SANDY: Fourteen-karat gold!

NICKY: Son of a bitch!

SANDY: Nicky!

BILL: What kind of a phrase is that, "professional inconsistency"?

SANDY: And your little arms were so skinny and waved every which way. Do you know what baby Nicky's arms looked like?

NICKY: Nicky was such a good baby, all blue and gold inside his plastic bag.

SANDY: French-fried potatoes, that's what your arms looked like!

[SANDY *and* NICKY *laugh.*]

BILL: *Gibberish!*

SANDY: And Nicky was such a hungry baby! Why, he drank fifteen bottles of sugar water only an hour after he was born!

NICKY: Oh, blue and gold Nicky was *sooooooooo* thirsty!

SANDY: [*Plugging an imaginary bottle in his mouth.*] The nurses on the floor had never seen anything like it! The stood around my bed and watched you drink one bottle after another: ten, eleven, twelve, thirteen...The head nurse lined up all the empty bottles in a row and took a picture with her camera!

BILL: There's talk around the office that Brill is going to ask for my resignation.

SANDY: Well, after drinking so much sugar water so fast, Nicky's tummy was all full of gas bubbles and Mommy had to burp him. [*Starts thumping his back.*]

NICKY: Oh, Nicky's tummy full of gas bubbles!

SANDY: So she swatted and pummeled him until Nicky exploded with such a loud burp that he flew across the room and landed in the sink!

BILL: It's quite subtle, don't you think?

NICKY: Baby firsty, baby still firsty!

SANDY: Such a hungry baby!

BILL: And this was over a week ago. [*Pause.*] *You're not even listening to me!* You don't give a good shit if I'm fired! All you care about is playing your moronic baby games with Nicky! [*He storms out of the room.*]

[*Long silence.* SANDY *takes off her mask.*]

NICKY: Daddy's mad.

SANDY: Daddy's mad.

[NICKY *sucks his thumb.*]

Just look at this mess!

NICKY: I don't like it when Daddy gets mad.

SANDY: God, Nicky, you have to destroy everything you touch, don't you?

NICKY: I want grape juice.

SANDY: I just don't understand you. One minute you're the sweet baby Mommy brought home from the hospital, and the next, you're a savage!

NICKY: [*Tearing off his mask.*] I said I want grape juice!

SANDY: We have company coming!

NICKY: [*Stamping his foot and whirling through all the wrapping.*] I want grape juice. I want grape juice. I want grape juice!

SANDY: You don't care if Jeffrey and Mia walk into a shit house! [*Starts cleaning again.*]

NICKY: [*Wailing.*] *I'm going to die if I don't have grape juice, and then you'll be sorry!*

SANDY: Well, you can't have grape juice. You'll spoil your appetite for your birthday cake!

NICKY: I want grape juice. I want grape juice. *I want grape juice.*

SANDY: [*Cleaning in a fury.*] Mommy said no grape juice.

NICKY: [*Hurtling into the middle of her cleaning.*] *Grape juice!*

SANDY: [*Shaking him, out of control.*] Mommy! Said! No!

[*Silence.* NICKY *makes a small strangled sound.*]

Oh, God.

[NICKY *faints flat out on the floor.* SANDY *stands over him, helpless.*]

Oh, God.

[*Nothing happens.*]

Billllll! Nicky's fainted!

BILL: [*Flying into the room, props* NICKY *up in his arms, and starts walking him.*] What happened?

SANDY: Oh, Bill, help him. [*Starts to cry.*]

[SANDY*'s and* BILL*'s reactions to* NICKY*'s fit are completely outrageous, a parody of parental panic.*]

BILL: *Quick, the ice!*

SANDY: [*Dashing to the refrigerator, takes out the ice, wraps it in a dish towel, and presses it to* NICKY*'s temples.*] It's all right, Nicky, Mommy's got some ice, Mommy will make you all better.

BILL: Come on, Nicker, move those legs of yours! Let's see some action! [*To* SANDY.] *Will you get more ice!*

SANDY: [*Trying to force the ice down* NICKY*'s mouth as* BILL *drags*

him around the room.] Open wide, darling, Mommy wants to
get some of this nice cold ice against your tongue and cool
Nicky off. Open wide...poor Nicky, did Mommy get mad
and shake her boy?

BILL: [*Trying to revive him.*] Keep that circulation going! Keep
those veins and arteries going! Come on, Sandy, for
Chrissake, will you get the tourniquet?

SANDY: [*Running around, panicked.*] Oh, Bill, help him, *help him!
The tourniquet! I forgot the tourniquet!* [*Wrapping a dish towel
around his head.*]

BILL: *Will you hurry up before he forms a blood clot!*

SANDY: Nicky...Nicky...

BILL: Come on, we'd better get him over to the sink! [*Dragging*
NICKY *to the sink, turns on the water full blast, shoves his head
under.*] That's the boy, let the water splash in your face. Now
try and open your mouth and take a deep breath.

SANDY: He isn't moving, Bill, he's still all limp...*Get him to open
his eyes at least! I want to see his eyes!*

BILL: *Will you please get me the goddamned flashlight?!*

SANDY: Oh, the flashlight...how could I have forgotten the
flashlight? [*Getting it, shines it in* NICKY'*s eyes.*] Oh, Nicky,
open your eyes for Mommy. Come on, honey, let Mommy
peek into your pretty eyes...

BILL: [*Lays* NICKY *on the floor and starts giving him artificial
respiration, pumping his arms back and forth. To* SANDY.] Get on
his legs, hurry up. [*Chanting.*] Up and back, up and back, up
and back.

SANDY: [*Pumping his legs.*] Maybe he needs more ice. I don't
think he got any in his mouth.

BILL and **SANDY:** [*Faster and faster.*] Breathe. In and out. In and
out. In and out.

[*Their chanting reaches a crescendo. Time passes,* NICKY *twitches.* SANDY *and* BILL *stop, sigh, wait. Silence.*]

NICKY: [*Weakly.*] Sing to me.

SANDY: [*Cradling him in her arms.*]
Hush, little baby, don't say a word,
Momma's gonna buy you a mockingbird,
And if that mockingbird don't sing,
Momma's gonna buy you a diamond ring.
[*Silence.*]

BILL: We got it in time.

[SANDY *keeps humming.*]

Jesus.

SANDY: What would I do if this ever happened when you weren't here?

BILL: Well, luckily, it only seems to happen when I *am* here.

SANDY: I don't know what I'd do without you.

BILL: *Nick Apple is four years old today!*

NICKY: It hurts being born.

SANDY: I know, honey, I know.

NICKY: It hurts Nicky's head and stomach.

BILL: Tell me, Nick, how does it feel being four? Do you feel any different?

SANDY: "Four" sounds so old.

NICKY: I feel…sweeter.

SANDY: [*Laughing, hugs him.*] Oh, Nicky.

BILL: And what else?

NICKY: Softer.

BILL: You nut.

NICKY: …and cuter.

SANDY: Oh, Nickyyyyy.

NICKY: ...and furrier!

BILL: Furrier?

NICKY: [*Sticking out his hands.*] When I woke up this morning, I saw fur on my hands, white fur.

BILL: *The kid's got white fur growing on his hands!*

SANDY: [*Mock-stricken.*] My baby!

BILL: [*Grabbing* NICKY'*s arm, inspecting it.*] The kid's got fur growing up his arm!

NICKY: Nicky's turning into a furry rabbit.

SANDY: Oh, Nicky!

NICKY: I like being a furry rabbit!

SANDY: My baby! What will we do?

NICKY: Look, there's fur on my tongue, too!

BILL: Well, son of a gun!

NICKY: And on my teeth...

BILL: We'll have to get carrots and lettuce...

SANDY: What will the neighbors say?

BILL: [*Whispering.*] They'll never know...We'll keep it a secret.

SANDY: Bill, I'm scared.

NICKY: [*Whispering.*] I'll only leave the house at night...

BILL: During the day he'll stay in his room...

NICKY: I'll hide under my bed.

BILL: We'll build vast underground tunnels...no one will suspect a thing...

NICKY: By day I'll hide under my bed eating carrots, and at night I'll roam the countryside.

SANDY: Ooooooh, Nicky!

BILL: For long periods of time he'll disappear altogether.

NICKY: I'll be known as...Rabbit Boy.

BILL: He'll become a champion of rabbits in distress.

NICKY: I'll learn rabbit magic.

BILL: He'll cast spells. He'll turn buildings into giant carrots!

NICKY: *Let's play Rabbit Says.*

SANDY: Oh, Nicky, not now.

NICKY: [*Standing on a chair.*] Rabbit says, "Raise your hands!"

BILL: Later, Nick.

SANDY: Please, honey.

NICKY: Rabbit says, "Raise your hands!"

BILL: We have the whole rest of the day.

NICKY: Rabbit says, "Raise your hands!"

> [SANDY *and* BILL *raise their hands.*]
>
> Rabbit says, "Scratch your nose."
>
> [SANDY *and* BILL *scratch their noses.*]
>
> Rabbit says, "Lift your right leg."
>
> [SANDY *and* BILL *do everything he says.*]
>
> Rabbit says, "Lift your leg." Rabbit says, "Stick out your tongue." *Reach for the sky!*
>
> [SANDY *and* BILL *do all these things;* NICKY *laughs, claps his hands.*]
>
> I tricked you, I tricked you! Rabbit says, "Rub your belly." Rabbit says, "Hop on two feet." *Hop on one foot!*
>
> [SANDY *and* BILL *do.*]
>
> You did it! You did it!
>
> [*The game gets faster.*]
>
> Rabbit says, "Lie on the floor." Rabbit says, "Get up." Rabbit

says, "Fart."

[BILL *makes a farting noise in his armpit.*]

SANDY: Not this again!

NICKY: Rabbit says, "Fart again."

[BILL *does.*]

SANDY: I'm not playing, it's disgusting.

NICKY: Rabbit says, "Fart three times in a row."

[BILL *does.*]

SANDY: It isn't funny, Nicholas!

NICKY: Rabbit says, "Run after Nicky and play Fart Tag."

[BILL *chases* NICKY, *making a farting sound every time he tags him.*]

SANDY: If this is the only way you can celebrate Nicky's birthday, it's just pathetic! [*Sits down and stares into space.*]

[BILL *and* NICKY *pantomime their game.*]

My front teeth feel loose… [*Leaning over, shakes a shower of sand from her hair.*] It's the strangest thing—ever since I got up this morning I've been smelling the sea. We're hundreds of miles away from it, but that bitter salty smell of low tide is unmistakable. I noticed it the moment I woke up… [*Inhales, shakes out more sand.*] Nicky, I'd like you to come back to the table now and open your cards.

BILL: [*Sits* NICKY *in his lap, rumples his hair.*] Nicky's four!

NICKY: I love you, Daddy.

SANDY: He got more cards than he did last year.

[BILL *starts tickling* NICKY.]

NICKY: [*Laughing.*] *Don't!*

SANDY: [*Opening a card, reads.*]

"This little pony comes galloping by,

With a smile on his face and a gleam in his eye.
Seems it's somebody's birthday, 'neigh, neigh, neigh,'
Somebody special who's four today!"
From Walt and Sally, and look, they sent five dollars.

BILL: [*Still tickling* NICKY.] Is Nicky ticklish?

NICKY: [*Screaming with pleasure.*] Stop…Stop!

SANDY: [*Reading another card.*]
"May God in his glory look down from the sky,
With a birthday blessing for a wonderful guy."
The Blys. How thoughtful.

BILL: I tell you, Nick, we're going to have a great party tonight!

SANDY: Will you look at this! Nicky got a card from Mrs. Tanner, his nursery school teacher, and they have a strict policy of not sending out individual cards on the children's birthdays. [*In a singsong.*] I guess someone is Mrs. Tanner's favorite! [*Long pause.*] It's important for a child to form attachments outside the home.

BILL: [*With* NICKY *on his lap.*] Children need guidelines!

SANDY: Self-discovery is key.

BILL: If a child isn't given love at home, he'll be emotionally crippled for life!

SANDY: *I* believe in discipline!

BILL: Children learn from observation!

SANDY: Tolerance comes from acceptance!

BILL: Self-respect is built on sharing!

SANDY: Reading readiness precedes cognition!

BILL: If I ever caught Nicky with matches, right out! I'd toss him right out of the house!
[*Silence.*]

SANDY: You know, Bill, I feel sorry for Jeffrey and Mia. I wish there was something we could do.

BILL: It's not our business!

SANDY: But not to have children…

BILL: You can't run other people's lives.

SANDY: *Neither* of them wants children!

BILL: Their careers are very important to them.

NICKY: I love birthdays!

SANDY: But they're missing so much.

NICKY: What I love most is blowing out the candles and making my wish.

SANDY: What if tonight…

NICKY: Sally told me all birthday wishes come true.

SANDY: …they changed their minds and decided to have a baby?

BILL: Jeffrey and Mia have been married for twelve years. I don't think they're going to change their minds about having children at Nicky's party.

SANDY: But what if they did?

NICKY: I know just the wish I'm going to make!

BILL: It won't happen.

SANDY: But what if they just…did…because of us and Nicky and how happy we all are.

NICKY: And it's going to come true because Sally told me it would!

SANDY: Oh, Bill, I bet they change their minds tonight, you wait and see!

BILL: What's going to happen tonight is that we're going to have one hell of a party for Nicky, and I'm going to show one hell of a movie!

SANDY: I have a feeling…

NICKY: When can I blow out the candles and make my wish?

SANDY: Imagine being a woman and not wanting to experience childbirth.

BILL: People are different.

SANDY: But never to have your own baby...

NICKY: When can I blow out the candles and make my wish?

SANDY: It would be so good for both of them.

BILL: As anthropologists studying children of primitive cultures, they see a lot of suffering.

NICKY: I want to make my birthday wish.

BILL: Once you've seen babies dying of starvation, I'm sure you think twice about bringing more people into the world.

SANDY: But their baby wouldn't starve!

NICKY: I want to make my birthday wish!

SANDY: They'd have such a beautiful baby.

BILL: They're not interested in having a beautiful baby, they're interested in primitive children!

NICKY: Mommy, can I make my birthday wish now?

SANDY: *No, you cannot make your wish now, Mommy's talking to Daddy and it's very important.* [*Pause.*] How can they understand primitive children if they don't have children of their own?

BILL: Just because I can articulate their reasons for not wanting children doesn't mean I agree with them!

NICKY: Daddy, can I make my birthday wish now?

SANDY: Well, you don't have to be so pompous about it. People do change!

BILL: It's very unlikely.

SANDY: But it could happen...

BILL: Well, anything *could* happen, but that doesn't mean…

NICKY: Please, Daddy, can I make my…

SANDY: *Shit, Nicky, can't you let Mommy and Daddy have a conversation?!*

BILL: Mommy and Daddy are talking now.

NICKY: [*Starting to cry.*] It's not fair…it's not fair…

SANDY: [*To* BILL.] He's impossible!

BILL: Can't you just wait…

[NICKY *cries louder.*]

SANDY: Keep this up, Nicky, and there won't *be* any birthday party!

NICKY: [*Putting on a mask to hide his crying.*] Go on, yell at me and be mean, I don't care because I still haven't made my birthday wish and when I make it, it will come true because Sally said so!

[*He exits. Long silence.*]

SANDY: [*Glancing at herself in the mirror.*] When I looked in the mirror this morning, I saw an old lady. Not *old* old, just used up. [*Takes off her slipper and dumps out a stream of sand.*]

BILL: Kids!

SANDY: [*Sighs.*] I don't know.

[*Silence.*]

BILL: [*Holding a party favor.*] Remember those surprise balls we used to get at parties when we were kids? Those endless ribbons of crepe paper rolled up with little metal toys inside?

SANDY: He has such a temper.

BILL: It's funny, you never see them around any more. [*Pause.*] We had some birthday parties in those days! One birthday I'll never forget, and that was my eleventh! *Shit, what a party!*

SANDY: My eighth was the best. I invited the entire class. It was on a Saturday afternoon and we strung white streamers from one end of the dining room to the other.

BILL: My mother let me invite the whole class. Thirty-three kids came!

SANDY: All the girls got pincushions for favors, and the boys got yo-yos that glowed in the dark. And instead of having cake and ice cream, my mother made this incredible baked Alaska.

BILL: We decorated the whole place in red: red streamers, red balloons, red tablecloth...

SANDY: When she brought it to the table, everyone gasped. It was three feet high and covered with peaks of egg white.

BILL: Shit, everything was red! My mother even put red food coloring into the cake.

SANDY: I can still remember the taste...like sweetened snow.

BILL: That was the birthday I got my red bike. And when we'd finished eating the red cake and red raspberry ice cream, we played games.

SANDY: I don't know where we got the room, but we actually set up twenty-seven chairs for musical chairs.

BILL: Darts, ducking for apples...

SANDY: We played it once, then twice.

BILL: Then we set up chairs and played musical chairs.

SANDY: By the fifth round we decided to alter the rules a little...

BILL: ...but after a while we changed the rules.

SANDY: When you sat down in a chair, you grabbed someone of the opposite sex and they sat in your lap.

BILL: It was getting boring with the same old rules.

SANDY: ...and then you had to...had to...

BILL: So you grabbed a girl and both sat on the chair together.

SANDY: ...you had to ...had to...

BILL: And you kissed the girl for as long as you could without coming up for air, and whoever got in a chair and kissed for the longest time played in the next round.

SANDY: We played musical chairs.

BILL: After the kissing part, we began unbuttoning the girls' blouses and putting our hands inside. [*He pulls* SANDY *onto his lap.*]

SANDY: We played it once, twice, then three times.

BILL: [*Nuzzling her.*] ...and feeling what there was to feel. Oh, it was nice, it was very nice.

SANDY: By the fifth round we decided to alter the rules a little.

BILL: [*His hands in her robe.*] And each time the music stopped, you grabbed another girl and reached down into another blouse...

SANDY: When you sat down in a chair, you grabbed someone of the opposite sex and he sat in your lap.

BILL: After a while we forgot all about the musical part of the game and everyone was just lying all over the chairs, kissing and feeling up.

SANDY: I don't know why the grownups didn't...

BILL: [*Caressing* SANDY.] Some of us even got our pants off.

SANDY: [*Laughing.*] *Bill!*

BILL: [*More and more amorous.*] ...and we pulled down the shades...

SANDY: Someone might come in...

BILL: Tommy Hartland and I got five girls under the table.

SANDY: [*Resisting.*] Oh, Bill.

BILL: But by the time we got our jockies off, the girls panicked and were back in the game with someone else, and there were Tommy Hartland and I, horny as hell, surrounded by all these goddamned red streamers and strawberry gumdrops.

SANDY: I remember, my mother made this baked Alaska. It was covered with egg whites...

BILL: Come on, give us a kiss.

SANDY: Don't, Nicky might come in...

BILL: Nicky's not coming in, just relax.

SANDY: Please, Bill, not now, I just can't...Nicky...

[*They struggle.* NICKY *bursts into the room, dressed up in* SANDY's *underwear. A slip trails off his shoulders, a bra is draped around his waist, a stocking hangs from his neck He's stricken with jealousy and confusion on seeing them so intimately involved.*]

[*Simultaneously.*]

NICKY: *Mommy!*

SANDY: [*Flying off* BILL's *lap.*] *Nicky!*

BILL: *You little prick!*

NICKY: *I want grape juice!*

BILL: *What in hell are you doing in your mother's underwear?*

SANDY: That's a seventy-five dollar bra you've got wrapped around your waist.

BILL: Boy, I never even *dreamed* of going through my mother's underwear!

NICKY: *I want grape juice! I want grape juice!*

SANDY: I just don't...

BILL: That child should be punished.

NICKY: [*Louder still.*] *And I...want...ice...in...my...grape...juice!*

BILL: Well, you can't have ice in your grape juice, you little—

SANDY: [*Shoving a glass of grape juice at* NICKY.] Here's your damned grape juice, without ice...nice and *warm!*

NICKY: [*Hurling the glass to the floor.*] Then I won't drink it!

SANDY: [*Rushing to her broom.*] *Look out, broken glass!*

BILL: Did you see what he just did? He deliberately threw his glass on the floor!

NICKY: [*Lunging headlong into the glass.*] *I want to make my birthday wish! I want to make my birthday wish!*

BILL: [*Pulling him back.*] *Mommy said look out!*

NICKY: [*Starting to cry.*] Daddy hurt me, Daddy hurt me.

SANDY: [*Sweeping.*] It's all over the floor. Don't anybody go near there until I get it cleaned up!

BILL: I didn't hurt him, for Chrissake, I was just trying to get him away from the glass before he cut himself.

NICKY: *You did so hurt me, you stupid idiot!* [*Kicks* BILL *in the shins.*]

BILL: [*Shaking* NICKY *with each word.*] *Don't...you...ever... hit...your...father!*

[NICKY *wails.*]

Did you see that? Your son just kicked me in the shin. [*Examines the wound.*]

SANDY: [*Sweeping.*] If you ever deliberately break a glass like that again...

BILL: He broke the skin...

SANDY: I've had enough. Take him up to his room, there'll be no party!

BILL: My own son drew blood.

SANDY: I'll phone Jeffrey and Mia and tell them to forget the whole thing.

BILL: You'd better get the peroxide to sterilize it with.

[NICKY *lies down in his wagon and makes his strangled sound.*]

SANDY: Come on, Bill, take him up to his room. We're calling the party off.

NICKY: But what about my cake?

SANDY: No birthday party for Nicky this year.

NICKY: ...and the candles?

BILL: You can spend the rest of the day up in your room.

NICKY: What about my wish? [*Starts to cry.*]

SANDY: The child must be punished.

BILL: It's your own fault, Nicky, we gave you every chance.

NICKY: You mean I won't have any party at all?

SANDY: We warned you.

BILL: It hurts us more than it does you.

SANDY: *You've got to learn some time, Nicholas!*

BILL: Maybe next year you'll be a better boy.

SANDY: *I asked you to wait and open your presents after the cards!*

NICKY: No party? No wish?

BILL: We certainly don't enjoy doing this, Nicky.

SANDY: No party, and that's that.

[*Crying,* NICKY *runs out of the room.*]

I'm sorry, Nicky.

BILL: We gave you every chance.

SANDY: We gave him every chance.

[*Curtain.*]

ACT II

Around 6:30 that evening. SANDY, BILL, *and* NICKY *sit around the birthday table all dressed up in party clothes. They wear little paper hats, and are blowing noisemakers and making barnyard sounds.* SANDY *clucks like a chicken;* BILL *howls like a coyote;* NICKY *grunts and oinks.*

BILL: *One, two, three—change!*

[SANDY *meows;* BILL *grunts like a gorilla;* NICKY *barks.*]

One, two, three—change!

[SANDY *whinnies;* BILL *whistles like a thrush;* NICKY *bleats like a goat.*]

One, two, three—change!

[SANDY *clucks like a chicken,* NICKY *hoots like an owl.*]

Stop! Mommy's out of the game! She already clucked before!

[BILL *roars like a lion;* NICKY *makes fish noises and faces.*]

[*Faster.*] *One, two, three—change!*

[BILL *hissses like a snake;* NICKY *gobbles like a turkey.*]

One, two, three—change!

[BILL *grunts like a gorilla;* NICKY *squeaks like a mouse.*]

Stop the game! Daddy already made gorilla grunts before, Nicky wins!

BILL and **SANDY:** [*Applauding and whistling.*] Yea, Nicky, yea, Nicky!

NICKY: Let's play again.

SANDY: [*Laughing.*] You're too good for us.

NICKY: Let's play again.

SANDY: They should be here any time now.

BILL: Is everybody ready for one hell of a party?

SANDY: The movie's all developed?

BILL: The movie's developed and ready to roll!

SANDY: Oh, Nicky, I can hardly wait!

BILL: They will eat their hearts out when they see this film!

SANDY: The whole day would be perfect if only Jeffrey and Mia changed their minds about having children. Tonight, with us.

BILL: I've always admired Jeffrey as a photographer, but frankly I think he overrates himself.

[NICKY *runs around the room making animal sounds.*]

SANDY: They have exciting careers now, but what about when they're sixty and retired and all alone in the world.

BILL: Just because he does a lot of traveling he fancies himself a professional photographer!

NICKY: [*Braying in their ears.*] Let's play again.

SANDY: If she waits too long, it will be too late. Remember Diane Oak? Diane Oak waited until she was forty-five before she had Jonathan, and by then her cervix had shriveled up and wouldn't even open for the birth.

NICKY: What's a cervix?

SANDY: She passed her ninth month, tenth, eleventh, twelfth...nothing happened. Finally they had to induce her in her fifteenth.

NICKY: What's a cervix?

SANDY: When that poor baby was finally pulled out by Cesarean section, he weighed thirty-six pounds and had a full set of teeth.

NICKY: What's a cervix?

BILL: It's a part of a lady.

NICKY: What part?

SANDY: The part the baby comes out of, sweetheart.

BILL: [*Whispering.*] The hole.

NICKY: The poopie hole?

BILL: Not the poopie hole! The baby hole!

NICKY: Where's the baby hole?

[BILL *indicates on himself where it is.*]

SANDY: I certainly wouldn't want Mia to go through what Diane Oak did. All her female plumbing was ripped to shreds by that child.

BILL: Babies come out of the baby hole, and poopie comes out of the poopie hole.

SANDY: Of course they could always adopt, but it just isn't the same.

NICKY: Where's the poopie hole?

[BILL *indicates on himself where it is.*]

SANDY: How she and Jeffrey can call themselves authorities on children when they've never had one of their own...

NICKY: Does Mia have a baby hole?

SANDY: She's never felt life moving inside her. It's sad.

BILL: Of course Mia has a baby hole. All women have baby holes.

NICKY: Then why doesn't a baby come out of it?

SANDY: Of course we don't get to travel like they do, we don't have their kind of freedom...

NICKY: Why doesn't a baby come out of Mia's baby hole?

SANDY: ...and we don't speak all the languages they do.

BILL: Maybe there is one in there, but he's stuck.

NICKY: [*Laughing.*] Stuck in with the poopie.

SANDY: They get out more than we do.

NICKY: [*Laughing.*] How does a lady tell whether she's going to have a baby or a poopie?

SANDY: Of course Mia looks younger than me...

BILL: Because if it's a baby inside her, her tummy swells up, and if it's a poopie inside her...

SANDY: She's missing the most basic experience a woman can have, and when you come right down to it, all she's left with are memories of other people's children.

NICKY: Why doesn't a baby come out of Mia's baby hole?

SANDY: Tape recordings and photographs of strangers...

BILL: Because she doesn't want it to.

SANDY: Slides of foreign urchins eating raw elephant meat. I feel sorry for her.

BILL: We all have different needs.

SANDY: [*Getting louder.*] It's pathetic. Trying to have her own family through other people's children, and not even American children but poor starving—

[*The doorbell rings.*]

BILL and SANDY: They're here.

SANDY: [*Whispering.*] Oh, God, they heard us!

BILL: [*Whispering.*] Don't be silly, they couldn't possibly have heard us.

SANDY: [*Head in hands.*] They heard us.

BILL: [*Going to the door.*] They didn't hear us.

SANDY: They heard us.

NICKY: *Heard what?*

SANDY: *Sssssshhhhhhhh!*

[BILL *opens the door;* MIA *and* JEFFREY *enter, out of breath.* JEFFREY *is professorial,* MIA *is a fragile beauty.*]

[*Simultaneously.*]

JEFFREY: [*Shaking hands with* BILL.] I'm sorry we're so late. Mia was delivering a paper at an anthropology convention and got tied up with a lot of questions at the end. [*Kissing* SANDY.] Sandy, I'm sorry. [*Sets down a slide projector and several boxes of slides.*]

MIA: [*Kissing* BILL.] Bill, forgive us. I was giving a paper at a convention and some visiting professors from Manila had all these questions...[*Kissing* SANDY.] Sandy, we finally made it!

SANDY: [*Kissing both* JEFFREY *and* MIA.] Jeffrey! Mia! It's so good to see you. Come in, please…

BILL: [*Slapping* JEFFREY *on the back.*] We were beginning to worry about you. Come in…

[*Simultaneously.*]

BILL: [*Kissing* MIA.] Mia, you look beautiful, as always. Come in!

MIA: [*Kissing* NICKY.] Nicky, four years old!

JEFFREY: [*Shaking hands with* NICKY.] Happy birthday, Nicky.

NICKY: I'm four today. Four!

BILL: [*Leading them into the room.*] Come on in.

SANDY: We were beginning to worry…

[*Pause.*]

MIA: Oh, Sandy, look at what you've done!

[*Simultaneously.*]

BILL: Well, folks, everybody ready for a great party?

SANDY: Nicky's been so excited…

MIA: *Jeffrey, look what they've done!*

[*Embarrassed laughter, pause.*]

[*Simultaneously.*]

BILL: *There's nothing like a kid's fourth birthday!*

MIA: We'll give Nicky his present at the table with the cake and ice cream.

[*They laugh, a pause.*]

[*Simultaneously.*]

SANDY: It just wouldn't have been a real celebration without you!

NICKY: I got a wagon and masks.

BILL: …and wait till you see the movie we made…

[*They laugh, a pause.*]

JEFFREY: When the Tunisian hill child turns four, he's

blindfolded and led into a swamp to bring back the body of a mud turtle for a tribal feast.

SANDY: How fascinating.

MIA: If he fails, he's expelled from the tribe.

JEFFREY: ...and left on the plains to be picked apart by giant caw-caws.

SANDY: How horrifying!

[*Pause.*]

MIA: In the Tabu culture, four is believed to be a magical age. I once saw a four-year-old Tabu girl skin a sixteen-hundred-pound zebra and then eat the pelt!

BILL: Son of a bitch!

NICKY: I can write my name.

MIA: How wonderful.

JEFFREY: I saw the same child nurse a dead goat back to life.

BILL: Jesus!

JEFFREY: With her own milk!

NICKY: I pulled Mommy in my wagon.

MIA: How wonderful.

SANDY: Come, let's sit down around the table.

MIA: [*Sitting.*] Sandy, everything is just...beautiful!

JEFFREY: [*Sitting.*] It's really amazing what you can do to a room with a little imagination and some crepe paper.

NICKY: [*To* MIA.] Do you have a baby hole?

SANDY: *Nicky!*

BILL: Nicky and I made a great movie this morning, didn't we, Nick?

NICKY: Daddy and I made a movie.

MIA: How wonderful.

SANDY: Bill and Nicky are very close. They've always been close.

Ever since Nicky was born they were close.

NICKY: [*To* MIA.] Do you have a baby hole?

SANDY: [*Fast.*] It's really quite unusual to find a father and son that are as close as Bill and Nicky.

BILL: I wasn't at all close to my father.

SANDY: I was very close to my father.

MIA: I was close to my mother.

SANDY: I hated my mother.

BILL: I don't remember my mother.

JEFFREY: My mother and father were very close.

BILL: That's interesting, because my mother and father weren't close at all.

[*Silence.*]

MIA: Sandy, this room is a work of art! I've never seen anything like it.

SANDY: Well, how often does your favorite son turn four?

NICKY: I got a lot of presents.

MIA: You must have been up all night.

NICKY: I got a wagon.

MIA: I'll bet you did!

SANDY: ...*and* birthday cards. Nicky got twenty-seven birthday cards this year, including one from Mrs. Tanner, his nursery school teacher. And they have a strict policy of not sending out individual cards on the children's birthdays. You know, they might forget somebody. So naturally Nicky was thrilled...I mean, to be singled out like that...[*Hands* MIA *the card.*]

MIA: [*Reading.*] "Happy birthday, Nicky. Sincerely, Mrs. Tanner."

SANDY: [*To* NICKY.] Mrs. Tanner sent that especially to you, breaking all the school rules!

MIA: [*Examining the card.*] That's funny, this looks like your handwriting.

SANDY: So, cousins, how long will you be with us before you disappear over the horizon again on the back of some camel?

MIA: Her Y's and N's are exactly like yours.

SANDY: [*Snatching the card away.*] People will start thinking you don't like American children, the way you're always running off to interview toddlers in Iceland and Nigeria.

NICKY: I pulled Mommy in my wagon.

BILL: He's very strong for his age.

JEFFREY: One of the interesting things about the Berbers is that parents regard spiritual strength much more highly than physical strength.

NICKY: I pulled Mommy and all my presents too!

MIA: Almost any Berber child can converse with desert vegetation.

SANDY: Really?

JEFFREY: To my mind, there are no children the equal of Berber children!

NICKY: I got instruments for my birthday.

MIA: That's wonderful, Nicky.

SANDY: I know we spoil him, but we just can't help it.

BILL: We spoil the living crap out of that kid and we love every minute of it, right, Nick?

NICKY: Daddy made a movie of me.

SANDY: Bill and Nicky are very close.

NICKY: [*Putting on a mask.*] I got masks for my birthday.

SANDY: Nicky and his masks…

BILL: Give that kid a mask, any kind of mask, and he's in seventh heaven!

MIA: We've always been fascinated by masks and the whole phenomenon of taking on the identity of someone else.

[NICKY *runs around the room, grunting.*]

JEFFREY: Remember those animal-head masks we were given in New Guinea?

SANDY: He gets so excited on his birthday.

BILL: He's been up since six this morning.

JEFFREY: Mia and I were given animal-head masks in New Guinea that were made out of a paste of dried insects.

MIA: You had the feeling that if you left one on too long, your face would slowly blend right into the mask and lose all human features.

SANDY: Uuuuuugh.

BILL: Nicky has an unusually vivid imagination.

SANDY: You should hear his dreams...

BILL: All about man-eating chairs and flying dogs.

SANDY: Really wild!

[NICKY *makes more and more noise running around the room grunting.*]

All right, Nicky, that's enough!

BILL: Come on, Nick, quiet down.

SANDY: He's been up since five-thirty this morning.

BILL: [*Chasing* NICKY.] Okay, Nicky, let's take off the mask and calm down.

NICKY: *I don't want to take off my mask!*

BILL: [*Wresting it away after finally catching him.*] You're being too wild!

NICKY: [*Wailing.*] I want my mask, I want my mask!

SANDY: Let him keep his mask on. Poor thing, he's exhausted. He was up at four-thirty this morning.

BILL: Okay, okay, you can have your mask back, but no more being wild...*understand?*

[NICKY *puts the mask back on, sits in his chair, and sucks his thumb through the mask. Silence.*]

[*Whispering.*] Take your thumb out of your mask.

[NICKY *doesn't.*]

SANDY: It's the strangest thing, but ever since I got up this morning I've been smelling the sea. [*Runs her hands through her hair; a shower of sand falls out.*]

[*Silence.*]

BILL: Tell us again, just how many languages can the two of you speak?

[*Simultaneously.*]

JEFFREY: Seventeen.

MIA: Thirteen.

SANDY: *Jeffrey and Mia can speak fifteen languages, Nicky.*

BILL: My maternal grandmother was Canadian and always spoke French around the house.

SANDY: My maternal grandmother was Dutch.

BILL: But us kids never learned it.

JEFFREY: Canadian French isn't considered a pure language, it's a dilution...

SANDY: I'm part Dutch on one side and Swedish on the other.

BILL: I'm pure Canadian and a little Irish.

NICKY: What am I?

BILL: No, wait, I forgot, I have some Greek blood in me too.

SANDY: Oh, Mia, say a few words in something for Nicky.

NICKY: What am I?

SANDY: Mia's going to say something in a funny language, honey.

NICKY: What am *I*?

BILL: [*Angry.*] *Canadian, Dutch, Swedish, and a little Greek!*
[*Silence.*]

MIA: Talla zoo zoo feeple zip.

NICKY: [*Laughing.*] What did you say?

SANDY: [*Laughing.*] Isn't it a riot?

BILL: [*Laughing.*] Jesus Christ!

NICKY: What did you say?

MIA: *Happy birthday!*

NICKY: Say something else.

SANDY: Oh, say more!

MIA: Dun herp zala zala cree droop soy nitch.

SANDY: [*Roaring with laughter.*] Stop, stop!

NICKY: Say it again, say it again!

BILL: Oh, God!

MIA: Dun herp zala zala cree droop soy nitch.

BILL: [*Laughing.*] What...what was it?

MIA: *Merry Christmas!*

[SANDY, BILL, *and* NICKY *howl with laughter.*]

SANDY: That was Merry Christmas?

NICKY: Say, "Nicky is four years old today."

MIA: Ooola oola zim dam zilco reet treet comp *graaaaa, Nicky!*
[*All laugh.*]

SANDY and NICKY: Again, again!

MIA and JEFFREY: Ooola oola zim dam zilco reet treet comp *graaaaa, Nicky!*

[*All laugh.*]

BILL: [*To* NICKY.] How would you like to be able to speak like that?

NICKY: [*Gravely.*] Lim biddle ree yok slow iffle snee buddle twee rat ith twank.

MIA: Nice...very nice.

BILL and SANDY: [*Laughing.*] Oh, Nicky, Nicky.

SANDY: We always have such a good time when you two come over!

MIA: We wouldn't miss Nicky's birthday for the world.

SANDY: Who else has cousins that speak fifteen languages?

BILL: Hey, I haven't told Jeffrey and Mia about Charley E.Z. yet, this crazy guy that works in our office.

SANDY: Oh, Bill...

BILL: Did I tell you about Charley E.Z.?

SANDY: He made the whole thing up.

BILL: There's a shakedown going on at the office, and several of the top-level guys are being let go. And the things they do to try and hang on. Unbelievable. I guess something comes over a guy when he feels his job threatened...

SANDY: Bill, really, I...

BILL: There's this guy Charles E. Zinn—Charley E.Z., we call him. He's a junior officer who recently lost an important account, so word came down that Charley E.Z. was going to be axed.

JEFFREY: I don't think I've ever heard you mention a Charley E.Z. before.

SANDY: He made it all up.

BILL: He'd been getting these letters accusing him of "professional inconsistency." Have you ever heard such a phrase—"professional inconsistency"?

MIA: [*Laughing.*] I have a feeling this is going to be another of Bill's wild stories.

BILL: So the word came down that Charley E.Z. was going to lose his job.

JEFFREY: Oh, no!

MIA: How awful!

JEFFREY: Poor guy.

BILL: So Charley E.Z. took action. And where did he take action? In the elevator! [*Lowering his voice.*] For the past few months between three and four in the afternoon Charley has been getting into the elevator and taking off his clothes, starting with his jacket, shirt, then pants, socks, shoes, and underwear. But the first time he did it, it was cold turkey.

[NICKY *pantomimes the action as* BILL *tells the story. He takes off his clothes except his underwear and stands in the closet facing the audience. At the appropriate moment, he opens the door as if he were in an elevator.*]

He changed in the executive men's room, stuffed all his clothes in a duffel bag, glided into the hall when no one was looking, rang for the elevator, stepped in…and began his long, lonely, naked journey.

SANDY: [*Laughing.*] Oh, Bill!

BILL: You see, there's a special control panel in the elevator that lets the operator open and shut the door whenever he wants. So if Charley E.Z. is cruising around between the fourth and fifth floors, say, and someone rings on Main and the door starts to open, and Charley sees someone he doesn't know, he just zaps the close-door button, the door slams shut and Charley zooms back up, safe with his secret.

SANDY: [*Laughing, to* MIA.] Isn't he crazy?

MIA: [*Laughing.*] Completely...

BILL: *Charley's first day in the elevator:* He's in there, cold turkey, nothing on, not even a cuff link. The bell rings on five. Charley braces himself, the elevator rises, stops, the door opens and in steps this account executive. He doesn't notice anything. Charley's cool, but by the time they're between two and Main, he looks at Charley. No one says a word, Charley lets him off at Main. One minute later, he gets another call. Guess who?

ALL: The account executive!

BILL: *The account executive!* Well, for the rest of the afternoon the two of them just kept riding up and down, down and up. One of the secretaries on two said when the elevator stopped at her floor she caught a fleeting glimpse of two naked men rolling around on the floor, laughing.

MIA: Amazing...

BILL: Lately he's taken to props: disguises, musical instruments, special effects.

[NICKY *opens and shuts the closet door, wearing a variety of masks.*]

Last week he was in there with a viola and the entire accounting department.

SANDY: And they all take their clothes off?

BILL: Take them off and throw them down the elevator shaft.

SANDY: Imagine businessmen doing that!

MIA: I never realized there was such an allure for the forbidden in business.

BILL: [*Whispering.*] I've heard that next week he's hired a string trio to play Schubert in the service elevator.

SANDY: Bill took a wonderful movie of Nicky opening his presents this morning.

BILL: The point is that everybody at Continental Allied loves

Charley E.Z. now. The letters about "professional inconsistency" have stopped coming...and he's doing just great.

[*Silence.*]

MIA: Don't you think it's time we gave Nicky his present, Jeffrey?

NICKY: [*Opening the door.*] Up, please. Elevator going up. Please move to the rear of the car to make room for the people getting on. [*Slams the door.*]

SANDY: [*Knocking on the door.*] Jeffrey and Mia want to give you your present now, honey.

JEFFREY: [*Puttering with his slides and projector.*] Nicholas, you've never gotten a present like this!

SANDY: Presents!

MIA: [*Helping* JEFFREY.] I just hope he likes it, you never know with children. But we put a great deal of thought into it.

SANDY: Nicky...

NICKY: [*Opening the door.*] Main floor, everybody off. [*Slamming the door.*]

SANDY: [*Lowering her voice.*] Please, Nicky, you're embarrassing us.

JEFFREY: You've got a movie screen somewhere, don't you?

BILL: [*Turns on a light, revealing an area set up with a screen, movie projector, tables, ashtrays.*] Say no more.

JEFFREY: Great! [*Pulls out the screen and sets it up.*]

SANDY: It's the strangest thing, but one of my front teeth is loose. People don't lose their front teeth, do they?

MIA: The Qua tribe starts out with all their permanent teeth and then at the age of sixteen every one falls out to be replaced with an entire new set of baby teeth. It's a complete mystery to dental science.

SANDY: How disgusting.

MIA: We were taping interviews with Qua mothers a few months ago. Wonderful people: highly resourceful. They used to prepare these aromatic banquets for us out of tree bark.

SANDY: Uuuuugh! I could never eat that native food. It always looks like human excrement.

MIA: Qua *women* have no teeth at all.

JEFFREY: They eat by grinding their food into a paste between large stones and then lapping it up.

SANDY: Uuuuuuugh!

JEFFREY: Okay, folks, we're ready to go. Get Nicky, his present is all set.

SANDY: He's always so thrilled to see you!

BILL: *Come out, come out, wherever you are!*

SANDY: Family means so much to him.

JEFFREY: [*Switching off the lights.*] The show is about to begin.

SANDY: Oooooh, Nicky, I wonder what it is!

BILL: [*Opening the door.*] *Nicholas, will you get the hell out of there!*

SANDY: You're being very rude, Nicky, Mommy isn't going to forget this.

BILL: [*Dragging* NICKY *out of the closet, now dressed.*] *Now come over here and sit down!*

[BILL *sits* NICKY *down. The birthday chairs have been rearranged to face the movie screen. The grownups sit. A silence.*]

JEFFREY: [*Rises, waves his hand over the slide projector and box of slides.*] Happy birthday, Nicky.

MIA: Happy birthday.

NICKY: What is it?

JEFFREY: Your own projector with slides of children from all over the world.

[*He starts showing slides of children in native dress doing all kinds of remarkable things. Every few seconds a new picture is flashed on the screen.*]

SANDY: Ooooooooh, Nicky!

BILL: What a present!

SANDY: Ooooooooooh, Nicky, look!

MIA: We took them all.

SANDY: They're just beautiful.

BILL: Son of a bitch!

JEFFREY: We figured this would be something he could work himself.

MIA: And learn from.

BILL: I've never seen such clarity of color. What kind of film were you using?

SANDY: And Jeffrey and Mia said you could keep them!

NICKY: Isn't there anything else?

BILL: Shit! That's color!

NICKY: ...something to unwrap?

JEFFREY: All you do is load the projector and then push this button when you want to see a new slide. Your mommy and daddy can help you with it.

NICKY: This is it?

MIA: These are some of the children we worked with last year.

SANDY: Jeffrey and Mia lead very special lives, honey, they travel all over the world studying poor children.

JEFFREY: Oh, look! The Io children. They decorate their faces with an iridescent paint made out of powdered giraffe hooves.

MIA: It's very bad for their skin, actually.

SANDY: I can imagine.

MIA: They're wonderful children. Highly motivated. Jeffrey and I got very close to them.

NICKY: I wish I could meet them.

MIA: Well, maybe someday, Nicky.

NICKY: I wish I could play with them. I don't have anybody to play with.

SANDY: That isn't true. You have Daddy and me to play with, and you go to nursery school three mornings a week.

JEFFREY: Actually, these slides don't represent the most amazing part of our trip last year...

NICKY: I don't have anybody to play with.

JEFFREY: ...our penetration into the Bush.

SANDY: I didn't know you were allowed.

NICKY: I wish those children could come to my house.

JEFFREY: We penetrated the Bush and saw things no human being has ever seen.

NICKY: Nobody plays with me.

SANDY: Oh, tell us everything!

JEFFREY: [*Turning off the projector.*] We encountered a civilization untouched by the Industrial Revolution. People living in the Stone Age.

[*The lights go dim and eerie.*]

SANDY: Ooooooooh, cave men.

JEFFREY: There are a Bush people called the Whan See who are still arboreal.

[SANDY *gasps.*]

BILL: Jeeeez.

NICKY: I'm lonely.

BILL: Ssssssh!

JEFFREY: They live in trees and never come down to the ground.

MIA: What was so remarkable about them was they were obviously Homo sapiens and not simian, yet they had this one extraordinary feature...

[SANDY *screams.*]

BILL: Christ, I hope you had your camera with you.

MIA: ...a freakish biological throwback.

JEFFREY: Each and every one of them had a tail!

[SANDY, BILL, *and* NICKY *gasp.*]

MIA: We couldn't believe our eyes the first time we saw them swinging through the trees. We'd been cutting our way through deep brush when we suddenly heard this chattering above us. It sounded like children giggling. We looked up. And there were these...people... swinging through the branches by their tails.

JEFFREY: Small boned with delicate features...

MIA: ...and covered with this silvery down that glittered so brightly we had to shade our eyes.

[SANDY, BILL, *and* NICKY *gasp.*]

BILL: *Did you get any pictures?*

MIA: And they had the most musical way of speaking...a kind of sighing almost.

[NICKY *picks up a cello and begins playing a Bach unaccompanied cello suite.*]

JEFFREY: We were afraid they'd run away when they saw us, but they didn't. They just became very still and stared down at us.

MIA: I had no idea Nicky could play the cello so well.

SANDY: Oh, yes, Nicky's always been musical.

JEFFREY: Because they exuded such docility, I reached up my hand to one and said, "We're American anthropologists, we come in peace."

SANDY: What a perfect thing to say!

BILL: Beautiful...beautiful.

JEFFREY: They became very excited and all started talking at once.

BILL: At least you had a tape recorder on you.

MIA: I've never seen such eyes...a kind of creamy pink...like looking into a strawberry parfait.

SANDY: Weren't you scared?

JEFFREY: You see, we, without tails and wearing clothes, were just as strange to their eyes. After Jeffrey spoke, I said a few words, and then our guide gave them chewing gum.

MIA: Then as a body, they furled and unfurled their long silvery tails and chanted, "Whan See." So we chanted it back.

JEFFREY and MIA: [Chanting.] Whan See, Whan See, Whan See...

JEFFREY: Then one of them motioned that we should join them. So we climbed a nearby tree, and they gingerly approached us, touching our hair and skin.

SANDY: I would have died!

MIA: They were an exceedingly gentle people who had no words in their vocabulary for hate, war or anger.

JEFFREY: We spent an entire week with them.

MIA: It's amazing how fast you can adjust to living in a tree.

SANDY: I would have died...

JEFFREY: And not once in all that time did we ever see one of them drop down to the ground, even though they could stand erect, run, and even dance on their hind legs.

MIA: *You should have seen them dance!* They'd wrap their tails around a branch and start rocking back and forth, swaying higher and higher, then they'd suddenly let go and spin off through the trees like meteors...

JEFFREY: While the older members of the tribe banged on drums made of hollow tree stumps.

MIA: Our last day there they asked us to join them, and the leader gripped me around the waist with his tail and started whirling me through the air. Everything was spinning and pulsating. There was this strong smell about him...cinnamon ... cinnamon dust sprinkled through his fur...he spun me higher and higher and then suddenly...let go. We went flying through the air...his arms holding me close...oh...it was...just...everything rushing by...the sun on my face...that fragrance of cinnamon...

BILL: Jesus...

SANDY: Oh, Mia...

JEFFREY: Other tribes in the Bush have repeatedly tried to capture the Whan See because of their great beauty and grace, but once a Whan See touches ground, they die. Something happens to their center of gravity, their balance goes haywire.

SANDY: [*Covering her ears.*] I can't listen...

BILL: Think of the shots you could have gotten with a Leica!

JEFFREY: In spite of their ignorance of science and technology, they displayed incredible artistic sophistication. They did these bark carvings with their teeth that were absolutely stunning!

MIA: It was a form of relaxation. They'd sit in the shade, tearing out the most intricate designs...

JEFFREY: Their virtuosity was astonishing. On the one hand, they did representational carvings depicting familiar Bush objects, but then they also did these highly abstract designs that resembled some ancient calligraphy.

MIA: And of course that constant gnawing on tree bark provided them with excellent dental hygiene.

SANDY: I've never heard anything like this.

JEFFREY: They also did exquisite lacework, tearing into large pawpaw leaves.

SANDY: You should write a book.

BILL: *Christ, I hope you got some pictures out of it!*

MIA: The whole thing was like a dream…except…

JEFFREY: Except…

SANDY: Oh, no, they do something awful you haven't told us.

MIA: We didn't find out about it until our last night, otherwise we'd still be there.

JEFFREY: Neither of us wanted to leave. We'd have given up everything to stay with them.

MIA: Our careers, our fieldwork, our publications…

JEFFREY: Sometimes at night we'd watch them make love, their silvery bodies radiating a kind of shimmering electricity. And everybody would watch: children, parents, grandparents…

MIA: But that last evening we saw a flaw…

JEFFREY: …the stye…

MIA: …the moral defect.

SANDY: No!

BILL: *They eat their young!*

[SANDY *screams.*]

I knew it.

SANDY: [*Covering her ears.*] Don't.

MIA: Our last evening there a young girl went into childbirth.

SANDY: Oh, no.

MIA: As usual, everyone gathered around to watch, since they had no awareness of modesty or privacy.

JEFFREY: No one doctor or midwife was in charge—the delivery was the responsibility of all the women of the tribe.

MIA: As the girl was in the final throes of labor, the older women reached out their hands to help her…

SANDY: I can't bear it, it will be awful!

MIA: Finally her moment came, the head appeared. She gave a shrill yelp of pain and joy…

[SANDY *gasps.*]

…and the baby was born…

SANDY: Oooooooh.

MIA: But the very instant it emerged, they lifted the tiny creature up and…and…

SANDY: [*Hands flying to her heart.*] No!

MIA: It's too awful.

BILL: *One of the elders popped it into his mouth!*

[SANDY *screams.*]

MIA: They lifted the tiny creature up and reinserted it back into its mother's womb.

SANDY and BILL: But that's impossible.

MIA: [*Upset.*] And they did it again and again and again and again…

BILL: Son of a…

MIA: And the mother kept urging them on. As soon as the baby came out, she'd motion them to…stuff him back in. It was obviously some ritual, there was some minimal number of reinsertions a mother had to withstand.

SANDY: I don't believe it!

BILL: Now, that's one thing I'd have to see with my own eyes…

SANDY: It's barbaric…unnatural.

BILL: Did. You. Get. Any. Shots?

JEFFREY: Only the strongest survive.

BILL: If you got any pictures at all, you could sell them to one of the national magazines and make a bundle.

SANDY: But why? Why did she do it?

JEFFREY: You have to remember, these were a highly primitive people who took things literally. When a civilized woman has a baby, she too is possessive, only in more subtle ways. She's possessive of her birth experience and delights in retelling it. She's possessive of her baby and tries to keep him helpless for as long as possible. Well, these Stone Age women were just acting out those same impulses by forcing the baby back into its mother's womb. Through fetal insertion, you see, the primitive mother could experience her moment of motherhood over and over again.

MIA: After the fourth insertion, her uterus went into profound shock. And how that baby squealed. It wasn't human after a while, but mangled…and drenched…like some rodent…some furry little…hamster.

SANDY: I'm going to be sick.

JEFFREY: [*Puttering with the slides, holding them up to the light.*] I've got to go through these and make sure I leave Nicky the right ones. Let's see—oh, yes, Caracas! What's this one of Nepal doing in here?

MIA: After a while they motioned me to join them, they pulled me over to where she lay.

SANDY: I wish you'd stop this.

MIA: It was such a beautiful night, the air was so warm…I didn't understand what they wanted me to do at first, so I just stood there.

SANDY: I haven't been feeling well today. When I looked in the mirror this morning, I saw an old woman.

MIA: Then someone gripped my hand, guiding it towards the girl's birth canal. I felt something warm and moist. I looked down, I was holding the baby's head. Such a tiny head, about the size of a softball and covered with that same silvery fur, except it was wet and matted down. It was so slippery I was afraid I'd drop it, but then this hand closed over mine and brought the baby up against his mother's birth canal, which opened again, receiving him...

SANDY: I've been smelling the sea ever since I got up...

MIA: Her body convulsed, the baby came out again and again: five, six, seven times...

SANDY: My front teeth feel loose...

MIA: After a while I noticed that I was doing it by myself, no one was holding my hands, *I* was inserting the baby...

SANDY: I feel so tired all the time.

MIA: You know what it felt like? Stuffing a turkey. Stuffing a fifty-pound turkey with some little...hamster.

SANDY: Nicky...oh, my Nicky...

MIA: And there was this overpowering cinnamon smell. I started laughing.

SANDY: Nicky is four today. My son is four years old.

MIA: ...and then everyone started laughing, with those light sighing voices. The women wrapped their arms around each other, threw back their heads and laughed.

SANDY: Oh, Mia! *You* should have a baby. It's so wonderful!

MIA: This great swell of musical sound rose up as the young mother stiffened and screamed, experiencing birth again and again.

SANDY: It couldn't have happened.

MIA: The baby died.

SANDY: Not even a Stone Age woman can withstand the abnormal.

MIA: The baby died.

SANDY: [*Whispering.*] You're afraid.

MIA: It died in my hands.

SANDY: You're afraid to have a baby.

MIA: It just stopped moving and went all stiff.

SANDY: You're afraid something will be wrong.

MIA: The mother didn't realize.

SANDY: We're all afraid...but...it...isn't...like...that...

MIA: I was responsible and it died. [*She starts to cry.*]

[NICKY *stops playing and puts his cello away.*]

SANDY: Of course there *are* sacrifices...

MIA: [*Rocking back and forth.*] She'd fainted, and when she came to, she bared her breast to him and cupped his tiny head in her hand...but he didn't move...

SANDY: There are sacrifices.

BILL: There are sacrifices.

SANDY: For the first few years you'd have to stay home. You certainly wouldn't want to bring a newborn into the Sahara Desert or anything.

MIA: His tiny body fit into hers so perfectly.

SANDY: *There are sacrifices, but you gladly make them!*

BILL: You couldn't take an infant into some mud village with no sanitary or medical facilities.

MIA: She kept drawing his little head closer and closer...

SANDY: Your child's welfare always comes first.

BILL: It's difficult to imagine the sacrifices you have to make until you've actually had your own child.

MIA: Suddenly she sensed something was wrong. She looked up into the semicircle of women and searched their faces.

SANDY: You'd have to forget about your career for six or seven years, maybe even longer.

BILL: There'd be great resentment on your child's part if you left him to visit other children.

SANDY: Strangers, people you don't even know.

BILL: It's perfectly understandable.

SANDY: I wouldn't trade motherhood for anything in the world!

BILL: Sandy and Nicky are very close.

SANDY: Of course you could always adopt, but it just isn't the same as having your own.

MIA: She lifted the baby off her breast and held him tightly in her hands.

SANDY: [*Leads* MIA *to the center of the room, eases her down to the floor.*] It isn't like that.

BILL: Sandy and Nicky are very close.

MIA: Nothing happened, he didn't move. She breathed into his mouth. She slapped his face. She pulled at the down on his arms. She dug at his closed eyes with sticks, but...*nothing happened...*

SANDY: [*Easing* MIA *on her back.*] It isn't like that...

MIA: *No life. Anywhere...*She understood at last and screamed this scream...

SANDY: I knew it would happen tonight. I told Bill you'd change your mind, that you'd want your own...

MIA: Then in one awful moment, she hugged him close, stood up and jumped...

BILL: [*Crouching next to* SANDY *and* MIA.] You can't really know about children until you've had your own.

MIA: Down they plunged and were lost in the night.

SANDY: It isn't like that. It just isn't like that. You'll see, Mia...

BILL: Sandy and Nicky are very close.

SANDY: Just relax and breathe. In...and out...In and out...In and out...

BILL: [*Attends* MIA *as a doctor, checking her vital signs.*] Her pulse is racing.

SANDY: Breathe with the contraction, then exhale. In and out...In and out...

MIA: ...lost in the night.

BILL: [*Breathes with* SANDY.] In...and out...In...and out...

SANDY: Nicky, we need you too.

[NICKY *joins the charade with great concentration and flair. He takes blood pressure, administers shots, writes on charts. Their voices are disembodied, as if heard through a haze of painkillers.*]

JEFFREY: [*Engrossed with his slides throughout.*] I'd completely forgotten about the Sook! They don't bury their dead, but prop them up against trees, like decorations. [*He looks through more.*]

SANDY: We'll help you. We won't leave you.

BILL: [*Breathing loudly.*] In and out...In and out...In and out...

NICKY: Blood pressure: 150 over 277. Heart racing, irregular cardiovascular pattern.

SANDY: Don't stiffen up...relax and breathe...relax and breathe... [*Breathes with* BILL.]

JEFFREY: [*Holding up a slide.*] Lahore! Remember that afternoon we took a walk in the foothills!

SANDY: It's the most beautiful experience a woman can have.

Breathe in...and out...In and out...

[MIA *starts breathing in tempo with* SANDY.]

Good girl...That's right...Hold it...Let it out slowly...

MIA: Oh! Something's happening...

NICKY: Pulse: 60 over 80. Blood pressure: 230 over 98. She should be dilated about seven centimeters by now.

[*They all breathe faster.*]

MIA: [*Screams in pain.*] Oh!...Oh! What's happening to me? I don't want this...please...I...Oh!

JEFFREY: The Brazilian nomad has a life span of a hundred and twenty years, give or take a few.

MIA: [*Breathing.*] In and...Oh...Oh!...God! Help me!

SANDY: [*Holding her hand.*] You're doing just beautifully. The first is always the hardest.

BILL: The first is always the hardest.

NICKY: The first *is* always the hardest.

SANDY: ...but the most rewarding.

BILL: Certainly the most rewarding.

NICKY: Absolutely the most rewarding...

MIA: *I...don't...want...this!*

SANDY: Concentrate on your breathing.

MIA: Can't you do something? *Can't you stop it? God!...Oh! Stop it!*

JEFFREY: Here's the skeleton of that goat we came across in Mexico.

BILL: [*Struggling to hold her down.*] You'd better give me a hand. She's fighting.

SANDY: [*Helping* BILL.] When you feel the contraction, push. Push...Breathe...Push...Hold...Push...Breathe...Push...

Hold. It's no good, she's fighting. Nicky.

NICKY: [*Sitting on her legs.*] She's going to pass out if she keeps up like this.

SANDY: She'll have to be put to sleep.

MIA: [*Screaming.*] *Let me up...Please stop this...I want to get...Please...Oh...Oh!*

JEFFREY: [*Looking at the slide.*] Lars Kronniger!

NICKY: *If you don't cooperate with us, you'll have to be put to sleep and miss everything.*

SANDY: That's right, you'll miss everything.

BILL: You don't want to miss everything, do you?

NICKY: Her pulse is 450 over 6 and her blood pressure is 6 over 450. That can't be right!

SANDY: You've got to relax.

BILL: We'll have to put her to sleep.

SANDY: Push, hold, breathe...Push, hold, breathe...

MIA: *I...don't...please...I...Oh!...You can't do this...I...Please... Leave me alone...Oh! You can't...Oh...Ohhhh!* [*She passes out.*]

[*Simultaneously.*]

SANDY: They'd have such a beautiful child.

BILL: It's no good when you fight.

NICKY: What a shame. What a shame.

[*Pause.*]

SANDY: Well, I guess some women just...can't have children.

BILL: You can't pass a camel through the eye of a needle.

NICKY: One man's meat is another man's poison.

[*Silence.*]

SANDY: Well! What do you say we bring out Nicky's cake?!

BILL: *Let's bring out Nicky's cake!*

NICKY: [*Racing to the table.*] My cake, my cake, my cake...

BILL: [*Prods* JEFFREY *away from his slides, escorting him to his seat.*] We're bringing out the cake.

JEFFREY: [*Holding a slide up to the light as he sits down.*] You know, it's funny about these slides of the Whan See. Not one of them came out. There must have been something in the down on their bodies that set off a toxic reaction to the film I was using.

BILL: Wait 'til you see this cake!

SANDY: [*Lighting the candles on the table.*] I just love candlelight.

NICKY: I get to make my wish now.

BILL: Sandy makes one hell of a birthday cake!

NICKY: I can't wait to make my wish.

SANDY: I wish Mia would get up and join us. It just isn't a party without her.

NICKY: I want Mia at the table.

SANDY: Why won't she get up?

BILL: I don't like this.

SANDY: Oh, Bill...

NICKY: [*Rises.*] What's wrong with Mia?

[*Silence.* JEFFREY *lifts* MIA *from the floor, drags her to the table and sits her in a chair.* MIA *sits upright for several seconds and then slumps over the table. She doesn't seem dead or seriously ill, rather, there's something vaguely comical about her collapse as with* NICKY's *fit in the morning.*]

JEFFREY: It happens all the time.

[*Silence.*]

SANDY: What have I done?

NICKY: Why won't Mia sit up?

BILL: [*Patting* MIA's *face.*] Come on, Mia...wake up...

SANDY: Oh, God.

JEFFREY: It won't do any good slapping her. When she's out, she's out.

SANDY: Oh, Bill...

BILL: Wake up, Mia!

NICKY: Is she dead?

[SANDY *screams.*]

BILL: [*To* SANDY.] Maybe you should get some cold water.

SANDY: [*Leaps up, gets cold water and sprinkles it on* MIA's *face.*] Mia? Mia?

BILL: [*Lifts* MIA *up, holding her under the arms.*] Come on, let's walk her.

NICKY: She's dead. *She's dead!*

SANDY: She is not dead, she just passed out, that's all!

JEFFREY: It's pointless to do anything. She'll wake up when she's ready.

SANDY: She's not moving, Bill.

BILL: I know she's not moving. What do you think I am, blind?

SANDY: You don't have to yell!

NICKY: Mia's dead. Mia's dead!

SANDY: *Will you shut up, Nicky!*

BILL: Maybe I should lie her down on the floor again. [*He does.*]

SANDY: Oh, Mia, I'm sorry.

NICKY: *You killed her!*

BILL: We did not kill her, she just fainted.

NICKY: *You killed her, I saw you kill her!*

JEFFREY: She'll pull out of it.

SANDY: I didn't mean to hurt you.

BILL: Isn't there any kind of medication that she carries with her?

JEFFREY: [*Angry.*] I *told* you. There's *nothing* you can do. You never should have started all this in the first place!

SANDY: [*To* BILL.] Prop her up again, she's so scary this way.

BILL: [*Leaning* MIA *against a chair leg.*] There!

NICKY: You killed her.

BILL: *Stop it, Nicky, or it's back to your room!*

NICKY: How could you kill somebody on my birthday? *I* wasn't even that bad.

JEFFREY: *Leave her alone!*

SANDY: I never should have said all that about having her own baby.

NICKY: I'd never...kill anybody!

BILL: [*Raising his hand to him.*] *Nickyyyyyy!*

SANDY: I shouldn't have forced her.

BILL: You'd think she'd carry some kind of medication.

[MIA *slides down to the floor again with a thud.* SANDY *and* NICKY *scream.*]

[*Peeling back* MIA's *eyelids.*] We must have some smelling salts or something...

JEFFREY: *I said take your hands off her!*

NICKY: [*Starts to cry.*] I'm scared.

BILL: Now what do we do?

JEFFREY: We finish the party so we can go home and forget the whole thing.

BILL: Yes! Let's bring out the cake!

NICKY: I don't want any cake.

BILL: Of course you want cake, it's your birthday, isn't it? Sandy, get the cake.

SANDY: How can we eat birthday cake when she's...

BILL: *Get the cake!*

NICKY: [*Cries.*] I don't like this party any more.

[SANDY *exits to get the cake.*]

BILL: [*Moving towards* MIA.] It would be nice if she could join us.

JEFFREY: [*Out of his seat, pushing* BILL *aside.*] Don't touch her! You've done enough.

[*He lifts* MIA *back to her seat, where she slumps over the table.* SANDY *enters carrying the cake, its candles blazing.*]

BILL: Isn't that some cake? Come on...let's sing!

BILL and SANDY:
Happy birthday to you,
Happy birthday to you,
Happy birthday, dear Nicky,
Happy birthday to you!

[SANDY *sets the cake down in front of* NICKY.]

BILL: Huhhhhh, is that *some cake?* Come on, Nick, let's hear your wish.

NICKY: I...can't.

BILL: Nicky can't make his fourth-birthday wish? I don't believe it!

SANDY: Oh, Nicky!

BILL: [*Whispering.*] Come on, try.

[*Pause.*]

NICKY: [*Concentrates, takes a deep breath.*] I wish...I had a brother. [*Blows out the candles.*]

BILL: Good old Nick, you never know what he's going to say.

SANDY: My Nicky…

JEFFREY: That's quite a wish.

NICKY: I wish I had…three brothers!

SANDY: [*Laughing.*] What about poor Mommy?

NICKY: I want three brothers to play with.

JEFFREY: All children need siblings.

BILL: Boy, that's all we need, three more kids.

JEFFREY: It would do Nicky good to have siblings.

NICKY: I'm lonely.

JEFFREY: The only child is more prone towards psychosis in later years…

NICKY: [*Stamping his feet.*] *I want three brothers for my birthday!*

SANDY: He's overtired. We never should have let him come down from his room this afternoon.

BILL: *Next time you'll stay in you room!*

[MIA *slides to the floor with a thud. Grim silence.*]

NICKY: I want five brothers! No, I want eleven brothers…thirty-seven brothers…a hundred brothers…six hundred brothers! I want nine hundred brothers!

SANDY: Oh, Nicky…

NICKY: Nine hundred brothers!

SANDY: But don't we have fun together? We play Babies with the masks. We play Rabbit Says. Daddy makes movies of us.

NICKY: [*Wailing.*] I want nine hundred brothers!

SANDY: I'd like to give birth to nine hundred more babies…but I can't.

NICKY: Why not?

SANDY: I've been trying.

BILL: We've been trying a long time.

SANDY: Ever since you were born.

NICKY: I'm lonely.

SANDY: There's nothing Mommy loves more than having babies, you know that, Nicky.

BILL: We've been to special doctors.

NICKY: I want someone to play with!

SANDY: No one can seem to find any medical reason why we can't conceive again, it's just one of those...

NICKY: I want to share my room with nine hundred brothers!

SANDY: The doctor said if you try too hard the mommy's eggs won't come down right.

BILL: Don't...

SANDY: [*Teary.*] You see, every mommy has all these unborn eggs inside her and...

NICKY: I want a sister!

BILL: [*His arm around* SANDY.] Stop...

SANDY: The timing has to be just right or else the egg won't turn into a baby.

NICKY: I want sisters!

BILL: He's too young to understand.

JEFFREY: The barren woman of the Gabon Tua tribe is considered a witch.

SANDY: It's such a wonderful feeling...life...fluttering...inside you...

NICKY: I want nine hundred brothers and nine hundred sisters!

JEFFREY: The barren Tot woman is taken out and drowned!

SANDY: [*In tears.*] Sometimes I imagine I can still feel you... turning inside me...

NICKY: I'm lonely.

BILL: We haven't given up, Nicky. We're still trying!

MIA: So big and strong.

JEFFREY: [*Taking her arm.*] Mia...

SANDY: [*Burying her head in* BILL'*s chest.*] I'm going to cry.

JEFFREY: It's getting late.

NICKY: [*Struggling to hold on to* MIA.] Don't go, don't go.

JEFFREY: [*Pulling* MIA *out the door.*] Our plane leaves in six hours.

MIA: Goodbye...goodbye...

JEFFREY: We'll send stamps...lots of stamps!

[*And they're gone. Silence.*]

BILL: That son of a bitch.

SANDY: They left.

NICKY: They left.

BILL: We sat through his lousy slides, but do you think he had the courtesy to watch our movie???! [*Imitating him.*] "A tribe of psychic toddlers is waiting for us." *Jesus!*

[SANDY *sighs. Pause.*]

NICKY: *I want to see the movie!*

SANDY: [*Her hand flying to her mouth.*] Oh no!

BILL: Well, shit on him, we'll see the movie without them!

SANDY: My front tooth just fell out!

NICKY: I want to see my movie!

SANDY: [*Showing it to* BILL.] Look!

BILL: [*Sets up the projector and screen.*] You'll see your movie, Nick, don't worry.

SANDY: I'll have to call the dentist tomorrow. I can't walk around like this. [*Flashes a smile with a blacked-out front tooth.*]

BILL: [*Dimming the lights.*] All right, folks, is everybody ready for one hell of a movie?

NICKY: Movie time, movie time!

SANDY: [*Showing* NICKY.] Look at Mommy's tooth, Nicky. What do you think?

[BILL *sings a fanfare.*]

It looks so…small…lying in my hand.

NICKY: Will the whole movie be just me?

SANDY: The other one is loose too.

[*Blurred images start up on the screen.*]

BILL: Hey, Nicky!

NICKY: Hey, Daddy!

BILL: Hey, Sandy!

NICKY: Hey, Mommy!

SANDY: Nicky on his fourth birthday…my Nicky…

BILL: *Four years old!*

NICKY: [*Throwing his arms around* SANDY *and* BILL.] Look! Look! Look! Look!

[*They freeze in an endless embrace.*]

SANDY: Four years ago today, you made us the happiest family in the world!

[*The curtain slowly falls.*]

Karen Malpede

US

So it is said, "all songs are Holy, the Song of Songs is the Holy of Holies." King Solomon composed three books, two of which, Proverbs and Ecclesiastes are full of moral sayings and the fear of God, and in them there is much talk of purity and devoutness. But in the Song of Songs such words do not occur. Because of the great power of its holiness, it does not appear to be holy at all.

—*Hasidic Tale*

In memory of Julian Beck & Jean Genet

Us was originally produced by Theater for the New City and The Living Theater at Theater for the New City, New York, NY, on December 17, 1987. Judith Malina directed; George Bartenieff and Crystal Field performed the six Roles; Lighting was by John P. Dodd; set by Ilion Troya.

CHARACTERS:

[*This memory play is written to be performed by two actors, who double in the six roles.*]

Tony, *Hannah's father, Italian-American*

Cora, *Hannah's mother, an assimilated American Jew*

Sylvie, *Michel's mother, of French extraction, living in Algeria, poor. Later, she marries, lives in France, has money*

The Man Who Comes in Through the Window, *Michel's father, an Algerian*

Hannah, *born with the bomb in 1945*

Michel, *child of the French/Algerian War*

Time: 1945-1985.

[*The original set for* Us *was 60 feet long, 18 feet high, and 3 feet wide. Different scenes were located in different parts of this large construction. For instance, Tony's car, in which he seduces his daughter, hung from the ceiling in the far upper right corner of the set. On this huge, narrow set, the actors, as they climbed about, appeared to be constantly in danger. In the original production, the two actors changed wigs and simple costumes as they switched from character to character.*]

SCENE 1: **Hannah's sudden recall of life in her parents' house in the United States, 1950s.**

[TONY *throws a female dummy* (CORA, *his wife*) *against a wall.*]

TONY: Filthy, fucking, pissing whore, cunt.

[*Bam. The "woman" is bashed against the wall.*]

I ought to spread your legs wide open and piss on you. You're not worth the goddamn money it takes to feed you dinner. Whore. Cunt.

[*He throws "her" against the wall again and again.*]

Slut. Fucking piss pot. Shit hole. Cunt. Whore. Nothing but a goddamned whore. You only stay with me for my money. Bitch. You're not worth the chair your ass is on. Cunt.

[*He beats the "woman" even as he yells at her. His rage increasing, he molests her every way he can.*]

Dirty Jew. Dirty, fucking, pissing Jew. Jew-girl. Whoring Jewish bitch. Jew-bitch. Fucking Jewish bitch. You're not worth an ass-hole fuck. Dirty Jewish bitch. Jew-cunt. Filth.

[*Again, the "woman" is slammed against the wall.*]

Sick, uppity bitch. Dirty, stinking, whoring, pissing, sick lady bitch. I ought to stick my prick so far up your cunt you crack in half, like a lobster, cunt. Rotten stink pot. Cunt.

[*The "woman" is thrown against the wall, again.*]

Whore. Rotten, stinking, fat, smelly cunt. I ought to suck the insides out of you. I ought to suck you until there's nothing left. Until you flatten out like a popped balloon. Piss pot. Ugly, stinking, flabby, fat-assed bitch.

[*Bam, the "woman" hits the wall. But this time, the rage is ended.* TONY *kneels at "Cora's" feet, holds her in his arms. He weeps.*]

Oh, baby, baby, forgive me. Please baby, please. Forgive me, please. I love you, baby, baby. I love you. I do. I'll make it up to you. I will. What do you want? What do you want? Dinner on the town. A red dress, made of silk? Those stockings with rhinestone studded ankles, what, baby, what? A new washer, dish washer? Diaper service? What? I won't hit you again. Oh, God, how could I hit you? How could I hit? How? Baby, baby, I love you. How could I hit you? I love you. Please, baby, please. Oh, yes, yes, yes. You know I do. Yes, help me. Help me. I need you. Please, baby, please. I need you. How could I hit you? I love you. How could I hit you? How?

[*He weeps at "his wife's" feet. Then takes off his hat, or wig, long hair falls down. He takes off his suit jacket and pants, revealing a woman dressed simply in skirt and top. "He" is his daughter,* HANNAH. *She stands.*]

I was a child in that house. I was a child watching that, hearing those words. I was a child behind closed doors, half asleep in my bed, alone at night, hearing those sounds. What was going on? Hiding behind chairs, choking down food, not hearing what I heard, lost in a book, doing homework, in bed, pillow between my legs, alone in my room for sixteen years.

[*She turns on the "woman," her mother, and beats her.*]

Cunt. Whore. Filthy, pissing, fucking, dirty, stinking Jew-girl, whore. Bitch. Cunt.

[*She composes herself.*]

I was born, born of ash. Born of ash borne across the sea, on a hot wind, smelling of death. A wisp of ash, a particle, a flake, infected my mother's womb. No egg. No sperm, but this odd smelling thing. Ash of my ancestors, Abraham, Sarah and the rest, beaten as they walked, beaten from the cattle cars, beaten as they choked, choked on prayers. I was born of ash into ash. Born of ash into a world of ash. Destined to become, to be, to reveal myself an insubstantial thing. World of ash which was, which once was hot, fire, hot, firey flesh.

[HANNAH *turns on "her mother," beating her again.*]

Bitch. Bitch. If it wasn't for you, I'd be free. Free. Free, do you hear it, bitch? Free. I'd be free. Healthy and free. Free, baby, free. Do you hear?

[*She rips open the dummy's stomach, pulling out the figure of a baby, herself; now she speaks words her mother might have spoken as she held the baby,* HANNAH.]

Oh, baby, baby, forgive me, forgive, forgive me, please. Forgive me, please, baby, please, forgive. Oh, somebody help me, please, someone come to me, please, someone help me, please, oh, please. Take her away. Take her away. Take. Take her. Someone come take her away. Away. Take her away from me. Before I...

[*She lifts "the child" high as if to smash her on the ground.*]

Before I. Before...

[*She brings the child to her breast.*]

Before I die. Take her away...before I...take her away. Take. Someone come take her away. Take her away from me. Take.

[*She holds the doll at arm's length, offering her to the audience.*]

SCENE 2: Michel's experience of Sylvie at her dressing table, France, 1958.

[*A middle-class home in France. A beautiful woman sits at a dressing table, her face reflected out toward the audience by a large mirror. She is slightly larger than life. Her face is a realistic, impassive mask. Her heels are very high; her shoulders are padded. Her hair, a wig, is a bright, artificial blond. But she is not grotesque. She is simply large as adults seem very large to young children, and very beautiful, stylish and somewhat cold in the way that a concern for self-image and style above all make someone cold.*]

SYLVIE: Don't tell me that because I don't want to hear it. I don't want to hear it because it is not true. It's not true because it could not possibly have happened. Because it could not possibly have happened it is not true and I don't want to hear it. Do you want to kill me? Do you want me dead? Please, if you want to amuse me tell me something funny. Tell me something funny that happened to you today. Tell me something smart. Something smart that you said or did. You are very smart, you know, very, very smart. Tell me something smart. Tell me something smart that you said. Show me something that you made. Or tell me how I look. Do I look nice to you, tonight? Do I look pretty? To you? How is my hair? Do you like the color? It's a new color, a new tint. Is it too light? Too dark? You are always so observant. Do you like my hair?

[*She takes off her wig and throws it on the ground. Now, turns toward the audience.*]

Do you like my face? Do you like my face today? I'm wearing a new lipstick, a new shade. I don't often wear such a rosy color, not in winter, in summer, perhaps, but not in winter. In fall? Yes, a rosy color in fall is all right, isn't it. A rosy color to remember by as the leaves drop. Do you like my eyes? It's sweet of you to say so. You like my face. I'm glad. I made it up just for you. It's true. I made my face up just for you. No one else is home tonight. Who else would I have made my face up for, if not for you?

[*She takes off the mask, revealing a man's face, with the features, only life-size and masculine, that were reflected in the mask, but "she" does not break character. In fact, it almost seems that as the mask comes off "her" character intensifies, as it might in a dream.*]

Look at my dress, darling. It's nice, isn't it? A little tight. My figure wasn't ruined until the second child. Until you came. You ruined my figure. Ruined it. But never mind, we won't talk about that tonight. I can still get away with a tight dress. Don't you think? It's just you and me. Just us. Help me with the zipper, dear, will you. Help me zip it up.

[*The actor reaches around his back and unzips the dress, stepping out of it. Now he is left with platform heels. Wig, mask and dress lie on the floor at his feet.*]

These shoes are killing me, really they are. I only wore them because you like them. You're always telling me how much you like these shoes. It's so adorable when you talk about my feet. Everybody thinks so. Really, it's so cute.

[*The actor takes off the shoes and puts them at the foot of the dress. The "mother" lies laid out, so to speak, on the floor; the actor is wearing light pants and a T-shirt, but still does not break character.*]

Now, give me a kiss, dear. Give me a kiss.

[*He kisses the mask.*]

That's a good boy. That's mama's darling boy. That's enough, now, enough. Don't smudge me, please, don't smudge.

[*He puts the mask back on his face.*]

Dont' rumple my hair. It took hours to get it right. Yes, dear, that's sweet, but don't rumple my hair, please, be careful, be careful, do you want to ruin my hair? You don't want to ruin my hair. Of course not.

[*He puts the wig back on his head.*]

You're such a handsome boy. You're mama's beauty boy, mama's little pet. You have such a pretty face. Yes, darling, yes. I just have to get out of this dress.

[*The actor puts the dress on.*]

Help me with the zipper, if you can, dear. Be careful. Be careful, don't catch my flesh. Be careful with your mother, careful. You know how much I love you. Be careful what you say.

[*The actor puts the shoes on and seats himself at the dressing table, as at the start.*]

You'll kill me if you talk like that. Andre is an angel. An angel, do you hear. Your brother did not put his finger up your ass hole. He did not masturbate you. He did not make you suck him off until he came. He did not sodomize you, over and over again. He did not make you promise not to tell. He did not hold you down and sodomize you. He did not say he'd kill you if you told. Don't tell me this because I don't want to hear it. I don't want to hear it because it is not true. It is not true because it could not possibly have happened. Because it could not possibly have happened it is not true and I don't want to hear it. Do you want to kill me? Do you want me dead?

[*She swings her perfectly coifed and made-up self out toward the audience and stares at them.*]

SCENE 3: **Sylvie's house in a poor workers' quarter of Algeria, 1949; Sylvie and the Man Who Comes in Through the Window; Sylvie's attempt to abort Michel's birth, 1950.**

[*The front room of a dilapidated house in a poor workers' quarter of Algiers.* SYLVIE *lives a crowded, uncomfortable life here with her first son, Andre. She is seen, leaning from a window, bathed in the green-white light of a full moon, as the* MAN *jumps in the window opposite.*]

SYLVIE: Turn around and go back the way you came. Get out.

MAN: Turn my back on you, Sylvie? You look too beautiful tonight.

SYLVIE: Don't flatter me because I don't want to hear it. Not from you. I don't want to hear it because you'll make me do something I don't want to do.

MAN: I only came to see the kid.

SYLVIE: You came in through the window.

MAN: I came in with the moonlight. There's a full moon tonight.

SYLVIE: So what?

MAN: I saw you leaning out the window the first time I passed. That's why I came back. I saw you sucking up that light, like a sea sponge. I saw you glittering in the dark.

SYLVIE: Andre is asleep.

MAN: Such a fancy French name you've given my son, Sylvie, like your own.

SYLVIE: Andre is asleep. Now get out.

MAN: Better he shouldn't see me. Better he shouldn't know who I am. With a name like that. I'll just look at him.

SYLVIE: If it was up to you "your son" would be dead.

MAN: That's why I found a good mama for him. I know who I am, the shadow light riding in and out on the dark side of the moon. Dance with me, Sylvie, dance.

SYLVIE: Don't give me those sweet words because I know what those sweet words mean. They're empty, just like you are. Get out. And do me a favor. Use the door.

MAN: Don't be mad a me, Sylvie. You know who I am. I said I loved you. I do. I said I'd come back. Here I am.

SYLVIE: Get out.

MAN: What do you want? A man who comes in every night through the door? A reliable man, who can't see into you? Who reads the paper all night and shakes his head but doesn't understand where he is, what is going on? A "good" man who falls asleep in his chair when he could be smelling you?

SYLVIE: Don't start with the fancy talk.

MAN: Sylvie, I'm the man for you. You know it. You do. You know where we've been. I'm the one who wakes you up. I've set you singing. Singing, Sylvie, with my touch. I've set your flesh to song. Sylvie, I've seen you turn wilder than the night sea, beautiful, so beautiful you take my breath away. If you want what we have, you have to stand a little pain. Dance with me, Sylvie, dance.

[*She walks away from him. He puts a record on the record player.*]

Hey, love, want a drink?

[*The tango music begins, as suddenly, furiously, inescapably, they fuse. The two bodies rush together, compelled by some inner cellular truth. They mate. The man is left, curled at her feet, but even as she speaks he disappears from her side.*]

SYLVIE: His lavender cock stuck straight out,
washed in the silver moon light.
Starved, I lept for that light.
I lapped it up with my thighs,
curled at his side. When I reached out again
he was gone. The empty moon hung in the sky
and I was ocean-drugged, trapped by the swollen sea.

[*His voice comes back to her, as if from a recurrent dream.*]

MAN: Hey, love, want a drink?

SYLVIE: I was walking away. I was walking away when his string snapped me back. I was almost safe. But it's done. Over and done. I'd better not give it another thought. He's gone for good this time and I'll spear the fish he left. [*She takes a long, difficult drink of abortificant, spitting out the remains on the floor.*] I paid good money for this foul stuff. She better have told me right. Feeling me like that. Clucking her tongue in my face. This better work. It better do more than make me sick. At least he's gone. He hasn't been back. Don't be afraid little one. Go back where you came from. Someone else will take you in. Turn around, now, go. Back over the window sill on that beam of light. Whiskey on his breath. Dark eyes flashing sex.

MAN: [*Again, he speaks as if from a dream.*] You know where we've been.

SYLVIE: Get out. Leave me alone. Prying myself open, open like a can of fish. Wouldn't do it herself. Not for me. I'm French. I told her. I told her who the father is. He's one of yours. She shook her head, afraid I'd turn her in. I begged. How I begged. She gave me this hook. It better be clean. This better not ruin me. I better come out whole. Like I was. I better come out all right. Now the cramps. Now the cramps and the blood. What a relief it will be. Squatting on the toilet, spitting it out. Let it hurt. Oh God, let it hurt. Let me go double with pain. But let it end.

MAN: That's how I am. If you want pleasure like we have, you have to stand a little pain.

SYLVIE: I was walking away.

MAN: Hey, love, want a drink? [*They fuse again.*]

SYLVIE: His lavender cock stuck straight out,
washed in the silver moon light.
I lept for that light.
Lapped it up. When I reached out again
he was gone. The empty moon hung in the sky
and I was ocean-drugged, trapped by the swollen sea.

[*This time, it's as if* SYLVIE *is giving birth to the man. She works him out from between her legs. She sits as if she holds the new-born baby-man in her lap. She speaks to the man-child who looks so trustingly at her.*]

So you don't want to eat. Who are you to turn up your nose? You think I like this any better than you? You're pulling me all out of shape. I can't afford fancy food. You look just like he does. Wouldn't you know. I'm giving you a good French name. I'm calling you, Michel. And you better stay out of my way. I've got to find a new man. That's easier said than done with two kids hanging around. So if you don't like the milk, you can starve. Come on, eat. I know how you feel. I could cry, too. Shut up, now, and eat.

[*The child in her arms is* MICHEL. *He escapes from her grasp, yelling at his mother.*]

MICHEL: I dream of hands. Hands clawing my eyes. The same dream all my life. Until I stopped dreaming at all. Andre told me. He told me the secret. He saw. You tried to get rid of me twice. He told me what you did. Things you put inside yourself, trying to hook me like a fish. But nothing you do ever works.

SCENE 4: Cora and Tony's suburban bedroom, U.S.A., 1946.

[*The woman,* CORA, HANNAH's *mother, is in bed. She holds her infant daughter at arm's length. The bed is perpendicular to the floor so that the actors, while leaning against it, are actually fully visible to the audience.*]

CORA: Someone come. Someone come, take her away. Take her away from me. Take.

[HANNAH's *father,* TONY, *enters.*]

TONY: Give her to me. Can't you do anything right? She's wet. She's been crying half the night. [*He takes the child, holds her to his chest, begins to walk, rocking, crooning.*] All right, piccolina. Daddy's little one. Daddy's little love. Hush, Hannah, hush, Daddy's here. Daddy's got you in his arms. Daddy's holding you safe. What do you want? A place in the sun? Music? Do you want music all around? Do you want to dance out under the moon? Dance under the stars in the night? Let Daddy hold you up. He'll pluck down a star for you. The brightest one. You'll sparkle. You'll shine. You'll fly so high. You can have anything, anything at all. You're Daddy's little girl. You can have all the things Daddy never had. Close your eyes, now, dream. Anything you dream of you can have.

CORA: Tony, she's quiet. Come to bed.

TONY: Shut up. She just closed her eyes.

[CORA *rolls over and sleeps.*]

Daddy's baby, yes. Yes. Dream of sweet things, a pink ruffled dress, teddy bears, a white Cadillac with the top down, long hair blowing in the wind. Daddy's girl, sleep, dream. You can sleep next to Daddy, but not if you cry. [*He puts the doll-baby in bed on one side of him. He is in the middle of the bed, his wife on his other side. To* CORA] Hey, baby, you awake?

[*She rolls away from him.*]

[*He turns to the child.*] You woke up? You little skunk. Hush, now, hush. Are you wet? Let me open up your diaper. Just to check. Oh, baby, baby, yes, yes. Once. That's all. Just once. Just once more. Baby, how good you feel. How good. So new, so warm, so wet. Daddy loves you. Yes. Daddy loves his little girl. Hush, now, hush. Go to sleep.

[*He turns to his wife.*]

Cora, wake up. Give me your mouth on my cock.

CORA: Tony, stop.

TONY: Come on. I just got the kid to sleep so we could have some time. Come on, baby, come on.

[CORA *rolls over on top of* TONY.]

Yes, baby, yes. Do me, do me, baby. Oh, baby, so good, so good. You do me so good. Yes. Yes. [*He runs his hands through her hair, pushing her head down between his legs.*]

CORA: Tony, what have you done? The child's in bed. Tony, what have you done, the child's in bed with us.

TONY: Shut up. She's asleep. What does she know? She's a baby. Shut up. Open your legs. Come on, baby, come on. I need you. You know I do. I need you. I need you, baby, please. I need you. [*He rolls on top of her.*] You're so good, baby, so sweet.

[*He rolls off of* CORA *and on top of the infant-doll at his other side.*]

Oh, baby, baby, yes, yes, open up, open up, just once, open up, now, once, open up. Yes. Yes. Just once. Just once more. [*He rolls back off of her.*]

CORA: What have you done, Tony, what? The child is in bed with us. Tony, what have you done?

TONY: Shut up. She's asleep. She's a baby. What does she know. Open your legs. Come on, baby, come on. I need you. You know I do. Please, baby, please. [*He rolls back on top of* CORA.] You're so good, so good, baby, so good.

[*He rolls back on top of the doll.*]

Oh, baby, baby, yes, once, just one time, open up, just once, open up, now, yes, yes. [*He rolls off of the doll.*]

CORA: Tony, what have you done? The child's in the bed. Tony, what have you done? The child's in bed with us.

TONY: Shut up. She's asleep. What does she know. She's a baby. What does she know. Open your legs. Come on, baby, be good to me, now. You're the best, baby, the best I ever had. [*He buries his head in* CORA's *lap.*]

CORA: Oh, Tony, what have you done? [*She reaches for the infant-doll, picks her up, holding her at arms length, the man's head buried in her lap.*] She's the only one you never hit. She's the only one you ever loved.

SCENE 5: **Michel with Sylvie at her dressing table, Algeria, 1958; Cora living in the basement, Tony in the kitchen, 1956; Tony and Hannah in Hannah's car, 1956.**

[MICHEL *outside the house in Algiers, 1958. He is eleven years old.* SLYVIE *at her dressing table inside.*]

MICHEL: We were leaving Algiers. She was going to take me away. I saw a man whistling at the window. Whistling at the window. Calling someone. Whistling a song. Then he was gone. Quick, through the backyard. Over the fence. Looking this way and that. I ran. I ran after that song.

[*Unseen by* SYLVIE, MICHEL *listens to her as, roaming the house, she begins to pack her things.*]

SYLVIE: That bastard came back again. Whistling at the window, like he's calling a dog. "I'm going out with Claude," I told him right to his face. "Claude is hard working, smart. Claude is steady. He comes home every night. If we get out of this country alive, if we get out of this war, if we get to France before we are killed, Claude will be a success." How he hated that. How he grew stony with rage. I laughed. I laughed in his face. Claude has a mechanical mind. Engineer, accountant, Claude could be anything. Money in our pockets. A private bedroom. I could open a shop. I'm marrying Claude. I told him that. Claude doesn't like Michel. He gets along with Andre, but he doesn't like Michel. Michel shakes when Claude is around. He stutters. He makes funny sounds, like motors, like guns. Claude can't stand that. Michel is stupid he says. Says he's trouble, like the other one. I'm lucky Claude will have me with two sons. Lucky he'll take me away. But he dosn't like Michel.

MICHEL: [*To* SYLVIE.] He came back. I know he did. He came back for me. He doesn't care about you. He came back for me. I know he did. I don't want to go with you and Claude. I want to stay here with him.

SYLVIE: How can you talk like that? How can you say those things? After all I've done? How can you threaten me? You'll be dead in the street. You'll be killed by one of their bombs. You stay away. You stay away from his kind. Claude is your father now. Claude will take care of you. The other one doesn't care if you're dead or alive. Say it. Say it for me. Call Claude "papa." Go ahead. Make me proud. Say it for me. I love you so. Call Claude "papa." That's my special boy. That's my Michel. Claude is your papa now.

[*Transition within the scene to* TONY's *house. He sits at the kitchen table. Underneath, in the basement,* CORA *is visible, camped out, she is frying an egg on a hot plate.*]

TONY: She doesn't love me. Never did. Married me because of the war. Whore. Neighbors saw them. They climbed into the window in broad day. Neighbors said, "Your wife. Your wife and the actor who was in that play." Climbed through the window of the empty house. In the middle of the day. She is the most beautiful woman I ever saw. Smart, too. Knows how to talk. How to talk sweet all right. Doesn't love me, never did. Married me because of the war. Thought I'd be rich. I'm rich all right. I'm killing myself for her and the kid. Jewish bitch. Her kind are all alike. "He was nice to me, Tony," Nice! Haven't I been nice. Haven't I tried. Look at this house. Closet full of clothes. Cleaning woman once a week. Beauty shop. I pulled at her hair. Pulled out a clump of her hair. "In the old country, you'd be dead." Bitch. "If you leave me, I'll take the kid. You'll starve if you leave me." Don't leave me, Cora, don't leave me. Can't you love me, if you try. "What kind of mother fucks around. You'll never see your kid again." Can't you love me? She doesn't answer anymore. Sleeps in the basement on a cot. Like she's hiding out. Cora, get the hell upstairs. I got to get to work. I got to eat.

CORA: [*From the basement. Meek, always meek when she speaks to* TONY.] Toast is in the toaster, Tony. Pop it down. Orange juice in a covered glass in the fridge. Hot coffee in the pot.

TONY: Get the hell upstairs. I want eggs.

CORA: Eggs are on the stove. In a pan with a lid. The way you like them, Tony, scrambled hard.

[*He looks around the kitchen for a moment, confused. Then slams down the stairs, going to work. He returns.*]

TONY: Getthehellupstairs. I'm home from work.

CORA: Dinner's on the table. Chicken. Potatoes. Peas. Key lime pie in the fridge.

TONY: Where's the kid?

CORA: I don't know where she is.

TONY: Whadaya mean, you don't know? She's eleven years old. Whadaya mean, you don't know. Get your ass up here.

[TONY *storms down the stairs again, to look for* HANNAH. *He comes back.*]

Cora, kid's at the neighbors. For Chrissake, come up from the basement. I want sex.

CORA: It's my time of month. I'm going to sleep.

[*In the basement,* CORA *lays down.* TONY *goes toward the bedroom. Morning comes and he comes back into the kitchen.*]

TONY: Get yourself up here. I need food.

CORA: Ironed shirts in the drawer. Breakfast on the table. Cut the banana into the cereal. Hannah's skirt hemmed. Her lunch in the paper bag. Coffee, strong, in the pot.

TONY: All right. Stay in the cellar. Stay there forever.

[*Again, he is down the stairs to work. He returns at night.*]

I don't care. Goddamned whore. Goddamned cunt. I'm going out. I got girls. I got girls. Girls at the office. Plenty of girls, I got.

CORA: Spaghetti and sausage in the pot. Bread warming up. Wine glass set out.

[TONY *sits, contemplating his situation. In a few moments, he has an idea. He calls excitedly to his daughter in her bedroom.*]

TONY: Hannah, baby, put your book down. You can't read all night. Hannah, baby, let's go to a show. Come on, baby, get your coat. Put your coat on. It's raining, baby. It's raining hard. Come on, Hannah, button up. Let's go, you and me. Let's go to a show. Come on, Hannah, let's go. It's raining hard. Watch out for that puddle there. Follow me. Come on, baby, get into the car.

[*They arrive at the car.* TONY *helps* HANNAH *in. Gets in beside her, starts the motor, off they go.*]

HANNAH: Daddy, go slow. You're driving so fast. Daddy, daddy, I'm scared. Daddy, listen to me. In school today, we had to hide. Hide in the basement, in the hall, under the big pipes, the pipes wrapped in tape, under the bandaged pipes. Hands over our heads, hiding out. Do you think the Russian's will drop the bombs? Daddy, do you think so? Will I live to be old like you?

TONY: Hannah, baby, let's stop the car. Let's stop the car on the side of the road. Don't be frightened, baby, don't be scared. Daddy will hold you in his arms. Once, baby, just one time, let me kiss you on the mouth. Let me kiss you, yes, yes. You love me, baby. I know you do. Daddy doesn't leave you. You know that. Daddy will keep you safe. Daddy doesn't let you down. Daddy's here for you all the time.

[TONY *slowly runs his hand down* HANNAH's *body, from her neck, between her two breasts, to her crotch. Silent and terrified,* HANNAH *stares straight ahead.*]

SCENE 6: Hannah and Tony at home, 1961; Tony's funeral, 1961.

[HANNAH, *at the back door of the house. She is pulled inside by* TONY. *She resists him. They argue.*]

HANNAH: We were watching TV. We were sitting in the TV room watching the late show.

TONY: Get your ass inside this house. What do you mean showing your face here at 3 a.m.? You should sleep in the street. You're just like your mother. A whore. Just like her.

[*She pulls away from him.*]

HANNAH: I'll sleep in the street. I'll never put foot inside this rotten house.

TONY: Get your ass inside this house. Don't you talk back. [*He grabs her, raising his hand, as if to strike.*] I'll kill that fucking bastard. I'll kill him before…You stay away from that bum. I'll kill him if you go near him again. I swear.

HANNAH: We were watching TV…

[*Now he is all remorse and gentleness.*]

TONY: Oh, baby, babe…be careful of yourself. You got to do that. I got no time left.

[*She is cradled in his arms.*]

HANNAH: Daddy, please…I…

TONY: Baby, help me, I'm scared. I'm sick, baby. Don't make it worse.

HANNAH: Daddy, please, I'm frightened, Daddy, please.

[*Her childish need makes him pull away. He begins to search the house for CORA. HANNAH trails behind him.*]

TONY: Cora! Cora! Help me, Cora, help. I heard what the doctor said. I'm dying. Cora, I got no hope. You got to help me, now.

HANNAH: [*Runs after him.*] Daddy, wait. We were watching TV. That's all. Daddy, please, forgive me, Daddy, forgive…

TONY: Cora, I'll make it up to you. I'll make it up, all of it, all. We'll be happy, now. Cora, Cora, we got to be happy now. Doctor says there's no time left.

[*He stops, for a moment. HANNAH rushes to him.*]

Baby, baby, baby…love… [*He caresses her. Then pushes her away and begins to search for CORA again.*] Cora, help me. I'm so scared. I'm scared. Cora, I'm scared. Cora, you're smart. You know how to behave. I love you, Cora. You know that. You're the only one I ever loved.

[HANNAH *follows him, but he pays no attention. All his focus is upon* CORA, *represented by the stuffed dummy who was battered in Scene 1.*]

You've got to help me, Cora. You're all I have. My own mother, she said, "It's all up for you, Tony. You're finished, you know that." She talked like I was already dead. "You got cancer, Tony, because you married out of your religion." You heard her say that, that's what she said.

Cora, what do you want? A diamond ring? A new car? Wall to wall carpet everywhere, a marble sink? What? What do you want while I can still do for you? Come on, Cora, let's go to the mall. I can still get around.

Cora, you're the only one for me. Yes, Cora, yes. Take me like you used to do. Talk to the doctor for me. Tell him to give us some time. Tell him we'll pay him anything. Stay with me, now, stay with me. Cora, stay. Read to me, Cora, read. Cora, sing to me, baby, sing. We'll be happy, now. We got to be happy now. You'll stay with me, now, stay with me, now, stay with me until I die.

[*He is dead on the floor at "Cora's" feet.* HANNAH *puts a black veil over "Cora's" face, and then puts a longer veil on herself.*]

HANNAH: I wanted to look beautiful at your funeral. Wanted to look more beautiful than she did. Wanted to look like your bride. I wanted to look like I belonged to you, was yours, I wanted to look like you. "Little Tony," they used to call me that. I wanted to look beautiful, pure. I wanted to look like a virgin bride. Dressed in black, following behind you, following behind, following behind you to the grave. I wanted to look radiant, wild. I wanted to throw myself into the grave. I wanted to look like I belonged to you, was yours, was you, was yours following behind you, following you. People whispered, they did, "oh, how lovely." "How lovely she looks." I wanted to be perfect. Radiant. On that day of days, day I followed you to the grave. Eyes, your eyes. Your eyes staring back from the mirror. I wanted you to see me. I wanted you to see me. I wanted you to see. I wanted you to know me, to know, to know me, to want me, to want, to want me to live. I felt, but I couldn't say how I felt. I felt you were jealous of me dating boys. You died because I grew up. You died and left me alone. You were jealous and you died. I wanted to be your bride. Dressed in black, following behind you, following behind you, following you back. I wanted to throw myself after you into the grave, I wanted to be, to be lost with you, like you, yours. I wanted to keep you, to keep you with me. I wanted you back.

SCENE 7: Michel at the sulpher lake, Algeria, 1956; Hannah at the stable, U.S.A., 1957.

[*The lovers meet. As* MICHEL *speaks, warm water showers over him.*]

MICHEL: On long, hot days, I went with my grandmother to the sulpher spring hidden in the hills, the spring where the Arab women bathed. I was a child to them, a skinny French child, ignored in their sovereign world. I swam in the hot, blue sulpher sea between the fat thighs of Arab women, heavy dresses pulled up, bright fabrics turned dark in the sulpher sweat, floating like lillies on the silken ledge, trunk legs planted in mud. Sharp talk drops hit overhead, fragments of family affairs, money exchanged, illnesses, marriages, births, broken now and again by a hot lava laugh flowing from an open throat, primeval flow from beneath the hot sea where I swim in and out of the folds of their flesh. They lift their skirts higher, plant flat feet deeper in the wet mud. I skitter between lush folds of fat. The harsh talk, talk, talk falls on the surface glass overhead.

Two full thighs close over me, squeezing me, wriggling helpless with delight. Flesh walls open above my skinny back, salt from the sea and salt. Seaweed hair and labia lips fall over me. Dizzy on the rhythm of blood rushing to the spot, the heart, the heart loud as a shot. I explode in the silver sea, filling it with fish sperming their way out. Mated with the wet underworld, spent and devoured. Quick, I slap tail-legs against the vice in which I am caught. I spurt up, I arrive, gulping air, born to two faceless breasts. Her hands slap me away with a blow that sets my water lungs hacking. "Nuisance," she yells, "nuisance," slapping at me like a fly. Bellowing out words, she is an elephant mare, standing calm. I dive down. Underneath, she convulses, writhes, glories in the lost underworld where pleasure survives. "Nuisance," she slaps and I dive, laughing between her fat legs. I set my sperm loose in the sulpher sea. For years afterwards, I look hard at the faces of fish, hoping to see my eyes or my mouth, a new creature spawned from those hot afternoons, alive in the hot sulpher sea.

HANNAH: I come to the stable late in the thick autumn dusk. Not used to the cotton pad between my legs or the hot blood collecting, I am walking clumsy, I think. I want to find others who smell as I smell, others who know the ragged edges of the flesh. I breathe in the horses, their deep dull eyes and their sweat, their golden urine mixed with the straw at their feet, and the sweet smell of decay rising between my legs. I am wrapped in this mist, grabbed, taken under the earth, like a root, determined and wet.

Cigarette smoke, stale and sharp, the hard laughs of the men exploding like bombs. Their muscular arms laced with blue veins hang on the rail of the ring while a dark stallion they've loosened seizes a mare between his forelegs and mounts her. They are yelling at him, laughing, urging him on. I put my hands to my ears. "Fuck the bitch. Fuck her." The two creatures crazed with desire abandon their shapes, becoming liquid and fire. I watch white light rise from the steam of their fusing. But I cannot block out the men's words, or their laughing. A clot of hot blood falls from me onto the thick cotton pad. Shame sends a hot current through me. Stallion and mare stand apart, heads hanging low. The men leave them there, turn, satisfied and go. There is no sound but our animal breathing. I enter the ring. The mare is quiet, pulled into herself, lost. I am drawn to the stallion. How did I not see he's been wounded. His long stalk utterly exposed. His soul spring reddened, wrinkled, sucked at and emptied. I want to kneel at his feet in the sawdust. I want to take his wound into my mouth, wrap my lips around his hurt flesh. I want to hold him there gently, while he gathers himself, while he mends. I lay my cheek against his wet neck, making low soothing sounds. I lead him into the barn. Slip a hard metal bit into the warm wet folds of his mouth.

[HANNAH *bridles* MICHEL, *who kneels and takes the bit, then she lays herself against his back.*]

Let's go, now, I whisper. We move out into the night. I give him his head, lay myself low on his back. Together we run through the deep autumn woods, leaves breaking under our weight, moon lighting our path, moon drenching us in white light. I sing into his ears because he cannot, because he runs for me as I sing.

Scene 8: Michel's war story, 1955.

[MICHEL *ties* HANNAH's *hands above her head with the reins of the bridle. He holds her bound as he speaks.*]

MICHEL: My grandmother tied rabbits to the spigot in the tin sink. She picked up a knife. With one stroke sliced them open, from chest to crotch. [*He demonstrates on her body.*] Their guts spilled out, long intestinal ropes, liver, kidneys, heart, singing against the tin sink. We come from the ocean, you know, our blood is the same as the hot sea water. Why, then, do we hold ourselves apart? [*He drops her hands.*]

HANNAH: My grandmother had chicken breasts delivered in cardboard boxes with the groceries. She cooked them for hours in their own fat in the high tin pot. During World War II, she ate chicken with her fair-haired German-Jew in-laws in Palm Beach restaurants beneath signs that said, "No Jews Allowed." What strong stomachs we human beings have.

MICHEL: I was coming around the corner, carrying the rabbit in the cloth sack. Waiting for the blood to spatter against my grandmother's big breasts, when I heard the animal cry. When I saw a man's guts spill against the hot stones, while he watched animal-like. I saw him go down on his knees. I saw him shovel his guts back into his belly with his hands. I watched while he held his wet self in his arms.

[HANNAH *goes down on her knees. She keeps trying to shovel her guts back into her stomach as she cries.*]

HANNAH: I don't know their names.
I am not a part of their group.
I don't know.
I don't know anything.
I never saw them before.
I'm dying. Oh, my god, I'm dying.
[*She speaks these works as a litany underneath the beginning of* MICHEL's *speech.*]

MICHEL: People were blown up in movie theaters, or cafes, mosques, churches or stores, on the streets, in their beds at home. Was it the Algerian Fellaghas or the French soldiers? Freedom fighters or mercenaries? You could never tell. Who were they? What had they done? What crime? Where they fighting for the people? Had they betrayed their own? Who did they leave? Who did they leave behind? That man, holding his guts in his hands, was that man my father? My father? Freedom fighter, night crawler, coward, jerk. In the resistance, the army, the police, plain clothes cop, terrorist chief, truck driver, liar, informer, waiter at the cafe where they met, did he know much, did he pass bombs? Once, I saw a hand, just a hand, lying in the gutter. Did that hand touch my mother? "Go on, get out, leave me alone." The head I saw on the fence post, did that head talk? "I only came to see my son." I pieced him together a hundred times from a hundred different parts. How I wanted to know, to know him, to know him, knowing me. How I searched, searched everywhere. The head of a doctor, the guts of a waiter, the heart of a worker, the long, thin, beautiful womanlike hand in the gutter so like my own. The legs of a farmer, the nuts and prick of a student, the eyes of a fighter, gouged out and left for the flies. The slippery noise of blood flooding the throat and the lungs, my father's song to his son.

[*He is on top of* HANNAH; *her legs wrapped around him.*]

One night, during an air raid, I made love for the first time. My aunt wrapped me between her strong legs. I made silent love on the cold floor, while the bombs exploded over our heads. I made noiseless love, careful not to move, careful not to move too much, careful not to bump my grandmother or anyone else who lay on the crowded floor, stiff and still. I felt myself swell while the bombs fell and I thought I would come apart in her arms, while she laughed her wild laugh in my ear.

[*Settled in* HANNAH's *arms, he speaks to her.*]

So you see, Hannah, why in the refugee camp when I was 11, I went immediately to the Red Cross tent and volunteered. I carried water to the wounded and told myself, when I grow up, I will become a healer.

And do you also understand, Hannah, why it is I cannot attach myself to anyone?

SCENE 9: Hannah and Michel, 1984.

[The lovers speak of their love.]

HANNAH: It's not a casual affair. Not to me, it's not. I've had them. It's not a casual affair.

MICHEL: I want only a casual affair. I want only someone to fuck. I need a little emotional diversion. I need some new emotional life.

HANNAH: Good morning, my love. I love you.

MICHEL: I found your note on my pillow. You are an exquisite lover, Hannah. We are having a great time.

HANNAH: When I look at you, I want to lick you all over. Your ass-hole tastes sweet to me.

MICHEL: The things you say. The things you cry in the night. "Take me. Take me." Yes, I will take you. I will take you as long as you want. But, you frighten me with your talk.

HANNAH: Don't fear, dear one. It will be over soon. Soon enough. Over and done. The flesh will stop straining to become. The two-throated pipe break on the song.

MICHEL: Hannah, can you come to me, now? Can you fly? I dreamt of you all night. I woke with such longing in my flesh. I woke feverish, in sweat. I woke with you in my blood.

HANNAH: Oh, my sweet, sweet one. You make love like a woman. Like a woman you lean into me. Like a woman, you moan in my arms, you give me your milk, rise and fall. In what silver sea, wrapped in what goddess's laugh, were you spawned? What blessing gave you to me?

MICHEL: Hannah, you are erotic everywhere. The hair on your ass, that soft, soft hair. Your feet, your toes, your toes kneeding my balls.

HANNAH: How did you become so fierce and so gentle?

MICHEL: Will you catch my balls in your mouth? Will you

swallow my balls?

HANNAH: Yes, of course, I will swallow them whole. I will sprout each seed you horde in your moist lavender sacks. I will drop a new race from between your legs. I will make you Abraham.

MICHEL: Your smell. I cannot get your smell off my hands. I shower. I wash. My skin smells of you, Hannah, all the time. I walk in your aura, your light, as if I were of you, formed by you, made, moulded inside, pushed out bearing your taste.

HANNAH: I write in the morning, in the morning, with my legs apart. I feel like I'm straddling a field, straddling the land, smelling the growing, smelling the growing of the grain. I breathe you in, breathe out an image, a thought. Effortless because the body already knows. In the beginning was the word. No. In the beginning was this rich scent. This lost memory of love.

MICHEL: I was so deep into you, from two sides, my cock and my hand almost met, but for a silk curtain of flesh. I wanted to draw the veil aside.

HANNAH: I am found. For the first time, I am seen.

MICHEL: I like to take you out of your mind. I work hard to free you from words, to set you free of yourself, free of us, free of me.

HANNAH: The taste. The taste of a man. As if I ate something unformed. As if I ate new-born flesh. As if I ate life.

MICHEL: I want to put my head inside you. I want to crawl into you. To be lost, spinning in space, the holiness dropping, dropping to earth in the dark.

HANNAH: Only let me lick you again. Before you become my own inside, let me taste. Before you vanish from my sight, leave your sweet taste in my mouth.

MICHEL: Why is it perfect with us, Hannah? Why is it better

than it has ever been?

HANNAH: Nothing we do sullies us, why is that?

MICHEL: Hannah, I go so deep inside you, I forget how to breathe. I am a fish underwater, searching your sea. I want to open you like a lobster. I want to crack you apart. I want to take a child out of you. I want to reach inside and pull a child out. I want to feel my fingers reaching, searching through mud, catching hold, catching hold of the first head, bringing up the first light, bearing the first sight. Hannah, I want life.

HANNAH: Look, look at your lavender cock, draped with my blood. A coat of many colors alive in the sun. Give me your cock. Put your cock in my mouth. I want to suck you dry. Suck you until I am full. Suck you until you melt on my tongue, in my mouth. Give me your wound, your hurt, your broken part. I want to suck you until you grow straight, suck you until I can hear you touching my voice.

[*Now they begin to speak in the other's voice. So that* MICHEL *says words that seem to issue from* HANNAH's *experience of their love and* HANNAH *speaks from knowledge of* MICHEL's *experience. Feeling with one another in this way, they are truly joined.*]

MICHEL: I want to make you sing. I want to give you my song. To put my song on your tongue, my taste, frothing sea-foam. I want to put the sea's song in your flesh. I want to give you the sound: the birth-cry, the lament, the uttering up, the belly-full shout.

HANNAH: I want to take you out of your mind, to feel you spinning as I reach into you. I felt you swirl overhead. I felt you in flight. Did you touch? Did you touch light?

MICHEL: I felt myself splayed apart, cut, like the sacrificed doe dripping blood. Did you taste? Did you taste god when you ate?

HANNAH: Nothing we do sullies us, why is that?

MICHEL: I want you inside. I want all of you. I want to give birth, to give birth to you. I want to birth you whole, whole and unhurt and alive.

HANNAH: You put such peace into me when we touch. Such peace when I rest in your flesh, when you leak your life into mine.

MICHEL: Are you here with me? Are you here?

HANNAH: Yes, I am here. I am here with you. It is all right. I am here.

MICHEL: Let me go where you lead. Let me open up. I will go. I will leap. I will be the corridor, the tunnel, the channel, the way. I will bring the blessing to earth. I will set it to root.

HANNAH: Yes, my one, yes. Bring me the light on your brow. The first sight. The smells the mother casts over the child. Oneness. The oneness of God.

[*They become themselves again.*]

Were you there with me? Were you there?

MICHEL: Yes, of course. I was there. We are twins. Placenta wrapped. Wet spots on the dark. Don't make me surface, Hannah, don't beach me. I die in the air, on the land. I die out of the sea.

HANNAH: Put your head inside me again, sweet, sweet prehistoric fish.

SCENE 10: **Hannah and Michel, 1985.**

[*The lovers wake.*]

MICHEL: How well we sleep together, Hannah. Without moving. Without moving once.

HANNAH: Where have you been while the flesh slept?

MICHEL: No, Hannah, I do not dream.

HANNAH: When you sleep you seem so utterly gone.

MICHEL: When I sleep, I am gone, Hannah, it's true. I cannot be for you all of the time.

HANNAH: I lay waking next to your skin. I lay tasting the moment you will come back. I cannot bear exile myself in a dream.

MICHEL: When I have a dream, Hannah, I will tell you. When I dream, I will do what the dream tells me to.

HANNAH: I must go…I have work…

MICHEL: Stay the morning with me.

HANNAH: I need…

MICHEL: I know what you need.

HANNAH: I need my work. I need myself back.

MICHEL: Hannah, I've read your book. It is not yet near what you will be. What you have inside. Stay the morning with me.

HANNAH: I need.

MICHEL: I know what you need.

HANNAH: I need your cock, your lavender cock, like a breast, lain in my mouth.

MICHEL: Yes, Hannah, of course.

HANNAH: No. I must dress.

MICHEL: Whatever you wish.

[*They dress as they speak, and, once dressed, they begin to move away from each other as they continue their debate.*]

HANNAH: You will leave me, Michel; you will go.

MICHEL: No, Hannah, I never leave anyone. I come back. I come back when I can.

HANNAH: Marry me, Michel.

MICHEL: If I said, "yes"?

HANNAH: I would run.

MICHEL: I am not constant, Hannah. I am not what you want.

HANNAH: Marry me, Michel.

MICHEL: You know the answer to that.

HANNAH: No, I don't.

MICHEL: If we are together all of the time, we will kill what we have.

HANNAH: No we won't.

MICHEL: I know how it is with passion like ours.

HANNAH: It will grow into something else.

MICHEL: It will die.

HANNAH: Michel, I am hurting this way.

MICHEL: But, Hannah, what can we do?

HANNAH: Work it out. Try.

MICHEL: Why do you always want more, my little Jew? Why do you like to suffer so?

HANNAH: How can we feel what we do and not want...

MICHEL: Can you make more money, Hannah? Can you give less time to your work? Can you help me in the office, Hannah? Can you send me to school, if that's what I have to do for myself?

HANNAH: I don't want to take care of you.

MICHEL: Why can't you be happy, now? You have a lover who loves you a lot.

HANNAH: This is hurting, Michel.

MICHEL: If it hurts, you must like it that way. See how your breathing is pinched from sitting all day over your books.

HANNAH: You disgust me, Michel.

MICHEL: Hannah, if you want to rage at how bad your life is, go out on the street, gather your bags full of garbage and sit, wailing into the gutter. Don't bother me with these words.

HANNAH: All right. We are having a love affair. That's all it is. We will watch it fizzle out. But why do we need it so much? Why is it like air in our lungs?

MICHEL: Hannah, think how lucky you are to have this.

HANNAH: With you.

MICHEL: With anyone.

HANNAH: With you.

MICHEL: With anyone.

HANNAH: Only you exist for me, Michel.

MICHEL: Then take what is here. Don't ask for what we can't have in this life. Hannah, stay the morning with me.

[*He begins to come toward her.*]

HANNAH: I have work to do.

MICHEL: Your work is this pleasure we have. Take it in.

HANNAH: I must go.

MICHEL: Hannah, you give me such joy. You put such peace into my flesh. Can't you be happy, now, with what you have?

[*She comes back toward him, now.*]

HANNAH: If you touch me like that...

MICHEL: Yes, Hannah. Leave your suffering behind.

HANNAH: You were so deep inside me.

MICHEL: My cock and my hand almost met. I wanted to draw the veil aside.

HANNAH: I wanted you to kill me, then.

MICHEL: No, Hannah, not this time.

HANNAH: When?

MICHEL: You want me to kill you, Hannah? But, of course, I have already killed you in another life. At an oasis, perhaps.

HANNAH: With a small silver knife

MICHEL: Before they stoned us to death.

HANNAH: You traced your mark on my womb.

MICHEL: I cut you then myself.
The Arab and the Jew.
Adulterer. Sodomite.
Before they stoned us to death.
The hot sand swallowed our blood.

HANNAH: I knew perfect trust.
I wanted you to kill me, then,
while I was death-blessed.

MICHEL: Hannah, let me take you again from behind.

HANNAH: Take me however you wish. I leave my flesh in your arms.

[*They speak the next speeches simultaneously, aria-like.*]

MICHEL: Let me take you. Let me take you, now. Yes, yes. Are you all right? Then shout, Hannah, shout. Shout as loud as you want.

Someone might come. Someone might. I watch you here on this ledge, this hard, white ledge where I squat, out of sight, watch you writhe, watch you squirm, watch you dance, dance in the palm of my hand. I want to be stretched on that wrack, to be pulled apart, to be looked at, looked up,

HANNAH: Yes. Michel. Yes. Take me. Take me however you wish. I leave my flesh in your arms.

I am lost in a body pile, stinking with shit that slips out after the breathing has stopped. Stinking Jew in a world of Jews, everyone marked, poisons seeping into each womb. Body piles, pits, the whole earth a pit for the dead who lie shitting their prayer: Hear, oh, hear. I crawl, crawling up. Then I know. Then I see. It is a soul pile in looked into, seen. Seen in the hollow spot. The rotting part seen. The stench taken in. What I want most of all as I hang here, spread, spread apart, pulled at and stretched, played with and left, is not to be shamed. I want to feel no shame. Stroked, dirtied and cleaned, smelled, powdered and washed. Shameless. Unashamed. Without shame. Without shame in your arms. Open and seen. Seen into. Held. Wanted. Wanted like this. As I am. I want to be whole, to be held. I want to heal. Hands reaching. Clawing at me. Don't. Don't make me feel. Don't. I land on the hot stones. Spilled open, crawling toward you. Begging. Don't. Don't hurt me again. Don't let me feel. Don't. Don't.

Love, oh my love, don't cry. Don't cry in my arms. Don't. Am I hurting you? Why do you cry, Hannah, why?

which I swim. In the midst of the flesh, rotten and wet, moulding like bread, bright souls are piled in a heap. Humming, humming their song. Souls ripe like round apples. Luminous, proud. I reach out. Reach, with my mouth with my tongue. Irresistible, sweet, soul fruit left by the dead. I am found. I am fed. Light spreads through my flesh, through my hollow self. Bright soul light. I am found. I am seen. Ash drops to the ground, like an old skin that I shed. While I cling, cling to the soul pile in which I sing. I am found. I am seen. Made whole on the ripe soul song. The sudden vibrating tone. The slow sound spreading. Everywhere spreading. Light seeping in, spreading through everything. Light giving light. Light drenching me in white light.

Yes, yes. Yes, I am crying. I don't know why I cry. Stop, Michel, stop. You are hurting me, now. Hold me, hold me. Hush, hush. Hold me gentle and close.

MICHEL: Are you here, Hannah? Are you back? Hannah, I like to take you out of your mind. But I want you back with me, now.

HANNAH: You reach so far inside me. You reach so far inside. You touch me where I have not been touched before. What is it with us, what? Why is it like this with us? Why is that?

MICHEL: Take what we have. Take.

HANNAH: It is a mystery.

MICHEL: Do not question it.

SCENE 11: **Michel's dream, 1985; Sylvie and The Man Who Comes in Through the Window, Algeria, 1955; Cora and Tony, 1949; Hannah's dream of her father, 1985.**

[HANNAH *and* MICHEL *in bed, asleep; he wakes, waking her.*]

MICHEL: Hannah, wake. I dreamt last night. I was led by a monk in a black robe along the ridge of the mountain range that runs across the top of the world.

"Am I dead?" I asked him. "Follow me," he said. "Have I died?" He led me across the mountain range. I could see the whole world from where we stood. He led me to the place where the water wells up from the earth and flows down the mountain from two sides, filling the oceans of the world. He waved his hand. "Look." I looked around. I saw everything. The whole world spread itself under my feet. And the water ran down. It bubbled and sang. The monk asked for my hand. I laid it down in his own. He drew a knife from his cloak. In one stroke, he punctured my palm. He squeezed the wound. Clots of my blood dropped into all the waters of the world. I saw the water turn red. "Will I be a healer?" "Will I heal or pollute?" I cried out to him. He didn't answer when I spoke. He was gone. I stood there alone. I watched my blood flow. Watched the water turn red as it spilled two ways down the mountain side, spilled into oceans, rivers and lakes. Red blood from my hand, turning the waters red.

Hannah, do you understand? I must become like a monk.

Shut the doors to my cell. I must give myself over to my work. I must study. I need to know more.

HANNAH: Michel, you remembered your dream. You found your dream life. And the dream is new.

MICHEL: It is because of you, Hannah, because of this, because of you filling me up. I used to say, "I have no brain." Remember, Hannah, how I spoke? "I have no brain. I have only the skin on my face, good for fucking and smoking dope." But, now, Hannah, I will work.

HANNAH: I love you, Michel.

MICHEL: Yes, Hannah, I know that you do. But I need energy, now. I need energy for my work. I need support. I need to be left by myself. I need money. Hannah, can you make more money, do you think? Give less time to your work? I'm going to go back to school. I'm going to get my MD. I'm going to be respected, Hannah. I won't be outside anymore. I need someone to help me through school. I need someone to give me support. I'm going back to my wife. She will let me have a mistress. Hannah, you would never do that.

HANNAH: Back to your cow. Something to milk everyday.

MICHEL: Hannah, don't talk like that. I need you in my life. You give me something I don't get. I don't find such passion with anyone else. You give me such peace. You put such peace in my flesh.

HANNAH: No, Michel, no. The feelings will start.

MICHEL: Don't talk. Let me be gentle, now. Once more. Let me lick you everywhere.

[*A transition within the scene occurs as the following scene between* SYLVIE *and* MICHEL's *father suddenly surfaces within* MICHEL's *unconscious. He is dragged back into the trap of his past.*]

SYLVIE: Once more. One more time. No one will know. Next week, we'll be in France.

MAN: See how good I am. How careful with you. How I need you, my fancy French girl.

SYLVIE: Hush up, your sons are in the next room. Be careful where you put your cock. Put your cock somewhere safe.

[*He begins to sodomize her.*]

MAN: She looked like you, Sylvie. Like you. Sitting in the cafe with her French army man. Flirting with French army men. I'd never seen her before. If you had money, Sylvie, you would look like that. Dressed in black. High heels. Big hat. I brought her plate. Napkin on my arm. Stupid smile on my face. I've been trapped wanting you. You running to France.

SYLVIE: I'll stop wanting your song in my flesh. I'll stop knowing how to want.

MAN: Listen to what I'm telling you. The bomb blew her soldier to bits. Tore open her face. The bomb tore off her face. Blood everywhere. I lifted her up. Lifted her up while she died. I was as deep into her as I am into you. She died singing my song. Fancy French whore.

SYLVIE: My God. Oh, my God.

MAN: You'll never be free. You'll never be free of me. You've got my smell on your thighs. You've got my blood in your blood. You've got my sons.

SYLVIE: Shut up. You woke up Michel. With your dirty talk you woke up your son. Get back to bed, Michel. Get back to bed. Won't you ever leave me alone? If you tell Claude what you've seen, I'll ring your neck. You want your father? Here he is. Blood on his hands. Good for nothing but killing and having sex. You want to be like that? Is that what you want? He kills everything, Michel. Kills everything he's ever touched. You've got to forget how to want.

[MICHEL's *flash-back ends. He is back in the present.*]

MICHEL: Hannah, can you come to me, now? Can you fly? Are you here with me, now? Are you here? Hannah, I need you in my life. You give me something I don't get. Don't leave me, Hannah. Hannah, don't leave me. I come back. I come back when I can. You know that. I come back. Hannah, I need you again.

[*Transition, now, to a scene imprinted in* HANNAH*'s unconscious.*]

CORA: I tried to do everything right. I didn't know what else to do. I didn't know how to cope. The child got sick. She got sick from it all. I went to my mother's house. Showed her my bruises, my cuts. I have a sick little girl. I have a sick child. And she turned her eyes. "This doesn't happen to our kind. This doesn't happen to women like us. Where would I put you and a child? I have my own life. Wear a high collar. Get him to buy you a fur. A fur with a cowl neck. Why did you marry an Italian man. Jews don't beat their wives. I love you and the child. I want you to do the right thing. It's a pity she's so dark. Looks just like him. Go home, Cora, go home. He makes good money. At least he does that. Be happy, Cora, with what you've got."

TONY: Baby, baby, your mother's gone. She's gone and left us alone. You're all I have, now. All I've got.

CORA: How you hold that child. So gentle. So close. How you rock her back and forth. Wipe her head with a cloth. She's the one, isn't she? She's the only one for you.

TONY: Cora, thank God. Thank God, you're back. I was frightened, Cora, I was scared. Cora, you look like an angel to me. The kid's asleep. Come on, Cora. I'll make you feel good.

CORA: No, Tony. Go on to bed. I want to stay here with the child.

TONY: I told you. She's asleep.

CORA: Go on, Tony. I'll sit awhile. I want to sit with the child. I want to sit with her, that's all. She's my child. She's my little girl.

[CORA *sits. Hesitantly, she begins to sing a Yiddish lullaby to the sleeping child. Her quiet, cracked voice begins to be filled with the song.* TONY *watches for awhile. Then he sits at her feet, his head in* CORA*'s lap.*]

TONY: Baby, haven't I held you soft? Haven't I sung you to sleep?

[TONY *joins his voice to* CORA*'s. They sing for awhile. Then the memory vanishes.* HANNAH *is back in the present.*]

HANNAH: Go on, now. Go. Go on, please. Either stay here forever with me or go back to your wife.

MICHEL: Because of you, Hannah, I go away full. I never want more. Then, in a few days or a week, I start longing again. Passion like ours Hannah, is worth the pain.

HANNAH: Michel, I don't want to see you again.

MICHEL: Hannah, why talk like this? We can still meet. I'll come to you when I can. You know that.

HANNAH: No, Michel. I need myself back.

MICHEL: Hannah, one day a week for an hour or two. What harm can come?

HANNAH: Michel, I can't tie myself up longing for you.

MICHEL: With passion like ours, Hannah, we have no choice.

HANNAH: No, Michel. I want to write it all down. While the smell still drips from my thighs and the ash coats my tongue, I want to give form. From perfect pain, perfect peace.

MICHEL: You're lying, Hannah. You're lying to me. You can't say "no." You don't know how. You'll be back. In a week or two or a month, you'll be calling me. Begging me to take you any way I can.

HANNAH: [*She walks away from him.*] No, Michel. Not this time. I've wanted you more than I have ever wanted anything. I wanted the past again. I wanted it all as it was. I wanted the start. To grow from the earth again. To be made new. Grown new on our love. I'm leaving you, Michel. I can't stay. I must go.

MICHEL: This is how you give, Hannah. This is how. You beg me to want you. You beg me. I do. I want you, Hannah. I want you. Now you step on me. Now you kill. I loved you, Hannah, I did. I loved you. But you had to hurt. You had to cut. You could never be happy with what you had. You never had enough. How does it feel, Hannah? Does it feel good? How does it feel to kill love?

[*Transition to* HANNAH's *dream of her father.* MICHEL *fades from* HANNAH's *life.*]

HANNAH: I dreamt of my father last night. He sat on a wooden bench spooning something into his mouth. What are you eating, Daddy, what?

TONY: Bone marrow from a can. I want to come back to you. I want it to be like it was.

HANNAH: I kissed him and he turned to ash. His flesh turned to ash on my tongue.

TONY: Baby, come closer to me. It's hard to hear. What are you saying to me?

HANNAH: What hurt you, Daddy, when you were young? I didn't know you then. What hurt you so bad?

TONY: Baby, baby, don't bother your head. Come on, let's go. You and me. Let's go for a ride.

HANNAH: You always looked so hurt to me. I wanted to help. I wanted to mend.

TONY: It's all right, babe. It's all right again. It will be like it was.

HANNAH: I kissed you and you turned to ash. Daddy, you're growing small. You're shrinking while we talk.

TONY: Baby, baby, don't cry. Let's sneak outside. Let's go for a ride.

HANNAH: You're so small, I can swallow you whole. Swallow you up. I swallowed you whole. You churn in me, belly-full.

TONY: Baby, baby, don't go. Don't leave me alone.

[*The end.*]

Maria Irene Fornes

WHAT OF THE NIGHT?

"... Watchman, what of the night?"
The watchman said, "The morning cometh and
also the night."

Isaiah 21.11-12

NADINE

CHARACTERS:

Nadine, *35 years old. A gaunt, wiry woman. She is tough and practical*

Charlie, *16 years old. Innocent, gentle, streetwise*

Rainbow, *9 years old. High strung and sensitive*

Birdie, *14 years old. Tough. Streetwise*

Leah, *35 years old. Nadine's friend*

Pete, *40 years old. Stupid and mean*

In an economically depressed place in the Southwest. 1938.

An empty lot. In back is a sunny sky with billowing clouds. Upstage, from right to left, is a sideboard, a bassinet, a rockingchair and a tree. On top of the sideboard there is a basin with water and some statues of saints. Center right there is a dining table with four chairs. On the left there is a mattress on the floor.

SCENE 1: *A live singer or a recording of Patsy Cline's "Leaving on Your Mind." As the lights come up, the music fades.* PETE *sits on a chair that has been placed to the left.* CHARLIE *stands by the table. He wears a pair of pants and a tattered shirt. He is barefoot.* PETE *wears a frayed suit and hat. He wears shoes.*

PETE: Did you get some stuff?

CHARLIE: Yeah.

PETE: Let's see.

CHARLIE: What?

PETE: The stuff, Charlie.

[CHARLIE *goes to the sideboard and takes out a cardboard box which contains clothing, empty cans, bottles, books, magazines, and other objects. He takes the box to* PETE. PETE *examines the contents of the box with disdain.*]

This is not good, Charlie.—You can throw that stuff out. [*Pause.*] I heard you got some good stuff.

[CHARLIE *looks down.*]

So?

CHARLIE: That's it, Pete.

PETE: Oh, yeah?

CHARLIE: …Yeah…

[PETE *gives* CHARLIE *a knowing look.*]

I got some other stuff.

PETE: That's what I said. Bring it out.

CHARLIE: It's not that good.

PETE: Bring it out.

CHARLIE: I thought I could keep some.

PETE: How come?

CHARLIE: I thought I could.

PETE: Who told you that?

CHARLIE: Maybe you did, Pete.

PETE: Never said that.

CHARLIE: Oh.

PETE: Better get it, Charlie.

CHARLIE: Yeah. [*He goes to the sideboard, gets a paper bag full of clothes and puts it on the floor.*] Here it is, Pete.

PETE: What's here?

CHARLIE: You can see for yourself, Pete.—It's not good.

PETE: Let's see.

CHARLIE: It's no good, Pete

[PETE *goes to* CHARLIE *and sends him flying with a punch in the jaw.*]

PETE: Show me, Charlie.

[CHARLIE*'s mouth is bleeding. He crawls to the bag. He takes out a garment.*]

What's that?

CHARLIE: A jacket.

PETE: Is it good?

CHARLIE: It's torn.

PETE: Did you do that?

CHARLIE: No, Pete.

[PETE *shows* CHARLIE *a fist.*]

Pulled it off him.

[*As* PETE *punches* CHARLIE *in the face.*]

No, Pete!

PETE: I said, don't be rough with the clothes. [*Pause.*] What do you say?

CHARLIE: Yeah, Pete.

PETE: I said to be careful.—What else?

CHARLIE: [*Pulling out a pair of pants.*] Pants.

PETE: Let's see.

[CHARLIE *hands* PETE *the pants.* PETE *looks at the pants. Then he looks at the pants* CHARLIE *is wearing.*]

Take them off.

CHARLIE: Pete.

PETE: Take them off.

[CHARLIE *takes off his pants and hands them to* PETE. PETE *puts the pants on the pile.*]

What else?

CHARLIE: There's a shirt.

PETE: [*Pointing to the pile.*] Put it here.

> [CHARLIE *does.*]

> Underwear?

CHARLIE: Yes.

PETE: Let's see.

> [CHARLIE *slides the bag towards* PETE. PETE *pushes the bag back with his foot.*]

> Take it out.

> [CHARLIE *takes out an undershirt and hands it to* PETE.]

> Undershirt?

CHARLIE: Yes.

PETE: Put it here.

> [CHARLIE *does.*]

> What else?

> [CHARLIE *takes out a pair of socks and puts it in the pile.*]

CHARLIE: Socks.

PETE: Are they clean?

CHARLIE: No.

PETE: [*Throwing them back at* CHARLIE.] Wash them!—Shorts?

CHARLIE: No.

PETE: How come?

CHARLIE: I left him that.

PETE: How come?

CHARLIE: He was cold.

PETE: He was cold.

CHARLIE: Yeah.

PETE: Was they yours to give?

[CHARLIE *doesn't answer.*]

Was they yours to give!

[CHARLIE *doesn't answer.*]

Was they yours to give!

[CHARLIE *doesn't answer.* PETE *punches* CHARLIE. CHARLIE *falls to the ground.* PETE *kicks him repeatedly and continues repeating the line through the following speech.*]

CHARLIE: [*Crying.*] He was naked! I didn't want to leave him naked! He was cold! I felt sorry for him! To be lying in the street cold and hurt. I wouldn't want it done to me! I wouldn't want it done to me! I wouldn't want it done to me! I wouldn't want it done to me!

PETE: Put the stuff in the bag.

[CHARLIE *starts putting the clothes in the bag.*]

This is junk. You hear! Get better stuff or your out! You hear! I try to place this stuff and it's crap.—You hear! Can't carry you any more. Shape up or you're out! I want good clothes. You mug bums! I want good stuff! Wallets with money! How come there's never any money. Wrist watches. Don't mug bums, idiot.—And if you ever keep something again you're dead! You hear! [*He takes the bag and starts to go.*]

CHARLIE: You didn't pay me, Pete.

[PETE *stops.*]

PETE: For what?

CHARLIE: For the stuff.

[PETE *walks to* CHARLIE. *He stretches his closed hand to him.* CHARLIE *reaches out.* PETE *grabs* CHARLIE's *hand and twists it.*]

PETE: You want to get paid?

[CHARLIE *lets out a scream.*]

CHARLIE: I need some money, Pete.

[PETE *presses harder on* CHARLIE's *wrist.*]

For Lucille, Pete.

[PETE *presses harder.*]

She needs medicine.

PETE: [*Pressing.*] You want money?

CHARLIE: Oh!

PETE: For what, Charlie? For this junk?

[NADINE *enters.* PETE *sees her and releases* CHARLIE's *hand. She looks at him a hard look.*]

He's stealing from me.

NADINE: Are you stealing from him, Charlie?

CHARLIE: No.

NADINE: He's not stealing from you. [*To* CHARLIE.] Did he hurt you?

CHARLIE: Yeah. [*Showing* NADINE *his hand.*] Look.

NADINE: I don't want you to be hurting the kid.

PETE: He's stealing from me.

NADINE: O.K., you don't hit him. He don't steal from you.

PETE: O.K. [*He starts to go.*]

NADINE: You paid for the clothes?

PETE: No.

NADINE: Why?

PETE: He tried to steal them.

NADINE: Yeah, but he didn't. So pay.

PETE: Says who, Nadine?

NADINE: Fair's fair.

[PETE *takes some coins from his pocket and throws them to* CHARLIE. *He exits.* NADINE *takes a few steps after* PETE.]

Come back here, Pete. I have to talk to you. Get lost, Charlie. I want to talk to Pete.

[PETE *re-enters.*]

Sit down.

[PETE *sits.*]

I just thought I'd discuss something with you.

[PETE *waits.*]

I think Charlie should get a bigger cut.

PETE: Who do you think you are, Nadine?

NADINE: I'm Charlie's mother.—And I have to look after him.

PETE: [*Starting to go.*] You don't say.

NADINE: Sit down.

[*He sits. She sits. She tries to be sociable.*]

I've lost the habit of talking to grown-ups. You get a little rough screaming at kids all the time. You forget to be civilized.—How about discussing something, Pete? Just sitting down and discussing something with another person. [*She waits.*] I have a sick kid, Pete. She's very sick. She's going to die. And I wanted to know if you ever had a kid. [*She waits.*] Have you ever had kids? [*She waits.*] Lost the habit of talking to grown-ups, didn't you.—Haven't you, Pete?

[PETE *stares at her.*]

Well, I wonder if you could lend me some money. I could buy some medicine for Lucille. And I could pay you back. [*She waits.*] Pete. [*She waits. A moment passes.*]

[CHARLIE *peeks in.*]

Scram!

[CHARLIE *exits.*]

Charlie goes out every day and risks his skin to get stuff for you. Sometimes he hasn't had a hot meal in days and you give him pennies for a full day's work even when you know he could get hurt doing it—or get arrested—for doing your dirty work. He doesn't ask so much but he needs more and you have to give him more. His kid sister's sick and she has to get medicine. Otherwise she's going to die. You're a nice man. You have a heart.—Give me the money for the medicine.—It's not that much.—You won't let the kid die. [*She waits.*] Pete? [*She waits. She swings at him and misses. She reaches over and grabs him by his shirt collar.*] I'm getting that money one way or another, Pete.

[*There's a pause. She releases him. He fixes his collar.*]

PETE: You're funny. [*He starts to stand.*]

NADINE: Sit.

[*He sits.* RAINBOW *and* BIRDIE *enter left.*]

What do you want?

[*There's a pause.* RAINBOW *and* BIRDIE *exit.* NADINE *walks behind* PETE. *She puts her hand inside his jacket and squeezes his breast. He grabs her arm to remove it but begins to shake. His eyes roll. She lowers her hand to his crotch. He quivers. He pants and grunts. His eyes roll.*]

You got to pay.

[*He shakes his head as he lets air out of his mouth.*]

You gotta.

[*He shakes his head. She grabs his hair and pulls his head back.*]

You gotta.

[*He whimpers and stamps his feet. He growls and drools.*]

You want some?

PETE: Yeah! Yeah!

NADINE: You got to pay!

PETE: No!

NADINE: You got to pay!

PETE: No!

NADINE: You got to pay!

PETE: No!

NADINE: Yeah!

PETE: No!

NADINE: Yeah!

PETE: No!

NADINE: [*Taking her hand off.*] You get none!

[PETE *snorts, pants and makes noises as if he is having a heart attack. He puts a dollar on the table. She takes the dollar and puts it on her cleavage.*]

More, Pete! Get it out.

[PETE *reaches for his fly.*]

Money!

[*He puts another dollar on the table. She puts it in her cleavage. He stands and pushes his pelvis against her.*]

More!

[*He puts a dollar on her cleavage. The lights fade as* PETE *moves his pelvis against* NADINE.]

PETE: Yeah! [*Moving his pelvis against her.*] Now! Now! Now! [*He pants.*] Now! Now! Now!

SCENE 2: CHARLIE *wears a pair of very large white pants over his own pants.* LEAH *sits to the left pinning the back of the pants.* BIRDIE *sits on the mattress sewing on a veil made from a black crinoline petticoat. She wears bright blue lipstick.* RAINBOW *sits next to her. She reads a comic.* NADINE *sits on the rocker. She holds* LUCILLE, *wrapped in a blanket, in her arms.*

CHARLIE: [*Pulling the pants out at the waist.*] They're too big, Mom.

NADINE: Take the other pants off, Charlie. You can't wear two pairs of pants at the same time and expect them to fit.—I hope your kids are smarter than mine, Leah.

LEAH: They're not any smarter. Kids are not smart nowadays.

CHARLIE: [*To* LEAH.] I don't see why you think you're so smart. You old folks always think you're smart.

LEAH: [*Turning* CHARLIE *around to pin the front of his pants.*] I'm not old. You think that because you're a twerp. You're not a person yet.

[CHARLIE *gestures hitting her on the head.*]

Stand still.—You're only half made.

CHARLIE: I'm grown up. I'm getting married.

LEAH: You're not old enough to get married. I'll bet you don't even have a peepee yet. You probably don't have a peepee yet.

RAINBOW: Don't let her talk to you like that, Charlie. I wouldn't let her talk to me like that.

CHARLIE: She's a crazy old witch. You think I listen to what she says?

NADINE: Show respect. Don't pay any attention to him, Leah. You can't teach kids respect nowadays. You think he listens to me? He don't. I tell him he should marry someone rich but he doesn't. Look who he's getting married to.

[LEAH *looks at* BIRDIE.]

Birdie!

CHARLIE: And why not?

NADINE: Look at her!

[*They look at* BIRDIE. *She continues sewing a moment. Then, she looks at them.*]

BIRDIE: What?

NADINE: See what I mean?

CHARLIE: And where would I find someone rich?

NADINE: Have you looked!

CHARLIE: If I had the right clothes...

NADINE: With your looks?

CHARLIE: I'd need a good suit.

NADINE: You don't need a suit.

[BIRDIE *puts the veil on. It covers her face.*]

BIRDIE: How does it look?

NADINE: See that?

LEAH: Let's see, Birdie.

[BIRDIE *turns to* LEAH.]

NADINE: Is there something you can do about that veil, Leah?

[BIRDIE *turns to* NADINE.]

LEAH: Let's see.

[BIRDIE *turns to* LEAH.]

I don't know, Nadine.

NADINE: [*Pointing to* BIRDIE.] Look at that... [*Pointing to* CHARLIE.] Then, look at him.—A prince.

CHARLIE: [*As he takes his pants off.*] Thanks, Mom.

NADINE: He could've married money.

CHARLIE: You hear that, Birdie?

NADINE: Sure.

CHARLIE: Oh, Mom.

NADINE: Oh, Charlie.

[BIRDIE *looks up.*]

Why are you wearing that lipstick?

BIRDIE: 'Cause I put it on. O.K.?

[NADINE *turns up her eyes.*]

NADINE: You see, Leah?

CHARLIE: It's O.K., Mom.

NADINE: Things were different when we were growing, Leah. Weren't they?

LEAH: Yes they were.

NADINE: Did you ever get married, Leah?

LEAH: No, Nadine. Did you?

NADINE: Never. Once I did. [*Touching her heart.*] Here.

LEAH: Who was that?

NADINE: Charlie's dad. He got inside my heart. And I couldn't pull him out. Then little Charlie come and I had to take care of him, so I couldn't work. I had to ask Charlie if he'd take care of us. He said yes but he didn't. The obligation. He'd go off and drink and stay away for days.—He got a woman.

LEAH: Did she give him money?

NADINE: Money?

LEAH: Did you?

NADINE: I never gave him money.

LEAH: You see him?

NADINE: Him?

LEAH: Yeah.

NADINE: In the street.

LEAH: Alone?

NADINE: Me?

LEAH: Is he alone?

NADINE: He is not alone. He's never alone.

LEAH: Was she pretty?

NADINE: She wasn't pretty.

LEAH: What did she look like?

NADINE: Like a dog. Worse. [*Pause.*] I had a baby.

LEAH: Rainbow.

NADINE: Before Rainbow. Ray. I was sick. I couldn't take care of him. I couldn't feed him. I thought I was going to die. I had no milk in my breasts. Charlie was older and he could fend for himself. But not little Ray. I had to give him up.—They thought I was going to die and I gave him up. He was cute. He had pretty eyes.—I don't know where he is. He's all right though. He's with a family, like his own. They say he's all right. He goes to school.

[RAINBOW *sits on* NADINE's *lap.*]

I should've give this one away too.

RAINBOW: Oh, Mom.

NADINE: Life with me isn't good. It's no good for the kids. I have nothing good to give them, nothing to teach them. I'm a whore. That's what I have to do to feed them. [*There is a pause.*] Did you know that? At least the kids don't see what I do.

LEAH: They can hear you, Nadine.

NADINE: They don't see it. At least they don't see it. [*She rocks* RAINBOW.] It's hard on them.

[RAINBOW *and* BIRDIE *do a little veil dance.*]

SCENE 3: BIRDIE *sits at the table. She wears a sweater. She is finishing eating a sandwich.* RAINBOW *sits on the mattress. She has just eaten. There are two plates and silver on the table.*

BIRDIE: My mother died of emphysema, couldn't breathe. They put tubes in her. Up her nose, up her private parts, up the veins in her arms. I wouldn't want any of that done to me. Even if I'm going to die. When I die I'll just die. That stuff doesn't save you. It just makes you look ugly. I'd rather just die. The uglier they keep you the uglier you look.—I don't think I'm ever going to be fat. I'm too skinny.

RAINBOW: Hm.

BIRDIE: In the home there was a girl who was nice. She never said anything unless she meant it. And no one could make her say anything she didn't mean. She had no teeth and she'd say to me, "Your problems are my problems." She meant that if I had a problem she'd help. And that was very nice but all the kids laughed at her because she had no teeth and they didn't understand her when she talked. [*She eats.*] I never did any whoring either. Not me. I wouldn't do anything like that. I can't stand someone telling me what to do. And I couldn't stand someone touching me unless I wanted it. I don't care how much they'd pay. Charlie's always telling me to do this and to do that because everybody bosses him. He thinks because he's married he should be bossing me. Nadine hates me and won't stop till she sees me out of here.

[NADINE *enters. She goes to the table, takes the silver from the table, goes to the sideboard, opens a drawer, gives a suspicious look to* BIRDIE, *counts the silver in the drawer, puts the silver in, closes the drawer, gives another suspicious look to* BIRDIE, *and exits.*]
Did you see that?

RAINBOW: What?

BIRDIE: Your mother. She thinks I'm going to steal something. I don't like that and I don't like being looked at weird either.

RAINBOW: I don't look at you weird.

BIRDIE: You don't, but she does. I'm getting out of here.

RAINBOW: Where are you going?

BIRDIE: I don't need a place.

RAINBOW: You don't?

BIRDIE: I can sleep in the street.

RAINBOW: Really?

BIRDIE: You can come with me if you want.

RAINBOW: And sleep in the street?

BIRDIE: Yeah.

RAINBOW: Uh uh.

BIRDIE: Well, I'm going even if you're not.

RAINBOW: You have money?

BIRDIE: No.

RAINBOW: You need money.

BIRDIE: What for?

RAINBOW: To eat.

BIRDIE: You call this eating here?

RAINBOW: It's better than nothing.

BIRDIE: It stinks.

RAINBOW: How about Charlie?

BIRDIE: He can leave too if he wants.—I was better off in the home. They didn't treat me like a criminal there. She's always watching me. She doesn't watch you! How many times is she going to count the silver? She thinks I'm going to steal her crummy forks. She's worse than the matrons in prison.

RAINBOW: In prison?

BIRDIE: Yeah, prison. No one there was as bad. Not even the torturer.

RAINBOW: Torturer?

BIRDIE: Sure. A big ugly torturer with a big ugly sore on her lip.

RAINBOW: Did she hurt?

BIRDIE: Sure. Plenty. She twisted our fingers and toes till we thought they were going to fall off.

RAINBOW: What for?

BIRDIE: Are you kidding? To hurt us.

RAINBOW: What for?

BIRDIE: Are you kidding? To find out something or to punish us for something. She liked to give us pain. Or else she tried to drown us.

RAINBOW: Drown you?

BIRDIE: Yeah. She'd put our head in the water and hold it there till we started to drown. Then she'd pull it up and said, "Ready to talk?" We couldn't talk because we had water coming out of our mouths and our noses and our ears. So she'd say, "O.K. If you don't want to talk, take this." And she'd push our heads in the water again. Someone said that Kitty was a dike and that she liked hurting us because she knew we wouldn't go for her. She didn't have to ask because she knew what the answer would be, "no, you pig." [*She laughs heartily.*] "No, you pig." That's what we'd say to her. [*She laughs.*] Some people said she had cancer on her lip. But no one gave a damn. That's how much nobody cared about her. Because she was so mean. We were not allowed to smoke but I smoked. They would catch me by the smell in my mouth. She was a pervert. She liked to put her nose in my mouth. She was always calling me in to smell my mouth. One day I bit her nose. She was going to report me but I paid her off.

RAINBOW: You paid her?

BIRDIE: I had money. I worked at the shop. We made shoes. I liked to work to keep my mind off how unhappy I was.

[CHARLIE *enters with* LUCILLE. *He sits in the rocking chair, rocks her to sleep and hums.*]

He's always telling me what to do because everyone tells him what to do.

CHARLIE: Who tells me what to do?

[PETE *enters left and hides behind the tree.*]

BIRDIE: Everyone tells you what to do. Nadine tells you what to do and Pete tells you what to do. So you think that getting married means that you get to boss me. But no one tells me what to do— [*To* RAINBOW.] He says he's the boss. But look at him, he's skin and bones. You see this sweater? It's too small for me. Well, I'm going to give it to Charlie because he's skinnier than me. He gets angry but that's a reality. Charlie said we're going to be on our own. But now he says he can't leave Lucille. Well, he cares more about Lucille and Nadine and the whole lot of them than he cares for me. [*Standing.*] I want something from life. Do something. [*She starts to walk left. She sees* PETE.] What's he doing! He's always staring at me! He just stands there and stares at me! You peeping Tom!

RAINBOW: Who's that!

BIRDIE: Pete.

CHARLIE: What are you looking at! Fuck head!

[*Going towards the tree.* LUCILLE *starts to cry.*]

Yeah, you! Fuck head! Yeah! Fuck head! You! Yeah, you! Fuck head! [*He returns to the rocking chair.*] Fuck head! [CHARLIE *rocks* LUCILLE. *To himself.*] Fuck head.

PETE: [*Shouting from behind the tree.*] I'm sick and tired of the whole lot of you!

CHARLIE: Shut your trap! I'm trying to put Lucille to sleep!

PETE: Always trying to get something for nothing! You hoodlums! Well, forget it! My money is mine and I'm keeping it! You won't get nothing for nothing! You hear that! Mine! You hear that! It's my money! And I get to keep it! And if you want it you're gonna have to send the pretty girl to get it! Come and get it, Birdie! I have a birdie inside my pants waiting for you!

CHARLIE: [*Starting to stand.*] You scum.—

PETE: Come here, girlie, tweet tweet!

CHARLIE: You take that back! [*Holding* LUCILLE *on the left arm and throwing punches with the right.*] Come out and fight!— Rainbow!!

[RAINBOW *runs to* CHARLIE'*s side.*]

Take Lucille!

[RAINBOW *takes* LUCILLE *and exits right.*]

I'm going to tear you to pieces , Pete!

PETE: Come on, Charlie! I always wanted to hear your tiny bones cracking! Crackle crackle! Come on!

CHARLIE: [*Shadow boxing.*] Come out you yellowed belly scum!

PETE: Take one more step and I'm gonna make you swallow your teeth.

CHARLIE: You're a coward, Pete!

PETE: Yeah? Say goodbye, Charlie. Say goodbye.

BIRDIE: Why don't you get yourself a date so you don't have to stand behind trees touching yourself?

PETE: Come a little closer you little slut! And I'll show you what I can put inside you!

CHARLIE: You blood sucker! That's my wife you're talking to! I'm going to push your face through your head! Come out! You coward! I'm not going to work for you any more!

PETE: Who're you going to work for, pee wee?

CHARLIE: [*Getting closer to the tree as* PETE *moves left.*] Don't make me lose my temper. Fuck head.

PETE: Sure.

CHARLIE: [*Reaching the tree as* PETE *moves further left.*] Scram!

[PETE *shadow boxes as he moves towards the tree.* CHARLIE *shadow boxes as he retreats. They freeze for a moment, then* CHARLIE *mumbles some words and sits on the rocking chair.*]

PETE: Yeah! You stay there, boy. And don't come too close to me or I may hit you hard. And don't ask me to feel sorry for you because I've had it with feeling sorry for you. I'm sick and nobody feels sorry for me. I'm going to die in the gutter and nobody's going to feel sorry for me or come and ask me if I need anything. The dogs will see me dead and they'll just come to eat me like dead meat. People eat animal dead meat and animals eat human dead meat if they can. They can tell you're dead because you get cold and also because you don't move when they get close to you and nudge you, or when they growl at you, or when they start digging their teeth into you. I'm saving money to buy me a cemetery lot so I don't have to lay in the street till the garbage collector comes to get me. I'm getting my corner in the cemetery and I'm getting myself buried when I die so no one can mess with me.

BIRDIE: Good bye, Charlie. I'm leaving now.

CHARLIE: Don't go, Birdie.

BIRDIE: You'll never leave, Charlie.

CHARLIE: I will, Birdie, I will.

BIRDIE: You'll never leave Lucille.

CHARLIE: I will.

BIRDIE: And you'll never leave Rainbow.

CHARLIE: I will.

BIRDIE: You'll never leave.

CHARLIE: I will, Birdie.

BIRDIE: Come now! Leave with me now!

CHARLIE: I can't!

RAINBOW: Get up and leave with me now!

CHARLIE: I can't now, Birdie. How can I?

BIRDIE: You'll never leave.

CHARLIE: Birdie. I'm tied down. I have to help Nadine. I gotta. I can't leave.

BIRDIE: Oh! Charlie! [*She starts to go.*] Good bye!

CHARLIE: Try to understand, Birdie.[*Going on his knees.*] I beg you, Birdie. Things will work out. You want to see me down? [*Going flat on the floor.*] My face is on the floor, Birdie. You want to see dirt on my face? [*He rubs his face on the floor.*] Here's dirt on my face. Birdie, don't leave. Don't go, Birdie, I can't stand it if you leave. Birdie.

[BIRDIE *exits.* RAINBOW *enters. She is wrapped in a blanket.* CHARLIE *mumbles and cries and sobs, his face still on the floor.*]

RAINBOW: [*Softly.*] Birdie...don't leave.

[PETE *comes out from behind the tree. He raises his hands after* BIRDIE *questioningly.*]

PETE: Birdie...?

SPRINGTIME

CHARACTERS:

Rainbow, *29 years old. Slim and spirited*

Greta, *26 years old. Slim, handsome and shy*

Ray, *27 years old. High strung and handsome. He wears a dark suit*

In a small Eastern city. 1958.

SCENE 1: Greta is ill

[RAINBOW'*s bedroom. A small room. On the left wall there is, up-stage, a small door; downstage of the door there is a small window. Downstage of the window there is a chair. In the up-right hand corner of the room there is a small bed with metal foot and headboard. On top of the bed there is a nightgown. To the left of the bed there is a night table. On the night table there is a book, a pitcher of water, and a glass. On the back wall there hangs a painting of a landscape.* RAINBOW *and* GRETA *have just entered.* GRETA *takes off her dress, sits on the bed, and starts to put on the nightgown.*]

RAINBOW: Don't worry, Greta. I know what to do.

GRETA: What, Rainbow? What can you do?

RAINBOW: I'll find some money. Don't worry.

GRETA: How?

RAINBOW: I'll find money, Greta. I can't tell you how.

GRETA: Why not?

RAINBOW: You won't love me anymore if I tell you how.

GRETA: Tell me.

RAINBOW: Please don't make me tell you.

GRETA: I don't want you to do anything that would make you ashamed.

RAINBOW: I've been in jail.

GRETA: Why? What did you do?

[RAINBOW *helps* GRETA *lie down. She covers her with the sheet.*]
Tell me.

RAINBOW: I've been in jail for stealing.

GRETA: Stealing?

RAINBOW: Yes. I haven't done it since I know you. But now I must do it again. You're ill and we must take care of you.

GRETA: No! I don't want you to steal for me. You'll be arrested. You'll go to jail. You mustn't.

RAINBOW: I must, my darling.

[*There is a silence.* GRETA *puts her face on the pillow and sobs.*]

SCENE 2: Stealing for Greta

[GRETA *is lying in bed.* RAINBOW *sits on the chair.*]

RAINBOW: I got it off his pocket. He came out of the store and put it in his pocket. I grabbed it and ran. He ran after me and grabbed me. He tripped. I yanked my arm off and I threw him. Look. He tore my sleeve. [*Putting a wristwatch on* GRETA'*s hand.*] He ran after me but I was gone. Went in a building and hid. Saw him pass. Went to the back of the building and got out through the yard. I was afraid to go in the street. I was afraid he may have gone around the block. There's no one there. I walk to the corner and grab a bus. I didn't look like a thief. Would anyone think I'm a thief? Wasn't out of breath. Sat calmly— [*Gettting the watch from* GRETA.] It's a good watch.

GRETA: Get rid of it.

RAINBOW: I'll sell it.

GRETA: To whom?

RAINBOW: I'll find a buyer.

GRETA: I'm afraid.

RAINBOW: Don't be.

GRETA: Just get rid of it.

RAINBOW: We need the money. For you. To make you well.

SCENE 3: Rainbow is caught

[RAINBOW *sits turned away from* GRETA. *Her hand covers her cheek.* GRETA *lies on the bed.*]

GRETA: Look at me! Who hurt you like that?

[RAINBOW *turns to face* GRETA.]

Who did that to you?

RAINBOW: The man whose watch I took.

GRETA: I knew you'd get hurt. I knew you couldn't do what you were doing and not get hurt.

RAINBOW: I got careless. I went back where I got the watch.

GRETA: Why?

RAINBOW: He came from behind. He grabbed me and made me go with him.

GRETA: Where?

RAINBOW: To his place.

GRETA: Oh!

RAINBOW: I tried to get away. He forced me. I resisted and he pushed me in. He said he'd put me in jail.

GRETA: What did he do to you!

RAINBOW: I had to agree.

GRETA: To what?

RAINBOW: To do something for him.

GRETA: What!

RAINBOW: Meet someone.

GRETA: Who!

RAINBOW: He didn't say.

GRETA: What for?

RAINBOW: He's nasty.

GRETA: Are you afraid?

RAINBOW: Yes.

SCENE 4: Greta wonders if Rainbow loves Ray

[GRETA *lies in bed.* RAINBOW *stands left.*]

RAINBOW: He's like a snake.

GRETA: Do you love him?

RAINBOW: Love him? I hate him. He hates me. He hates me for no reason. Not because of the watch. He never cared about the watch. Just for no reason. He never cared about the watch. That was nothing for him. He hates me. Just because he wants to. —I hate him but I have a reason. [*She goes to the chair.*] I understand him though.

GRETA: You do?

RAINBOW: Yes.

GRETA: How can you?

RAINBOW: I think in his heart of hearts he's not the way he appears to be.

GRETA: What is he like? He couldn't be good and do what he does.

RAINBOW: Well, he's not what he appears to be.

[*Pause.*]

GRETA: …Could I have some water?

[RAINBOW *pours water. She lifts* GRETA's *head up and holds the glass to* GRETA's *lips. When* GRETA *drinks,* RAINBOW *puts the glass down and sits.*]

Didn't you already do what you had to do for him? Didn't you already pay—for the watch? Why do you still have to work for him?

RAINBOW: He's a friend.

GRETA: If I die…Will you love him then?

RAINBOW: …If you die?— [*She goes to the side of the bed and kneels.*] If you die I'll love *you*—whether you live or die it's you I love. And if I ever loved anyone else, it would not be Ray. Not Ray. Never Ray.

[GRETA *laughs.*]

SCENE 5: *Heute sind Kleider eng*

[RAINBOW *sweeps the floor.*]

GRETA: You never wear clothes that fit.

RAINBOW: This?

GRETA: That's a size too small.

RAINBOW: It's my size.

GRETA: Clothes should be looser.

RAINBOW: Not any more, madam. Now clothes are tight—how do you say that in German?

GRETA: What.

RAINBOW: What I just said.

GRETA: What?

RAINBOW: Now clothes are tight.

GRETA: *Heute sind Kleider eng.*

RAINBOW: [*Mispronouncing.*] *Heute sind Kleider eng.*

GRETA: [*Impatiently.*] *Heute sind Kleider eng.*

RAINBOW: How do you say, "You lose your temper too easily"?

GRETA: Who?

RAINBOW: You.

GRETA: I lose my temper?

RAINBOW: Yes.

GRETA: I don't.

RAINBOW: How do you say it?

GRETA: That I lose my temper?

RAINBOW: Yes.

GRETA: I don't lose my temper.

RAINBOW: How do you say it?

GRETA: *Ich werde niemals heftig.*

RAINBOW: *Ich werde niemals heftig...*I love German. [*She swoons to the floor.*] ...I love German.

GRETA: That means "I don't lose my temper." Ha!

SCENE 6: Ray gives advice to Rainbow

[RAINBOW *stands right fluffing the pillow.* GRETA *sits up against the headboard.*]

RAINBOW: Can you imagine?—And I said to him, "It's you who places too much importance on whether I like men or I like women. For me it's not important. What's important is that since I met Greta it's only she I love. [*Placing the pillow behind* GRETA.] That's what's important. [*Taking the bedspread off the bed.*] Why should it be important whether I like men or women? Does it make any difference to anyone?— [*Taking the bedspread out the door to shake it.*] If it doesn't make any difference to anyone, why should anyone care?" [*Turning to* GRETA.] He said, "If it doesn't make any difference why don't you choose to love a man?" And I said, "It doesn't make a difference to anyone else, but of course, it makes a difference to me." [*Placing the cover over* GRETA.] If I don't like men why should I pretend that I do? Why should I try to love someone I don't love when I already love someone I love? And besides, do you think it makes a difference to anyone?

GRETA: I suppose it doesn't make any difference to anyone.

RAINBOW: That's right. Why should I force myself. [*Sitting next to* GRETA.] And he said, "What difference does anything make? Live, die, it doesn't make any difference." And I said, "Live or die makes a difference. I want to live and I want to be happy but I don't care about the things you care about." And he said, "What things?" And I said, [*Walking to the chair.*] "The way you see things." And I said that I'm not going to pretend to see life the way he does. And he said, "Why not?" that he thought I should. And he said that I should care about those things and if I don't I should pretend that I do. And I said, [*Sitting.*] "Why?" And he said that he talks to me as a brother would, for my own good. And I said I thought he had some nerve because I thought his life was far from impeccable—far from it.—And I told him that.

GRETA: His life is far from impeccable.

RAINBOW: I told him he had some nerve.

GRETA: Your life is impeccable now. —I don't see anything wrong with it.

RAINBOW: ...Neither do I.

GRETA: Your life was peccable when you were working for him. But now that you've paid your debt to him and you don't work for him anymore your life is impeccable. It was he who made your life peccable.

[RAINBOW *laughs.*]

Why do you laugh?

RAINBOW: How do you say peccable in German?

GRETA: Why?

SCENE 7: Greta wonders how Rainbow sees things

[GRETA *lies in bed.* RAINBOW *sits by the window looking out into the yard.*]

RAINBOW: With time and money they look better and better.

GRETA: What, honey?

RAINBOW: The flowers.

GRETA: How could that be?

RAINBOW: Maybe it's the fertilizer I put on the soil.

GRETA: What looks better?

RAINBOW: The colors. They look healthier.

GRETA: How do you see things? Do you see things different from the way I see them?

RAINBOW: Why do you ask?

GRETA: [*Smiling.*] I just wondered.

RAINBOW: Why?

GRETA: I worried…

RAINBOW: That we see things differently…?

GRETA: Yes.

RAINBOW: We don't.

SCENE 8: **Greta discovers what Rainbow does for Ray**

[GRETA *is standing on the chair. She is opening an envelope. She takes out some pictures and looks through them with alarm. She throws them on the floor and stares into space.* RAINBOW *enters. She looks at the pictures on the floor. Then, she looks at* GRETA.]

GRETA: Is that what you do for him!

[RAINBOW *kneels down to get the pictures.* GRETA *tries to reach for the pictures.*]

Why! Why!

[GRETA *starts pounding on* RAINBOW. RAINBOW *tries to hold her down.*]

Why! Why are you doing that when I asked you not to! Why do you do that!—Why do you do that!—Why do you do that! You're lying naked with that man! Who is that man! What is he doing to you! Why do you do that! Why do you take your clothes off! Why do you take such pictures.

RAINBOW: I'm sorry! I'm sorry!

GRETA: Why do you do that!

RAINBOW: I have to.

GRETA: Why!

RAINBOW: Because you must have treatment.

[GRETA *cries.*]

I don't mind. It's for you.

[GRETA *sobs.*]

It's for you.

SCENE 9: **Greta admires the sunlight**

[*The shutter is closed.* GRETA *sits upstage of the window. The chair faces front.* RAINBOW *stands next to her.*]

GRETA: Could you open the window?

[RAINBOW *opens the window.*]

I like to sit here and see the sun coming in. I like to let it come in through the open window. The sun is brighter that way—or so it seems to me. There are times when I feel disturbed. I feel restless. I feel nasty. And looking at the sun coming in makes me feel calm.

SCENE 10: Greta thinks that Ray is in love

[GRETA *stands left of the bed straightening the bed.* RAINBOW *sits on the chair.*]

GRETA: Ray was here this afternoon.

RAINBOW: What did he want?

GRETA: He didn't say—He waited for you and then he left— [*She starts moving down as she straightens the side of the bed.*] Does he sound to you like he's in love?

RAINBOW: No.

GRETA: He sounds to me like he's in love.

RAINBOW: Who with?

GRETA: I don't know, but he sounds to me like he's in love.

RAINBOW: How does a person in love sound?

[GRETA *sits on the right side of the bed.*]

GRETA: A person in love holds his breath a little after inhaling or while they inhale. They inhale, stop for a moment and inhale a little more.

RAINBOW: I haven't seen him do that. [*She lies on the bed.*]

GRETA: I have.

RAINBOW: He seems preoccupied to me.

GRETA: Yes, I think he sounds preoccupied. Maybe he's lost money in the Market.

RAINBOW: Maybe he has. Why are you concerned about him?

GRETA: I'm not.

RAINBOW: You sound concerned.

GRETA: He's preoccupied.

SCENE 11: **Rainbow doesn't feel loved anymore**

[GRETA *lies in bed.* RAINBOW *stands by the door facing her.*]

RAINBOW: Something's wrong. Something's wrong because you're not happy, because you have to keep things from me. I know you don't tell me what you think—not everything. Did you ever keep things from me before? Is this something new or have you always kept things from me? [*Pause.*] Is it that you don't love me anymore?

GRETA: [*Shaking her head.*] No.

RAINBOW: For me to love is adoring. And to be loved is to be adored. So I never felt I was loved before. Till I met you. But I don't feel loved anymore.

SCENE 12: **Ray wants something from Greta**

[GRETA *lies in bed.* RAY *stands to the left of the bed by her feet, facing her. She is frightened like a trapped cat.*]

GRETA: I lash out at you because I can't deal with you. I can't even understand what you are.

[*In the course of the speech* RAY *moves closer and closer to her and starts to lean towards her, she recoils.*]

You're like some kind of animal who comes to me with strange problems, to make strange demands on me.

[*She pushes him off. He persists.*]

You come in all sweaty and hungry and you say you want this and you want that. Take your hands away from me! Not again! Not again! Never again! Don't touch me! Leave me be! I have nothing to give you. Don't tell me that you want these things. Talk about something else. What else can you talk about?

[RAINBOW *enters. She is obviously alarmed. She looks at* GRETA, *then at* RAY; *then at* GRETA *again.* GRETA *turns her head away and sobs.* RAINBOW *and* RAY *look at each other.*]

SCENE 13: Rainbow leaves Greta

[RAINBOW *stands at the door looking out.* GRETA *sits on the bed looking at her. "Melancholy Baby" is heard:*]

Come to me, my melancholy baby.
Just cuddle up and don't be blue.
All your fears are foolish fancy, baby.
You know, honey, I'm in love with you.

[GRETA *moves to the chair. She sits facing* RAINBOW. *She looks down.*]

Every cloud must have a silver lining.

[GRETA *looks at* RAINBOW.]

So wait until the sun shines through.
Smile, my honey, dear,
While I kiss away each tear.
Or else I shall be melancholy too.

[GRETA *reaches out and takes* RAINBOW'*s hand.* RAINBOW *allows her to hold her hand, but does not respond.*]

Come sweetheart mine
Don't sit and pine.
Tell me all the cares
That made you feel so blue.
I'm sorry, hon.

[RAINBOW *faces* GRETA.]

What have I done.
Have I ever said

An unkind word to you.
My love is true.

[RAINBOW *leans over and puts her head next to* GRETA*'s.*]

And just for you.
I'll do almost anything
At any time.
Hear when you sigh
Or when you cry.
Something seems to grieve
This very heart of mine.
Come to me my melancholy baby.
Just cuddle up and don't be blue.

[RAINBOW *walks to the door and stands there looking out for a while. Then she exits while the song plays to the end.* GRETA *lowers her head. Then, she looks to the back. As the song is coming to an end, she looks down again.*]

SCENE 14: **Greta reads Rainbow's letter**

[GRETA *walks to the chair holding a book. She sits down and opens the book. An envelope falls from it. She opens the envelope, takes out a letter and reads it.*]

GRETA: "My beloved,—I'm sometimes obliged to do things that are dangerous,—and to do things that I hate. To befriend people and then betray them. Someday I may be hurt. If this happens, and I'm not able to tell you this, I hope one day you'll open this book and find this note. I love you more than anything in the world and it is to you that I owe my happiness. I always felt that I didn't want to love only halfway, that I wanted to love with all my heart or not at all and that I wanted to be loved the same way or not at all. With you, I had this and if anything happens to me I wanted you to remember this: that you are my angel and I will always love you. Even after death. Forever yours,—Rainbow."

LUST

CHARACTERS:

Ray, *37 to 52 years old. Passionate and driven*

Joseph, *55 to 70 years old. A self-contained businessman*

Helena, *25 to 40 years old. A beautiful and sensitive upper-class woman*

Jim, *a car mechanic*

She, *a woman with a loud mouth*

Lorraine, *a woman in a house dress*

Wang, *a Chinese man in traditional embroidered clothes*

Girl, *a girl in Victorian clothes*

Wing, *a Chinese woman in traditional embroidered clothes*

Boy, *a boy in black satin Chinese clothes and cap*

Birdie, *49 years old. Subdued, honest, and well-meaning*

In a major city. 1968 to 1983.

On the right side of the stage is RAY *and* HELENA'*s bedroom, on the left is* JOSEPH'*s office. The two rooms are divided by a couch that faces left and two easy chairs that face right. The furniture suggests a futuristic or art deco style. Behind the back wall there is a platform that runs the width of the stage.*

The bedroom. On the back wall of the bedroom there is a door. In the up-right side there is a bed with a satin cover. There is a straight chair to the left of the bed and two easy chairs on the left facing right.

The office. On the back wall of the office there is a door. In the up-left corner there is a desk. On the up-stage side of the desk there is a chair facing front. There is another chair against the right side of the desk facing front and another against the left wall facing right.

Scene 6—The Dream: The back wall of the set is removed exposing the platform.

> *a.—The car-repair shop. This is played on the right side of the platform.*
>
> *b.—A bathroom door in a working-class apartment. On the left of the platform there is a door with a full-length mirror.*
>
> *c.—A fire escape. A scaffolding against the left wall. There is a milk crate on it.*
>
> *d.—A Chinese restaurant. On the down side of the platform, between the steps, there is the window of a Chinese restaurant. A sheet of plastic is stretched on it. There is a small wooden box on each side of the window. On the stage floor, up-center, there is a dining table. On the down side of the table there is a chair that faces up.*
>
> *e.—The restaurant basement. This is performed down-center stage.*
>
> *f.—The streets of Bolivia. This is performed on the platform.*

Scenes 7-11: The stage is restored to its original setting.

SCENE 1: *In* JOSEPH's *office. There is a blanket on the down side of the sofa.* JOSEPH *stands to the left of the desk.*

RAY: The boy's eleven. He has difficulty at school. He can't concentrate. He gets distracted and he has a problem with discipline. Not discipline in the sense that he's unruly. He's well behaved. [*He sits on the sofa.*] But he doesn't do his work well. He's fallen behind and he keeps falling behind. He's small for his age and he's thin and underdeveloped.

JOSEPH: Why are you telling me this?

RAY: Because I want you to help him. He's been expelled from school. His parents are very poor. The kid's undernourished. He should stay in a boys' residence. He's bright. He'll do well if he gets financial help.

[*While* RAY *speaks,* JOSEPH *sits next to him. He reaches for the blanket and covers their middle. He puts his arm around* RAY's *waist and twists him around so* RAY's *back is to him. He pulls* RAY's *pants down and begins to move his pelvis against him.*]

He needs nourishment and physical therapy. I'm asking the foundation to help him financially. Can the foundation pay his tuition in a live-in school that can handle learning problems, to give him that chance and perhaps to save his life?

JOSEPH: How can I help?

RAY: With a scholarship and additional funds for medical expenses.—Is this ordinary, is this the way you conduct business?

JOSEPH: Yes, frequently. This is frequently the way I conduct business. It doesn't interfere with business. Yes, we can continue our discussion as we do this.

RAY: I may not be able to speak clearly as you do what you're doing.

JOSEPH: I would prefer not to stop now.

RAY: No, —I'm not asking you to stop.

JOSEPH: Yes. What should I do for the boy?

RAY: He needs help.

JOSEPH: What kind of help?

[*They both climax.*]

How old is he?

RAY: Eight.

JOSEPH: Put in a request to the foundation. I'll advise them in his favor. I'm sure it's a good investment.

[*He zips himself up and stands up.* RAY *adjusts his pants and removes the blanket.*]

RAY: By the way, I enjoyed that very much.

JOSEPH: I did too. Any time you feel up to it again, give me a ring. I thought it was quite pleasant. Very natural.

RAY: I thought so too.

HELENA: [*In a low voice from offstage.*] ...Father.

JOSEPH: Come in, Helena.

[HELENA *enters.*]

HELENA: I didn't mean to interrupt. It's two and you had asked me to come at two. Would you prefer it if I came later?

JOSEPH: No, Ray and I are finished. Do you know each other?

HELENA: Yes, Father.

RAY: How are you, Helena?

HELENA: I'm very well, Ray. I am so glad to see you. [*She sits behind the desk.*] Ray has a savage nature, Father. Have you found this out about him yet?

JOSEPH: ...No.

RAY: I never thought I did.

HELENA: You do.

RAY: How?

HELENA: You're wild, Ray.

RAY: How?

HELENA: You're wild like earth full of worms. Worms that shout.—If you can imagine that. And so are you, Father. You're also wild. I'm not. My earth doesn't have living creatures in it. I am like milk. I have milk in my veins. That's perfectly all right. I don't mean that I'm dead or anything like that. Milk is a good substance. I am clear and liquid and fine. I enjoy your being the way you are. It amuses me and delights me. There is something dear about wildness. [*She falls to the floor. She remains still for a moment.*] It's a bitter thing.

[RAY *kneels next to her and helps her up.*]

JOSEPH: Are you all right?

HELENA: [*To* JOSEPH.] Yes, Father. I love you. I have always loved you. Even if I've never been close to you. I tell you this now, so strangely, like this because I feel a strange urgency to tell you that I love you. That you are the person who has enriched my life and that I feel grateful to you and will be grateful to you as long as I live. I'm sorry to behave this way. I know I'm acting very strangely. Perhaps it's because I'm going to die. Perhaps I'm going crazy.—I'm going up now. Don't worry about me. I am happy and I'm very well. Even if I sound as if I am perfectly insane.

[*She starts to move.* JOSEPH *stops her and kisses her on the cheek. His movements are clumsy. She exits.* JOSEPH *and* RAY *look at each other.*]

RAY: Do you think she's all right?

[*Pause.*]

JOSEPH: Would you marry Helena, Ray?

[RAY *thinks a moment.*]

RAY: Yes.

JOSEPH: Thank you.

[RAY *looks at* JOSEPH *for a moment, then he looks away.*]

SCENE 2: *In* RAY *and* HELENA's *bedroom.* HELENA *is lying in bed under the covers.* RAY *sits on the chair to the left of the bed. His jacket and necktie are off. They hold hands as they speak. They both look front.*

RAY: I was two or three. I remember some things. My parents, my adoptive parents came to the agency and took me to their home. They were kind but I felt very strange and isolated at first. They were dutiful, honest, and gentle and they provided for my needs. Modestly. But I never lacked anything material or emotional. What I got from them would have sufficed but I came to them with a fever, a fever placed in my heart by my mother. A fever that has never left me.

HELENA: An illness?

RAY: ...a hunger.

HELENA: For food?

RAY: . . . Yes. . . For food.

HELENA: How I wish I knew what I hunger for.

RAY: I remember her voice. Husky. I remember her arms. Being in her arms. And I remember the fever we all shared. . . The hunger.

HELENA: Who were the others?

RAY: My brother, my sister.

HELENA: Have you tried to find them?

RAY: No.

HELENA: Why not?

[*He is absorbed in his thoughts.*]

RAY: I never have. [*Pause.*] Never have. . .

HELENA: Do you love your adoptive parents?

RAY: I do. Yes, I do. [*There is a pause.*] But can you ever forget the arms that first held you?

HELENA: . . . No.

RAY: Your mother's?

HELENA: She never held me. Hardly ever.

RAY: Who did?

HELENA: I remember the arms that didn't hold me. [*Pause.*] Come to bed.

[*He is thinking of something else. She looks at him. She lets go of his hand, turns from him and cuddles up on her side of the bed.*]

SCENE 3:   *In* JOSEPH's *office.* RAY *sits on the chair to the right of the desk.* JOSEPH *stands in the up-right corner.*

RAY: The human being is sinister. It's morbid. It's morbid. It's morbid. It's perverse. It's serving a devil.

JOSEPH: Why do you say that?

RAY: It's serving another species. Is there a species that controls us? That seeks revenge upon us?—A species that aims to destroy us? Are we doing this ourselves? Are we suicidal? Are we aiming to destroy ourselves?

JOSEPH: Why do you say that?

RAY: Don't you think we're destroying ourselves? We live in the future. We're robots. Have you realized that? Who thinks of the present? Our present is no use to us. Our present is a thing of the past. Our past is no use to us either. We have no reason to remember. If we think of something new, God loves us. It's an addiction. A daily dose. What's new? What's new? What's new? What's new? What's next? What's next?

JOSEPH: Ray. How long since you've had a vacation? A holiday.

[*Pause.*]

RAY: It's been some time.

JOSEPH: You should take one. [*He walks left and looks out.*] I make myself do it. Twice a year. Last time I went to Paris. I forced myself to stay. And I tried not to do too much. I hardly did any business. I did what other people do. I looked around. I saw some earrings that I wish I had bought for Helena. She would've looked good wearing them. She's elegant, like her mother. She is well made. Like a horse or a piece of art. You look at her from a distance and you know it took time and craft and breeding to make it. There is something wrong with her and I don't know what it is. But I don't understand women. I've never understood them. They're a different species. Don't you think, Ray? But I know there's something further wrong with her beyond what is wrong with women.—This business with technology. What do you have against it?

RAY: It will destroy us, Joseph. Can't you see that?

JOSEPH: Why don't you and Helena go away on a holiday?

SCENE 4: *In* RAY *and* HELENA'*s bedroom.* RAY *is sitting on the downstage easychair.* HELENA *is standing on the right side of the bed. She wears a slip and is putting on a dress. She continues dressing through the rest of the scene.*

RAY: I see people drunk, unclean, unshaven, their clothes torn, their foul smell polluting the air. They don't know enough to wash. Mindless. Toothless. Their eyes in a daze. And I wonder, "When do you ever see an animal like that?" If they're physically ill. If they can't find food and they're undernourished and ill, perhaps. But no animal would ever be passive if there is food within their reach. No animal would leave a stone unturned if their survival, or their health is at stake. Humans don't learn much in a lifetime. They unlearn what has been learned by others.

HELENA: Humans can't find food under stones. Humans can't just sniff and find food. That's ridiculous. Food is many steps removed from man's reach.

RAY: You can figure out how to find it.

HELENA: It's harder for some.

RAY: Why is it harder?

HELENA: For some people it's not so easy. It's not so clear. [*Under breath.*] For some people, survival is not so clear.

RAY: How can anyone live and grow in such a state where survival is not clear.

HELENA: I would be at a loss if I had to earn my own living—

RAY: Oh, Helena, you. Of course you would.

HELENA:—if I were not dependent on someone else's earning ability. [*Pause.*] I was talking to you. I was telling you something and you never answered.

RAY: What were you saying?

HELENA: You never heard me?

RAY: I did but I don't remember.

HELENA: I said I didn't like the play.

RAY: You didn't?

HELENA: No.

RAY: That's odd.

HELENA: Why odd?

RAY: I liked it.

HELENA: I didn't like the words.

RAY: What words?

HELENA: The words the author used.

RAY: The writing you mean.

HELENA: I guess the writing. Some words in particular.

RAY: Which words?

HELENA: Words which are not real words. Like "likewise." False words which have nothing behind them.

RAY: Those are words that help get a thought through.

HELENA: No thinking goes into words like that.

RAY: New times need new words.

HELENA: Maybe so, for practical uses. But a lot of these words are a hoax. People feel good using them but they feel a little cheated later, debilitated. If you speak without meaning you feel debilitated.

SCENE 5: *In* JOSEPH's *office.* RAY *enters holding a briefcase. He is walking hurriedly.* HELENA *is right behind him.* HELENA *stands upstage of the desk. She wears a jacket and hat. She carries a purse.*

HELENA: I asked you a question and you didn't say anything.

RAY: [*Standing upstage of the chair and opening the briefcase. She stands to his right.*] I didn't.

HELENA: Why not?

RAY: [*Looking through papers in the briefcase.*] Because.

HELENA: Don't because me. I'm talking to you!

RAY: [*Slamming shut the briefcase and walking around the left of the desk to down-right.*] What do you want?

HELENA: I asked you a question.

RAY: What was it?

HELENA: You didn't hear me?

RAY: [*Turning to her.*] No, I didn't.

HELENA: Why not?

RAY: I was thinking about something else.

HELENA: What were you thinking about?

RAY: [*Turning to her.*] Work! That's what I was thinking about! That's what I'm always thinking about. Work! [*Walking around the desk to her.*] That's all I think about. [*Through the following speech he grabs her by the wrist and twists her arm gradually.*] I don't need you for anything whatsoever—I go home to you each day. But I could go to an empty apartment as well—I go home to think about my work. About what I did during the day. What I did in the last ten years and what I'm going to do in the next ten years—I don't pretend to be thinking about anything else. I never did. I've never lied to you. I never said I would be thinking about anything else. I've never said, "I love you." I said, "The only thing I care about is my work." You never believed me when I told you. But I did tell you. Stop insisting, Helena. I don't hear you. You are like an insect smashing itself against my windshield. I don't hear you. And I don't see you! And I don't want to hear you! Or see you!

[*Pushing her on the chair.* HELENA *lowers her head. She is desolate.*]

HELENA: What are you doing?

RAY: You're submissive!

HELENA: [*Reaching to him.*] ...What do you mean?...Why do you say that?...What have I done?

[*He grabs and pushes her on the floor behind the desk. She starts crawling on all fours around the right of the desk towards the couch.*]

RAY: "What do you mean. Why do you say that." Why don't you say something! Your eye shifts! You fret but you say nothing! Why does it make you uncomfortable to hear me speak? Why is it hard for you to breathe.

HELENA: [*As she reaches the couch, she climbs on it and sits.*] Because I don't know what you mean or how to talk about it. I don't understand what you mean. I don't know what you're saying—What do you mean? How does one talk about such things? I can't even understand what you're saying. It makes me very unhappy. I feel very unhappy.—I live in a fog and I can't even talk about it. I don't know how to talk about it.— Do you? Can you talk about it? Can you help me?

[*Pause.*]

RAY: ...I can't help you.

[JOSEPH *enters. He takes a couple of steps in. He looks at* HELENA.]

Animals are beautiful and refined and delicate. They are poised and elegant and intelligent. All their senses are put to use. They are delicate when they need to be and fierce when they need to. They know how to obtain sustenance and shelter. They not only exercise when they need to chase after prey or get away from an animal that gives them chase, but they know when they need exercise and run and play for no reason other than to keep in shape. [*Turning to* JOSEPH.] Haven't you seen animals playing in the fields? [*He looks at* HELENA *again.*] Human beings disintegrate morally unless they are under someone's constant surveillance. They need to be under constant commands, praise, penalties, abuse, rewards. They are slaves. There's nothing in them that lets them know if they're straying. They don't know if what they do is something that will destroy them. So they become slaves to whatever will take command of them,—instead of being guardians of their own self. [*Pause.*] How can anyone be so unworthy of her own life?

[HELENA *weeps.* JOSEPH *goes to her. The lights go to black.*]

SCENE 6: *The following occurs simultaneously: Upbeat music is heard; color lights whirl all over the stage; the back wall of the set is removed; and the furniture is moved to the left and right creating a clearing in the center. A projection on the rear wall reads: "Ray has a dream."* WANG *walks across to up-center, then down-center. His appearance and behavior mimic a traditional Chinese prototype.*

WANG: Ray has a dream. [*He walks up, then left and exits.*]

[*Dream—a: A projection reads: "In a car-repair shop." There is a piece of wood on the floor.* RAY *is waiting left. He feels his crotch. He shakes his leg. He feels his crotch again.* JIM *enters from the right. When he sees* RAY, *he becomes cautious.* RAY *turns to him.* JIM *picks up the piece of wood and holds it up in position to attack.*]

RAY: Easy...

[JIM *tightens up.*]

I'm just waiting for someone.

JIM: Who're you waiting for?

RAY: My girlfriend. She's working across the street.

JIM: And what's she doing there?

RAY: She's rehearsing. She'll be down in a few minutes.

JIM: What's she? A dancer?

RAY: An actress.

JIM: Really.

RAY: Yeah.

JIM: Is she in the movies?

RAY: She was in one.

JIM: You're pulling my leg.

RAY: I'm not.

JIM: [*Walking closer to* RAY.] And she's coming here?

RAY: Yeah.

JIM: I'll be damned.

[JIM *looks front.* RAY *looks at him.*]

RAY: I'm an actor myself.

JIM: [*Getting closer to him.*] Really.

RAY: Yes.

JIM: You've been in movies too?

RAY: T.V.

JIM: T.V.?

RAY: And some small parts in movies.

JIM: Really?

RAY: Wanna dance?

JIM: Dance?

[*A tango is heard at a low volume as* RAY *holds* JIM *in a dance position. Facing front,* RAY *moves sinuously in an eccentric and bizarre manner then he stops.*]

RAY: [*Indicating towards the right.*] Is there anybody in there?

JIM: In the office?

RAY: Aha.

JIM: No.

[*They dance right as the volume of the music increases, and exit. A moment later, offstage,* JIM *lets out a sound half pain and half pleasure.* RAY *enters wiping his hands with a gray cloth and stands in the same spot where he stood earlier. The music fades.*]

[*Dream—b: A projection reads: "At the bathroom door."* RAY *faces the door and leans on it. Both his hands are on the doorknob. His head leans against the mirror.* SHE *is behind the door.*]

SHE: Do you think I'm one of those exotic flowers!

RAY: Don't you fuck with me again!

SHE: Do you think I'm going to sit in my place waiting for you with my little legs crossed while you fuck half the world!

RAY: You're going to stay in there till you change your mind! You hear! [*He presses his lips against his own image and moves his pelvis against the mirror.*]

SHE: Who's going to change his mind, you son of a bitch! You open up or I'll cut you up in little pieces when I get out! [*Pause.*] Open up!

[*He reaches climax.*]

RAY: Ahhh…!

SHE: What are you doing!

RAY: Ahhh. . .

SHE: What are you doing?

RAY: Shut up!

[*"Harbor Lights" is heard.*]

[*Dream—c: A projection reads: "In the fire escape."* RAY *sits on the fire escape. He looks out over the roofs.*]

RAY: [*Singing.*] Tra tra tra ta ta-ta. [*He looks at his shoe.*] Tra tra tra ta ta-ta. I have to shine my shoes. [*Short pause.*] Honey!

LORRAINE: [*Offstage.*] What!

[*Short pause.*]

RAY: Measure my cock.

LORRAINE: [*Offstage.*] Get off it!

RAY: [*Singing.*] Tra tra tra ta ta-ta.

[LORRAINE *enters and sits on the box.*]

LORRAINE: Do you know why they call me Mary?

RAY: What else should they call you?

LORRAINE: By my real name.

RAY: What's your real name?

LORRAINE: Lorraine. Mary's a nickname.

RAY: For Lorraine?

LORRAINE: Yup.

RAY: Like "Lefty"?

LORRAINE: What do you mean like "Lefty"?

RAY: It's a nickname.

LORRAINE: For what?

RAY: For nothing. For an arm—

LORRAINE: I'll be darned.

RAY: So why do they call you Mary?

LORRAINE: For Mary Magdalene.

RAY: Why?

LORRAINE: Because of how... [*Pointing with her head to his feet.*] ...you know.

RAY: What?

LORRAINE: [*Pointing with her head.*] You know…I…

RAY: What?

LORRAINE: You know…feet.

RAY: Oh yeah… sweety, do my feet while I sing.

LORRAINE: You want?

RAY: Yeah. [*He sings and she starts to take off his shoes.*]

    Ta ta ta ta ta-ta

    Ta ta ta ta ta-ta.

    [*He looks at the roofs.*] Jesus Christ, everyone's fucking tonight.

    [*The following occurs simultaneously: Fake Chinese music is heard; color lights whirl all over the stage; the window of the Chinese restaurant is lowered; a table is brought up-center on the lower level; a chair is placed on the down side of the table, facing up.*]

    [*Dream—d: A projection reads: "In a Chinese Restaurant." RAY sits at the table facing up. He wears an emboidered Chinese robe. He wears a long, narrow, white beard held by white strings, and a bald cap with some scraggly hair around the edges. He is holding an open menu. He looks out the window at the GIRL who is playing with a stick, cupped at the end, with a ball attached by a string. On the upstage side of the window, WANG stands to RAY's left. He also wears a narrow white false beard and a bald cap. He looks outside. Crows land on the pavement. The GIRL shoos them. When RAY and WANG speak they move their mouths and WING's voice is heard. When WING speaks she moves her mouth and WANG's voice is heard. Each time RAY speaks he moves his head and torso in a manner resembling a mechanical toy. WANG moves his arms and legs up and down and makes sounds to express anger.*]

WANG: They leave home too young.

RAY: Who does?

WANG: The young.

[RAY *looks at the* GIRL *with a fiendish smile.*]

RAY: [*Laughing.*] Huh huh huh huh huh huh. Ya ya ya ya ya.

WANG: …What was that…?

[RAY *looks at* WANG. *Then, he looks at the* GIRL *and slurps.* WANG *is annoyed.*]

You leady to oldel? You look at the gill all night?

[RAY *looks at the menu closely and makes slurping sounds.* WING *enters upstage of the window. She writes "Merry Xmas" and draws a bird and snow using a spray can on the window.* RAY *chews on the menu.*]

Now you eat menu! You-oldel-food!

RAY: What do you have? [*He makes slurping sounds.*]

WANG: [*Pointing to the menu.*] It's in menu!

[RAY *licks the menu.*]

Don't *eat* menu! *Lead* menu.

[RAY *makes sounds resembling a Chinese language as he moves his head from left to right.* WANG *indicates with head as he speaks.*]

You don't lead flom side to side! You lead up and down!

[WANG *turns the menu on the side.* RAY's *head vibrates and moves up and down as he continues making sounds resembling Chinese.* WANG *takes the menu from* RAY. *He opens it and looks at it.*]

We have hundled yeal old egg.

[RAY *belches.*]

O.K. We have fish fin soup.

[RAY *translates what* WANG *said into sounds that resemble Chinese. Then he belches.*]

Why you go like that!

[RAY *makes throwing up sounds.* WANG *wipes the table.*]

You have no table mannel.

[RAY *laps his tongue.* WANG *looks at the menu again.*]

O.K. We have Chinese pickle vegetable.

[RAY *starts to speak words resembling Chinese. He coughs.* WANG *pats him on the back and points to the window.*]

Chlistmas.

[*There are Chinese voices singing "Jingle Bells." Snow starts falling on the* GIRL. RAY *stretches his arms toward the window and starts to stand. The* GIRL *looks at* RAY *for a while through the window while snow falls on her. She enters the restaurant.*]

GIRL: Someone was accidentally wounded.

[RAY *stands, puts his head on the* GIRL'*s chest and slurps.* WING *enters the restaurant and looks at the window.* RAY *cries. The* GIRL *helps* RAY *to the chair.*]

WING: [*Pointing to the window.*] The bild didn't come out light. This little wing is sholtel than this little wing. And the little left leg of the little bild is not as good as the little light leg, and this little "a" is not good. We have to fix it.

WANG: Wing is sad. She failed. At the picture.

[*Crows alight. The* GIRL *runs outside. The following occurs simultaneously: Music is heard; colored lights whirl; the* BOY *enters up-right, walks to the center, and turns front. There is a crow on his shoulder. He carries a tray with four lit candles;* WANG *goes up the left steps, takes the box from the right, and a candle from the tray and stands to the right of the* BOY *facing left.* RAY *stands and pretends to lose his balance. The* GIRL *puts her arms around him to support him. He puts his lips to her neck, his head drops to her chest, his hand drops to her buttocks as they go up the right steps. The* GIRL *takes a candle.* RAY *and the* GIRL *stand left of* WING *facing left. They all walk around the window to the main platform.* WANG *places his box down center while* WING *places hers two feet up of* WANG'*s. They take paper bags from the boxes. The* BOY *places the tray on the downstage box.* WING, WANG, *and the*]

GIRL *place their candles on the tray. The* GIRL *helps* RAY *sit on the upstage box.* WING *and* WANG *stand behind* RAY. *The* BOY *stands down-left and the* GIRL *stands down-right.*]

[*Dream—e: A projection reads: "In the basement." The* BOY *takes two one-hundred dollar bills from his pocket and holds one on each hand. The voice-over continues.*]

WANG: He's going to buln the money.

[*The* BOY *lights both bills and lets them burn.* RAY *contorts and convulses.*]

RAY: Buln money? Buln money? Buln money? [*Pulling his hair.*] Can't beal it! Can't beal it! Can't beal it! Why! Why!

WANG: Yes.

RAY: Why buln them?

WANG: Is a leligious act. Not to explain.

RAY: [*His left hand is holding his right hand back and his right hand is resisting.*] Difficult fol me to watch. [*He tries to pull his eyelids open. His right hand takes his left hand and puts it in his pocket. He puts the right hand in his pocket.*] Difficult to keep hands in pocket. Difficult not to knock down boy! Put out file! Glab money!

WANG: Vely difficult.

[*The* BOY *holds the crow towards* RAY. WING *and* WANG *flap their paper bags to create the sound of flapping wings.*]

BOY: [*Imitating the sound of a crow.*] Take me to him! Take me to him! Take me to him!

[*The* BOY *steps closer to* RAY, *holding the crow up.* RAY's *eyes open wide.*]

I resemble him! He is like my mirror! He is like my mirror! I am like him! Take me to him!

[RAY *touches his chin, nose, ears, eyes.*]

Take me to him! Take me to him!

[*The crow starts pecking at* RAY's *face.* RAY *covers his chin, nose, ears, eyes.*]

Take me to him! Take me to him! Take me to him!

[*Music is heard. Lights whirl all over the stage.* RAY *exits up-right.* WANG, WING, *the* BOY, *and the* GIRL *hurry to the back. They scatter and run back and forth on the platform.* WING *and* WANG *flap their wings as if invisible crows are attacking from above. In the meantime, the set is restored to its position at the start of "Lust."*]

[*Dream—f: In the streets of Bolivia. A projection reads: "In Bolivia." Music still plays. Lights still whirl.* RAY *enters left running. He wears a suit jacket. He joins the others in their running. When the set is restored, the others exit.* RAY *runs back and forth a few more times.*]

SCENE 7: *In* RAY *and* HELENA's *bedroom.* HELENA *is lying in bed.* RAY *stands right facing right. He is in shirt sleeves looking in an imaginary mirror as he combs his hair and puts on a necktie.*

HELENA: I was with a young boy.

RAY: You were?

HELENA: I already mentioned it to you.

RAY: So what about it?

HELENA: I was with him intimately.

RAY: So what about it?

HELENA: He asked me if I was sick.

RAY: He didn't use a condom?

HELENA: He did, but I asked him to kiss me.

[RAY *does not answer.*]

I asked him to kiss me. [*Pause.*] Ray, I asked him to kiss me.

RAY: Yes, I heard you.

HELENA: He asked me if I was sick.

RAY: What did he mean?

HELENA: A venereal disease. [*Pause.*] I thought it should be I who asked.

RAY: Asked what?

HELENA: If he was sick.

RAY: [*Putting on his jacket.*] I agree with you. If you sleep with a whore you should ask if he's sick.

HELENA: But instead of me it was he who asked me.

RAY: It's you who should've asked him—because you sleep with whores.

HELENA: I'm not a whore, Ray.

RAY: I know. I said you *sleep* with whores.

HELENA: You know why I do it.

[*He walks to the up-chair.*]

RAY: You could have a venereal disease.

HELENA: Do you think I have a venereal disease?

RAY: I think you should be tested.

HELENA: That's humiliating. It's humiliating to have you think that of me.

RAY: You should be tested. You could have a venereal disease.

HELENA: You think that boy is right, then? You think he has a right to ask me if I'm sick when he's a whore? You think I could have a venereal disease.

RAY: You could.

SCENE 8: *In* RAY *and* HELENA's *bedroom.* HELENA *stands by the bed holding a dress.* BIRDIE *sits on the downstage easy chair. There are several dresses on the bed and on the floor.*

HELENA: ...What would you like to eat?

BIRDIE: Nothing, thank you.

[*They pick up the dresses.* HELENA *looks at one of the buttons on a dress.*]

HELENA: This one here is too big.

BIRDIE: What is?

HELENA: Well, the button, or maybe the buttonhole is too small. The buttons are all the same, I think. The buttonhole is too small. I already had one fixed. I don't know if I can do anything about it now.

BIRDIE: Maybe you can get a smaller button.

HELENA: That wouldn't look right. [*Sitting on the bed.*] It would look uneven to have a button smaller than all the rest.

BIRDIE: [*Standing.*] Can't you cut the ends. One end. [*Going to* HELENA.] All you have to do is cut one end and then stitch it.

HELENA: What do you mean?

BIRDIE: [*Taking the dress and looking at the buttonhole.*] One corner of the stitch on the buttonhole.

HELENA: It's sewn too tight.

BIRDIE: If you get a pair of scissors with a very fine point you could push it down between the threads and cut some of the threads. [*Returning the dress to* HELENA.] Do you have one of those cuticle scissors with a fine point?

HELENA: I don't have any scissors.

BIRDIE: Not any at all?

HELENA: [*Shaking her head.*] They don't let me have them.

[*There is a sound offstage. They both look in the direction of the sound, then at each other.*]

How long have you known Ray?

BIRDIE: Not very long.

HELENA: Is he your lover?

BIRDIE: No.

HELENA: How did you meet him?

BIRDIE: I met him when he hired me.

[HELENA *stands still holding the dress.*]

HELENA: How did he know you wanted the work?

BIRDIE: Someone sent me.

HELENA: Who did? An agency?

BIRDIE: A friend.

HELENA: What did he hire you for?

[BIRDIE *looks down.*]

You can't tell me?

BIRDIE: To look after you.

HELENA: [*Walking around the bed to the right.*] Do you understand Ray? Do you understand him when he talks?

BIRDIE: No.

HELENA: Well. Now he wants me to meet his brother. He's going to bring his brother here, for me to meet him. He's found a brother and he wants me to meet him.

[BIRDIE *makes a move to stand.*]

You stay—Can you understand that? Why does he want me to meet him?—You can have that dress if you want.

BIRDIE: ...Thank you...

HELENA: Helena— [*Putting the dress on the bed.*]—you can call me Helena, why be formal. What's the point.—How does he know if he's really his brother? [*Returning to the left of the bed.*] How does he know if this Charlie's really his brother? He never even saw him. How does he know if he's not a crook?

BIRDIE: How does he know?

HELENA: He thinks he is.

RAY: [*Offstage.*] Helena!

HELENA: [*To* BIRDIE.] See?

RAY: [*Offstage.*] Helena!

HELENA: The way he speaks to me.

RAY: Are you here! Charlie's here, would you come down!

[HELENA *goes to the entranceway.*]

HELENA: [*With a polite smile as if he could see her.*] Your brother?

RAY: [*Offstage.*] Yes.—Please, come.

[HELENA *looks down at her dress, adjusts it and adjusts her hair.*]

HELENA: [*To* BIRDIE.] Do I look all right?

BIRDIE: Yes.

HELENA: Do you hate me?

BIRDIE: No. I don't hate you at all.

[HELENA *goes to the door. She pauses.*]

HELENA: He's seen his mother, hasn't he? [*Walking down.*] I know he's seen his mother. I know he has. Didn't he mention it to you? Did he tell you anything about it? He doesn't tell me anything anymore. He doesn't want to talk to me. —You knew his mother, didn't you, Birdie. You knew Nadine.

BIRDIE: Yes.

HELENA: You're one of them, aren't you?

BIRDIE: Yes.

HELENA: You love him too, don't you?

[BIRDIE *lowers her head.*]

I don't mind if you do. I feel sorry for you.

BIRDIE: I'm sorry.

HELENA: Don't be sorry for me, Birdie. Don't be sorry for me. I don't mind that you love him. You're not a bad person. I feel sorry for you.

[BIRDIE *cries*. HELENA *shakes her head.*]

Pour soul.

SCENE 9: *In* RAY *and* HELENA'*s bedroom.* RAY *is in bed. He wears an undershirt.* BIRDIE *enters. She stops at the door. She carries a cup of coffee. She takes a couple of steps down. He looks at her. She moves her hand with the coffee cup towards him.*

RAY: I'll take it.

[BIRDIE'*s hand starts to shake. The coffee cup rattles. Her arm stretches toward him. She takes a step toward him. She waits with her head down. He takes the coffee. She starts to exit.*]

Please wait.

[*She stops.*]

Sit down.

[*She sits. He drinks some coffee. He looks at her. She looks at him. He nods. She lowers her head.*]

BIRDIE: Yes.

[*The lights go to black. Then they come up.* BIRDIE *is straddling* RAY. *They make violent sounds.*]

SCENE 10: *In* RAY *and* HELENA'*s bedroom.* JOSEPH *sits on the upstage easychair.* BIRDIE *straightens the bed from the up left side of the bed and stands there through the rest of the scene.* HELENA *sits on the floor facing* JOSEPH.

JOSEPH: I've never talked to you about the things that are important to me. I've never talked to you about my work. You may not realize what I do—because my work is not something you can see. It's in my head. My work is my life. It's my universe. I have not loved anything the way I love my work. I don't know that I could think of my life without it. I don't know that I could live without it. I don't know that I could exist without my work.

[HELENA *looks in the direction of the door.* JOSEPH *also looks. There is a pause.*]

Come in, Ray.

[RAY *takes a step in.*]

How are you?

RAY: I'm fine. [RAY *stands behind the straight chair.*]

JOSEPH: I believe Ray is taking over my business, Helena.

HELENA: Is he?

JOSEPH: Why don't you ask him?

[*She looks at* RAY. RAY *looks away.*]

HELENA: [*To* JOSEPH.] What does this mean?

JOSEPH: It means he's taking over my business.

[JOSEPH *looks at* RAY. RAY *is still looking away.*]

What do you say, Ray? [*Silence.*] Is there anything I can do to prevent it? Your taking my business from me? Taking everything away from me?

[RAY *looks at* BIRDIE. *He then sits on the straight chair.*]

You have a cold heart, son. [*Pause.*] Well, I'll be going now. [*He stands.*] You are the master of your own life, Helena. [*There is a pause. He waits for a response.*] Exercise your free will. Animals can do better than you, Helena. Animals are not our slaves even if they appear to be. Even when they wag their tails they're not dependent on us. We're not their masters and they're not our slaves. Animals manage to work their way around us even if it appears that they are dependent on us.—They don't need to bemoan their lack of freedom.— We also don't need to bemoan our lack of freedom in regard to any other human being. [*Pause.*] Haven't I taught you to love yourself?

[HELENA *looks at* JOSEPH.]

HELENA: No,—Father. [*She looks down.*]

SCENE 11: *In* JOSEPH's *office.* JOSEPH *enters abruptly. He is visibly frightened. He opens the drawer of his desk and starts to look among his papers frantically. He hears a sound. He turns to the entranceway.*

JOSEPH: Here they come.

[RAY *enters.* JOSEPH *reaches into his breast pocket.* RAY *rapidly moves to stop* JOSEPH's *action. They struggle.* RAY *pulls a gun from* JOSEPH's *hand.* JOSEPH *is shaking. He lowers his head.* RAY *puts his hand on* JOSEPH's *back affectionately.*]

What a mistake I've made. What a mistake. What a mistake.

[JOSEPH *sits and rests his head on the desk. As the lights whirl the following occurs simultaneously: the scenery is carried out;* HELENA *enters;* RAY *walks right.* HELENA *helps* JOSEPH *up. They walk around the stage. He is leaning on her and makes plaintive sounds. With* HELENA's *unnoticed help, his clothes come off his body as if they were peeling off. He becomes more and more debilitated until he falls to the ground inert and naked but for his shorts.*]

SCENE 12: HELENA *walks to up-center.* RAY *sits on a chair down-right facing down. She looks at him.*

HELENA: He told me he always wished for a son and not a daughter. That he loved me but that he wanted a son. He said he wanted a son just like me because he loved me. He knew it was possible that a son could have resembled you instead of me. He said he knew his son could have been like you. That he could have been a misfit. A crazy son. Someone who, like you, is distasteful in every way. But he said that he still wished I had been a boy.

HUNGER

CHARACTERS:

Charlie, *a portly man 76 years old. He has a scar on his forehead. He is pensive. He seems to place the same value on all things. He wears a worn and stained suit and necktie*

Birdie, *74 years old. She is inquisitive and reserved. She wears a black crepe dress, high heeled black shoes, and carries a clutch purse*

Ray, *67 years old. He is high-strung and obsessed. He suffers from nervous ticks and tremors. He is in rags*

Reba, *50 years old. Ray's mate. She is detached and pensive. She has a dry wisdom. She is in rags*

The Angel, *a stone-like gothic figure. One of his wings is broken and hangs behind him. He carries a wooden box strapped around his neck containing animal entrails*

After an economic disaster. Some time in the future.

A warehouse. Against the back wall there is a platform two and a half feet tall, eight feet deep and the width of the stage. At each end of the platform there are archways that lead to other rooms. On the platform there are two sets of steps left and right that lead to the stage. On the upstage end of each side wall there are archways that lead to other rooms.

SCENE 1: Room 1.

[*In the dark there is the sound of a bell struck at about six second intervals. There is a desk and a chair up-left and a second chair against the center of the left wall. The lights are dim.* CHARLIE *enters left on the platform. He moves slowly. He takes a few steps and stops.* BIRDIE's *steps are heard. She enters.* CHARLIE *proceeds to walk in front of her. They reach the archway on the right and walk*

around to enter through the right archway on the floor level.
CHARLIE *stops half way and lets* BIRDIE *proceed to the chair on the left.*]

CHARLIE: I'm sorry he's not here. He said he couldn't come today, that he didn't think he'd be here. That he had things to do.

BIRDIE: Did you tell him I was coming?

CHARLIE: Yes.

[*She sits.*]

BIRDIE: What did you say?

CHARLIE: I said you wanted to see him.

BIRDIE: Did you tell him who I was?

CHARLIE: ...No.

BIRDIE: What did you tell him?

CHARLIE: [*Walking to the desk and sitting.*] I told him a woman had been here to see him. And he said he didn't think he'd be able to come.

BIRDIE: Did he say why?

CHARLIE: Yes. He said there were things he had to do.

BIRDIE: What?

CHARLIE: He said he had to look for things.

BIRDIE: What things?

CHARLIE: Things he could find.

BIRDIE: What for?

CHARLIE: To exchange or to eat, or things to sell, or to use for himself. Sometimes he gets things he can sell.

BIRDIE: Where does he find these things?

CHARLIE: In the street. In the rubble. Empty buildings, I guess. I don't know. Maybe he burgles sometimes. Although I doubt that. He doesn't come up with anything too costly. He goes out at night. Hunting. Then he spends the day here, he sleeps or sits or paces waiting till it gets dark again to go out again. Resting. It's safer then.

BIRDIE: Safer?

CHARLIE: To go out. At night no one can see you. Not as easily.

BIRDIE: Stealing?

CHARLIE: Not stealing. I don't think he steals. He finds things. In the streets. In the rubble.

BIRDIE: What can he find?

CHARLIE: Many things. A piece of ribbon, a button, an old handle, a spool, nails, if they're not too crooked. Sometimes he's spotted something, a good pile, some place where he thinks there may be some stuff. But he doesn't go to it right away. He waits till dark. —It's too dangerous to do it in the daytime. If someone sees him looking and putting something in his pocket he may be followed and he may be jumped, hurt badly, if the person thinks he has found something of value, or killed. When you're in the street, you should never put anything in your pocket. If you do, someone may think you're carrying something of value.—Why are you looking for him?

BIRDIE: I was asked to talk to him.

CHARLIE: ...To talk to him?

BIRDIE: It seems he took something with him when he left the Compound.

CHARLIE: Did he?

BIRDIE: It seems that he did.

CHARLIE: What?

BIRDIE: I don't know. There's something he may have taken.

CHARLIE: I hope that if he took something, that he still has it, and that you want to buy it from him. If he has it, he'll sell it to you. I'm sure he will, if you want to buy it.—Then he may get back on his feet again. If what he has is worth something. He's sinking lower and lower. [*Pause.*] Once you're outside you can't get in again. There's never a reason to go in. That is, one has a reason, but they don't see that you do. [*Pause.*] Once you're out it is not likely they'll want you in. That's why you have to leave. [*Pause.*]

BIRDIE: Is Nadine here, Charlie?

CHARLIE: ...Nadine?

BIRDIE: Do you remember Nadine?

CHARLIE: Yes...She's old. She doesn't remember things too well.—I think Nadine died.

BIRDIE: When?

CHARLIE: When?

BIRDIE: Did she die a long time ago? [*There is a silence.*] You don't remember things too well. Do you?

CHARLIE: What.

BIRDIE: Do you remember who you are?

CHARLIE: Not too well.

BIRDIE: You didn't remember me, did you—when you saw me.

CHARLIE: No, I didn't.

BIRDIE: And now, do you know who I am?

CHARLIE: No.—Things are very different now. I don't think that much anymore. Not often. I was hit on the head when I was little. [*Pause.*] A moment ago I was thinking I used to be skinny. Was I?

BIRDIE: Yes.

CHARLIE: Did you know me before?

BIRDIE: Yes.

CHARLIE: It's different now. The way a person thinks. The way a person is.

BIRDIE: Yes.

CHARLIE: Who'd believe that I'd end up having a good position. I've gone far and I never thought I would. And yet Ray, who went so far when he was young, is scrambling for a piece of bread. Do you know that?

BIRDIE: [*Standing and walking left.*] Yes.

CHARLIE: Did you know him then?

BIRDIE: [*Walking toward the desk.*] Yes.—

CHARLIE: Did you know him well?

BIRDIE: Yes.—

CHARLIE: Did you know me?

BIRDIE: Yes.—Do you help him now?

CHARLIE: Who?

BIRDIE: Ray.

CHARLIE: …What do you mean?

BIRDIE: Do you help Ray? Do you give him something now and then?

CHARLIE: Ray?

BIRDIE: Do you give him food?

CHARLIE: No.

BIRDIE: Why not?

CHARLIE: I don't have that much to give.

BIRDIE: He's your brother.

[*Pause.*]

CHARLIE: Is he? I don't remember that.

BIRDIE: Ray is your brother.

CHARLIE: I remember Rainbow. Did you know her?

BIRDIE: Yes, I knew her once.

CHARLIE: Ray met Rainbow once.

BIRDIE: He did?

CHARLIE: Yes. He didn't know she was his sister. Did she know she was his sister?

BIRDIE: I don't know.

CHARLIE: Did you know me?

BIRDIE: Yes, Charlie.

CHARLIE: It's harder for some.

BIRDIE: What is?

CHARLIE: To settle down. When is he going to settle down? It's harder for Ray? It's taken him too long.—He's never quiet. He's never quiet at all. He's too restless. Sometimes he doesn't even come to sleep. He stays up all night. [*He puts his hand to his forehead.*] Someone hit me on the head, and it still hurts sometimes. [*He stands and walks right.*] Sometimes he comes up in the middle of the night and he wakes up everyone. He sleeps in the daytime but the others sleep at night and he doesn't let them sleep.

[*She looks around the room.*]

BIRDIE: What do you do here, Charlie?—What is your work?

CHARLIE: My work? I look after the place. I see to it that things are in order. There's always a problem...sometimes. Sometimes someone wants to get in. Someone who doesn't belong.—I see to it that they don't get in. Sometimes there are fights among the people who live here. [*He walks toward the desk.*]

BIRDIE: Do you receive payment for your work?

CHARLIE: Why do you want to know?

BIRDIE: ...I don't know how things work here.

CHARLIE: I get paid in goods. Some food. Sometimes. I got this suit.

BIRDIE: How do the others live?

CHARLIE: We get food...sometimes. [*Pause.*] You talk different. You don't sound like anyone I know. Your voice sounds different. The color of your skin is different. You are of a different time. [*He walks to her. He takes her hand. Her purse falls to the floor. He examines her hand.*] Your hand is like an object of art. Why is your skin so perfect? What is it made of?

[*She touches the side of his face.*]

BIRDIE: ·...Charlie...

CHARLIE: [*Putting his arm around her waist and bringing her body against his.*] I would like to know what it feels like to put my body against yours. I knew you'd feel fresh. Like water. Like I've had you in my arms.

[*She moves away from him gently.*]

BIRDIE: Please don't.

[*He releases her. She takes a few steps back. He lowers his head in shame. He picks up her purse and hands it to her. He returns to the desk, sits down, folds his arms on the desk and rests his head on his arms. She takes a photograph from her purse, walks to him and puts the photograph on the desk. Putting her hand on his back.*]

Look at this.—

[*He starts to look up.*]

Do you remember this?

[*He takes the picture and looks at it. His mind travels through time.*]

CHARLIE: A picture... [*He puts the picture down. His head starts to move down again.*] Would you like to take a nap now? I'm very tired. I would like to rest.

[*He rests his head on his arms. She slides the picture towards her and looks at it.*]

BIRDIE: [*Putting her hand on his head.*] Yes, Charlie. You rest. [*She puts the picture in her purse.*] I'll come back later.

SCENE 2: Room 2.

[*The same structure as the first. There are bodies shrouded in blankets lying down or sitting against the walls.* RAY *and* REBA *lie center-right. They are covered with blankets. He holds a cloth sack which contains several small objects he has collected in the street. He mumbles.*]

RAY: Why wouldn't it work?

[*Pause.*]

REBA: What.

RAY: It would work.

REBA: What.

[*Pause.*]

RAY: Reba, I told you time and time again.

REBA: I forgot.

RAY: [*Hurt.*] Reba... [*Pause.*] ...You forgot? [*Pause.*] ...How could you forget?

REBA: I don't know, Ray.

RAY: It didn't matter to you?

REBA: It did.

RAY: How could you forget?

REBA: I had other things on my mind.

RAY: Other things?

REBA: Other thoughts.

RAY: What thoughts, Reba?

REBA: Different thoughts.

RAY: Like what, Reba?

REBA: They change, Ray.

RAY: Every day?

REBA: Not every day of the year, but there are a few things that I think about and I think about them on different days.

RAY: You don't remember the things I tell you?

REBA: I know there are things you tell me but I don't remember them from day to day.

RAY: You don't remember the things I dream about?

REBA: I know there are some things you dream about but I don't remember what they are.

RAY: How could you forget those things I want—and dream of?

REBA: It's been a while since we last talked about them.

RAY: How long?

REBA: I don't remember.

RAY: I thought you loved me and I thought to love a person is to know what their dreams are, and the things they think about. And that thinking about those things makes the person get through each day. And I thought to love a person is to know those things and to think of those things too and to know when the person is thinking of those things. [*He empties the contents of the sack on the floor. A stone, a piece of wood, a bottle top and a piece of metal. He lines two pieces on the floor and holds the other two.*] Look at this, Reba. You see this? [*Pointing at the pieces.*] This is you. This is me. [*He picks up the pieces and gives* REBA *her piece. Then, as he puts a third piece down:*] This person comes and puts his piece down. Then you come and you put your piece down.—Put it down.

[*She puts her piece down. Putting his own piece down:*]

Then, I come and I put my piece down. This person is first, you're second and I'm third. We can go sit in the sun or go for a walk or do something we have to do. When it's time to come in the shelter we stand in line. Like this. We know our place because we know what our piece is. You see what I mean?—Reba, do you see what I mean?—This here is me...this is Nadine...This is Helena...This is Birdie...This is Rainbow... [*He starts to cry.*] This is Helena. [*Pause.*] Helena...poor Helena.

[CHARLIE *enters from the upright archway. He carries a clipboard with a printed form. A pencil and an eraser are attached to the clipboard by strings. He stops to write on the form.*]

...Charlie, [*Pause.*] look at this.

[CHARLIE *moves closer and looks at the piece.*]

This is what I wanted to show you. This is what I was talking to you about. [*Pointing.*] This is someone who came first. This is Reba. This represents her. This is me and this is someone else.

[CHARLIE *sits down.* RAY *waits a moment for* CHARLIE'*s reply.*]

Charlie, someone comes first and puts his piece down. Then Reba comes and puts her piece down. She's second. Then, I come and put my piece down. Then, someone else puts his piece down. It's clear in what order we came in. We don't have to stand in line. We can go somewhere else, sit down someplace, or do something we have to do. Then when it's time to come in we stand in line in the order of our pieces. [*Pause.*] See?—A person may have to go to the toilet. They can go to the toilet and come back because their piece is on the floor in place. When your piece is on the floor it means you're around and you're coming back.

[CHARLIE *looks at the pieces.*]

This is what I was telling you about; a way to save us from standing in line. You see what I mean.

[CHARLIE *looks at the pieces.*]

Charlie, it's a way for us not to have to wait in line such a long time.

CHARLIE: I don't have a form for that, Ray.

REBA: I didn't think it was going to work, Ray. I didn't tell you because I didn't want to say when I wasn't sure. But I didn't think it was going to work. Things like that don't usually work. I don't know why but they usually don't work. [*She sits up. Her arm is in a sling.*] You see, my arm is broken. I think my arm is broken. Last week I fell and I hit my elbow. Now it hurts. I put it in a sling because it doesnt hurt as much if I keep it like this. If it hangs, it hurts. But I need help because it may be broken. And I wondered, Charlie, if I could get some help.

CHARLIE: What kind of help?

REBA: I thought that I may get some food because I'm disabled or that I may get something to make a cast.

CHARLIE: ...with plaster?

REBA: Or some sticks and gauze to make a splint.

CHARLIE: You want me to put in a requisition?

REBA: Might as well.

[CHARLIE *writes on the form.*]

Are you going to put my name on that?

[CHARLIE *continues writing.*]

CHARLIE: You have to sign this.

REBA: ...I don't know, Charlie.

[CHARLIE *continues writing, then hands the clipboard to* REBA. *She takes the clipboard and looks at the form.*]

RAY: [*Pointing to the objects on the floor.*] Are you going to put in a requisition for this?

CHARLIE: I don't know Ray...I don't know what kind of forms you'd use for this kind of thing. That requisition would not go in this form. You have to have a form that has the right questions.

REBA: I'd prefer it if you didn't put my name on this.

CHARLIE: What do you mean?

REBA: [*Handing the clipboard to* CHARLIE.] My name here, Charlie.

CHARLIE: Well, I can't put in this requisition unless I put your name on it.

REBA: I don't like to have my name on that paper. I don't like it when my name is down on paper. It's better if you don't put my name there. Don't put your name down on paper. If you see something happen you say you didn't see it. And if you didn't see it, you say you saw it. It's better that way. Always say the opposite. Otherwise they think you're lying. If you lie you sound better to them. You don't sound so stupid to them. People don't like it when you tell the truth. You can't go inside any place if you tell the truth. If you tell the truth you have to stay outside. They don't let you in. You stay in the cold. They won't let you through the door. If you tell the truth you end up arrested.

CHARLIE: [*Annoyed.*] What do I do with this now?

REBA: I don't know, Charlie.

CHARLIE: You have to sign it.

[REBA *shakes her head.*]

Didn't you know you had to sign a requisition?

REBA: No, I didn't know that.

CHARLIE: You never made one

[REBA *shakes her head.*]

You did, Reba.

REBA: When?

[CHARLIE *looks at the clipboard.*]

CHARLIE: You have. I know you have.

REBA: No, Charlie.

CHARLIE: You better sign it.

REBA: No, Charlie.

CHARLIE: I know you have.—Now I'm going to have to erase this.

[*He erases what he wrote and starts to walk left.* BIRDIE *walks into the archway to the left. She carries a shopping sack and a loaf of bread.* CHARLIE *stops and looks at her for a moment.*]

Here's that woman, Ray.

[RAY *turns to look at her.*]

She's looking for you. Do you know her? [CHARLIE *walks to* BIRDIE.] Ray's here.

[CHARLIE *exits.* BIRDIE *crosses to the right and stands against the wall.*]

BIRDIE: Now they're calm, but something is seething inside them. Something that may ignite without much provocation. Something swelling inside them. I feel the stench in the air. I must be careful. I must not provoke their rage. I must not let them notice I'm different from them. If they do I'm sure they'll blame me. What's happening to them is not my fault. How could it be? If they think it is *they* will vent their rage on me. I must be careful. [*She walks to* RAY *and* REBA.] Ray...

RAY: How are you, Birdie?

BIRDIE: I'm fine.

RAY: I'm going back soon. I've been getting ready to go to the Compound. I've been working on some ideas. Some people blow their wad, but I haven't. I assure you, Birdie, I have some very good ideas. I'm going back soon. I'm sure they'll appreciate my going back. Because I've had time to work on some ideas that are of value. Useful.

BIRDIE: I brought you some food.

RAY: Thank you. This is Reba.

[BIRDIE *sits.*]

BIRDIE: Hello, Reba.

REBA: Pleased to meet you.

[BIRDIE *hands the shopping sack to* RAY.]

BIRDIE: This is for you. It's still hot.

RAY: Thank you.

[BIRDIE *breaks the loaf of bread in half.*]

BIRDIE: [*As she hands a piece to* RAY.] Here is some bread.

RAY: Thank you.

[REBA *starts to walk to the up left archway.*]

BIRDIE: I'm going to take this to Charlie.

RAY: Why him?

[REBA *stops.*]

BIRDIE: Why not?

RAY: Why is the bigger piece for him?

BIRDIE: I didn't realize it was bigger.

RAY: You're lying.

BIRDIE: Me? [*She turns to him.*] Why would I?

RAY: How could you not know which piece is bigger?

BIRDIE: I didn't notice.

RAY: That's a lie.

BIRDIE: [*Coming closer.*] Why do you say that?

RAY: The way you say "I'm going to bring him this" or "This is for him."

[BIRDIE *sits.*]

The way you say "This is for him," as if you cared for him more than you cared for me. While before you used to say how I did this or that better than him. Now you want to bring him the bigger piece. As if you still cared for him. Because he has a better position.

BIRDIE: [*As she exchanges the pieces of bread.*] Take this one. [*As she turns upstage.*] I'll bring him the smaller piece. [*Walking to the up-left archway.*] I did it without thinking.

[*When* RAY *speaks,* BIRDIE *stops without turning.*]

RAY: [*Hysterically.*] You didn't do anything without thinking, Birdie! You think about everything!

BIRDIE: [*As she exits.*] That's how you always used to talk.

RAY: [*Shouting.*] I think about you each day! [*Turning front and sobbing.*] I think about her each day!

[RAY *sobs. He moves to the down left corner carrying the sack and bread as he sobs. His movements resemble those of a monkey. When he reaches the wall his sounds become louder, more plaintive like a torn animal.* BIRDIE *reenters.*]

REBA: That doesn't matter anymore, Ray. You can't think about those things anymore.—He has to forget that. We all have to forget where we came from. I can't remember where I came from. I have a hard time remembering that.—Sit down Birdie.

[BIRDIE *sits.*]

Make yourself at home. You're among friends. You're welcome here.

[CHARLIE *enters carrying a folded blanket.*]

CHARLIE: [*Offering* BIRDIE *the blanket.*] This is for you, Birdie. To keep you warm.

[BIRDIE *stares at the blanket.* CHARLIE *puts the blanket on her lap. She pushes it off her lap and looks at* REBA. CHARLIE *picks up the blanket.* BIRDIE *moves up-right.* CHARLIE *moves towards her offering her the blanket. She takes a few steps backwards. She then runs around him and stands next to* REBA. REBA *holds her hand. There is the sound of a bell.*]

REBA: It's time for our rations. [*She stands. She turns to* RAY.]

CHARLIE: Come, Ray. It's time for our rations.

[RAY *joins them. They walk upstage left and turn to face right. The* ANGEL *enters from the up-right archway. He walks, shuffling his feet with short wide steps. When the* ANGEL *reaches center right, they walk to the* ANGEL. *They stand facing him in a semicircle.*]

REBA: Soon you'll feel like us. It won't take too long. A moment ago you felt you were different. But it won't take too long before you feel just like us.

[*All but* BIRDIE *kneel. The* ANGEL *empties the contents of the box on the floor.*]

Come, eat something.

[BIRDIE *kneels on the floor as* REBA, CHARLIE *and* RAY *bow their heads.* BIRDIE *gags and faints. The* ANGEL *begins to exit.*]

She fainted. She's not used to this.— [*To the* ANGEL.] Next time would you bring her something she can eat? Something she likes. [*To* BIRDIE.] What would you like? [*To the* ANGEL, *who continues walking.*] Bring her some bread and coffee and some juice and cream! Cheese and crackers instead of bread. And some fruit! I think fruit is good—when you feel the way she does—listless. She feels very weak. Perhaps she should have some red meat. Some roast beef!—Rare! So it puts some blood into her system. And some milk.—She should not have sugar, because that isn't good for you. But she should have honey, which is good for you. And I think she should have something hot. Instead of coffee she should have something more nourishing! Pea soup, or perhaps chicken soup is more digestible. With potatoes because the starch of the potato will restore some of her lost strength!—And fish. Fish is good for the brain, because when you faint the brain feels as if it's disintegrating, either baked or a fried patty, or some tuna and canned sardines. She should have some vegetables, carrot sticks! and raw cauliflower! or any raw vegetables they may have! Although cooked vegetables are also good! If they are not over-cooked! And also a little red wine. I understand it's good to pick you up. Or sherry's better, I think. It is better to pick you up. [To BIRDIE softly.] Would you like a little liqueur?

[RAY *turns to* BIRDIE *sobbing. He stretches his arm to her. His head starts coming up still sobbing. He looks up to the heavens. He is now wailing. The lights fade to black. The bell is heard once.*]

Suzan-Lori Parks

THE DEATH OF THE LAST BLACK MAN IN THE WHOLE ENTIRE WORLD

> When I die,
> I won't stay
> Dead.
> —**Bob Kaufman**

THE FIGURES:

Black Man with Watermelon
Black Woman with Fried Drumstick
Lots of Grease and Lots of Pork
Yes and Greens Black-Eyed Peas Cornbread
Queen-then-Pharaoh Hatshepsut
Before Columbus
Old Man River Jordan
Ham
And Bigger and Bigger and Bigger
Prunes and Prisms
Voice on thuh Tee V

The action takes place in the present.

OVERTURE

BLACK MAN WITH WATERMELON: The black man moves his hands.

[*A bell sounds twice.*]

LOTS OF GREASE AND LOTS OF PORK: Lots of Grease and Lots of Pork.

QUEEN-THEN-PHARAOH HATSHEPSUT: Queen-then-Pharaoh Hatshepsut.

AND BIGGER AND BIGGER AND BIGGER: And Bigger and Bigger and Bigger.

PRUNES AND PRISMS: Prunes and Prisms.

HAM: Ham.

VOICE ON THUH TEE V: Voice on thuh Tee V.

OLD MAN RIVER JORDAN: Old Man River Jordan.

YES AND GREENS BLACK-EYED PEAS CORNBREAD: Yes and Greens Black-Eyed Peas Cornbread.

BEFORE COLUMBUS: Before Columbus.

[*A bell sounds once.*]

BLACK MAN WITH WATERMELON: The black man moves his hands.

QUEEN-THEN-PHARAOH HATSHEPSUT: Not yet. Let Queen-then-Pharaoh Hatshepsut tell you when.

LOTS OF GREASE AND LOTS OF PORK: This is the death of the last black man in the whole entire world.

[*A bell sounds three times.*]

BLACK WOMAN WITH FRIED DRUMSTICK: Yesterday today next summer tomorrow just uh moment uhgoh in 1317 dieded thuh last black man in thuh whole entire world. Uh! Oh. Dont be uhlarmed. Do not be afeared. It was painless. Uh painless passin. He falls twenty-three floors to his death. 23 floors from uh passin ship from space tuh splat on thuh pavement. He have uh head he been keepin under thuh Tee V. On his bottom pantry shelf. He have uh head that hurts. Dont fit right. Put it on tuh go tuh thuh store and it pinched him when he walks his thoughts don't got room. Why dieded he huh? Where he gonna go now that he done dieded? Where he gonna go tuh wash his hands?

YES AND GREENS BLACK-EYED PEAS CORNBREAD: You should write that down and you should hide it under a rock. This is the death of the last black man in the whole entire world.

LOTS OF GREASE AND LOTS OF PORK/PRUNES AND PRISMS: Not yet—

BLACK MAN WITH WATERMELON: The black man moves. His hands—

QUEEN-THEN-PHARAOH HATSHEPSUT: You are too young to move. Let me move it for you.

BLACK MAN WITH WATERMELON: The black man moves his hands.— He moves his hands round. Back. Back. Back tuh that.

LOTS OF GREASE AND LOTS OF PORK: (Not dat).

BLACK MAN WITH WATERMELON: When thuh worl usta be roun. Thuh worl usta be *roun*.

BLACK WOMAN WITH FRIED DRUMSTICK: Uh roun worl. Uh roun? Thuh worl? When was this.

QUEEN-THEN-PHARAOH HATSHEPSUT: Columbus. Before.

BEFORE COLUMBUS: Before. Columbus.

YES AND GREENS BLACK-EYED PEAS CORNBREAD: Before Columbus.

BLACK MAN WITH WATERMELON: HHH. HA!

QUEEN-THEN-PHARAOH HATSHEPSUT: Before Columbus thuh worl usta be *roun* they put uh /d/ on thuh end of roun makin round. Thusly they set in motion thuh end. Without that /d/ we coulda gone on spinnin for ever. Thuh /d/ thing ended things ended.

YES AND GREENS BLACK-EYED PEAS CORNBREAD: Before Columbus.

[*A bell sounds twice.*]

BEFORE COLUMBUS: The popular thinking of the day back in them days was that the world was flat. They thought the world was flat. Back then when they thought the world was flat they were afeared and stayed at home. They wanted to go out back then when they thought the world was flat but the water had in it dragons of which meaning these dragons they were afeared back then when they thought the world was flat. They stayed home. Them thinking the world was flat kept it roun. Them thinking the sun revolved around the earth kept them satellite-like. They figured out the truth and scurried out. Figuring out the truth put them in their place and they scurried out to put us in ours.

YES AND GREENS BLACK-EYED PEAS CORNBREAD: Mmmm. Yes. You should write this down. You should hide this under a rock.

LOTS OF GREASE AND LOTS OF PORK/PRUNES AND PRISMS: Not yet—

BLACK MAN WITH WATERMELON: The black man bursts into flames. The black man bursts into blames. Whose fault is it?

ALL: Aint mines.

BLACK MAN WITH WATERMELON: Whose fault is it?

ALL: Aint mines.

BLACK WOMAN WITH FRIED DRUMSTICK: I cant remember back that far.

QUEEN-THEN-PHARAOH HATSHEPSUT: And besides, I wasnt even there.

BLACK MAN WITH WATERMELON: Ha ha ha. The black man laughs out loud.

ALL (*Except* HAM): HAM-BONE-HAM-BONE-WHERE-YOU-BEEN-ROUN-THUH-WORL-N-BACK-UH-GAIN.

YES AND GREENS BLACK-EYED PEAS CORNBREAD: Whatcha seen hambone girl?

BLACK WOMAN WITH FRIED DRUMSTICK: Didnt see you. I saw thuh worl.

QUEEN-THEN-PHARAOH HATSHEPSUT: I was there.

LOTS OF GREASE AND LOTS OF PORK: Didnt see you.

BLACK WOMAN WITH FRIED DRUMSTICK: I was there.

BLACK MAN WITH WATERMELON: Didnt see you. The black man moves his hands.

QUEEN-THEN-PHARAOH HATSHEPSUT: We are too young to see. Let them see it for you. We are too young to rule. Let them rule it for you. We are too young to have. Let them have it for you. You are too young to write. Let them—let them. Do it. Before you.

BLACK MAN WITH WATERMELON: The black man moves his hands.

YES AND GREENS BLACK-EYED PEAS CORNBREAD: You should write it down because if you dont write it down then they will come along and tell the future that we did not exist. You should write it down and you should hide it under a rock. You should write down the past and you should write down the present and in what in the future you should write it down. It will be of us but you should mention them from time to time so that in the future when they come along and know that they exist. You should hide it all under a rock so that in the future when they come along they will say that the rock did not exist.

BLACK WOMAN WITH FRIED DRUMSTICK: We getting somewheres. We getting down. Down down down down down down down down—

QUEEN-THEN-PHARAOH HATSHEPSUT: I saw Columbus comin./I saw Columbus comin goin over tuh visit you. "To borrow a cup of sugar," so he said. I waved my hands in warnin. You waved back. I aint seen you since.

LOTS OF GREASE AND LOTS OF PORK: In the future when they came along I meeting them. On thuh coast. Uh! Thuh Coast! I—was—so—polite. But in thuh dirt, I wrote: "Ha. Ha. Ha."

ALL: Ha. Ha. Ha. Ha. Ha. Ha. Ha. Ha. Ha. Ha. Ha. Ha. Ha. Ha. Ha. Ha. HHHHHHHHHHHHHHHH.

BLACK MAN WITH WATERMELON: Thuh black man he move. He move he hans.

[*A bell sounds once.*]

PANEL I: THUH HOLY GHOST

BLACK MAN WITH WATERMELON: Saint mines. Saint mines. Iduhnt it Nope: iduhnt. Saint mines cause everythin I calls mines got uh print uh me someway on it in it dont got uh print uh me someway on it so saint mines. Duhduhnt so saint: huh.

BLACK WOMAN WITH FRIED DRUMSTICK: Hen.

BLACK MAN WITH WATERMELON: Huh. Huh?

BLACK WOMAN WITH FRIED DRUMSTICK: Hen. Hen?

BLACK MAN WITH WATERMELON: Who gived birth tuh this I wonder. Who gived birth tuh this. I wonder.

BLACK WOMAN WITH FRIED DRUMSTICK: You comed back. Comin backs somethin in itself. You comed back.

BLACK MAN WITH WATERMELON: This does not belong tuh me. Somebody planted this on me. On me in my hands.

BLACK WOMAN WITH FRIED DRUMSTICK: Cold compress. Cold compress then some hen. Lean back. You comed back. Lean back.

BLACK MAN WITH WATERMELON: Who gived birth tuh this I wonder who.

BLACK WOMAN WITH FRIED DRUMSTICK: Comin for you. Came for you: that they done did. Comin for tuh take you. Told me tuh pack up your clothes. Told me tuh cut my bed in 2 from double tuh single. Cut off thuh bed-foot where your feets had rested. Told me tuh do that too. Burry your ring in his hidin spot under thuh porch! That they told me too to do. Didnt have uh ring so I didnt do diddly. They told and told and told: proper instructions for thuh burial proper attire for thuh mournin. They told and told and told: I didnt do squat. Awe on that. You comed back. You got uhway. Knew you would. Hen?

BLACK MAN WITH WATERMELON: Who gived birth tuh this I wonder. Who? Not me. Saint mines.

BLACK WOMAN WITH FRIED DRUMSTICK: Killed every hen on thuh block. You comed back. Knew you would. Knew you would came back. Knew you will wanted uh good big hen dinner in waitin. Every hen on the block.

BLACK MAN WITH WATERMELON: Saint mines.

BLACK WOMAN WITH FRIED DRUMSTICK: Strutted down on up thuh road with my axe. By-my-self-with-my-axe. Got tuh thuh street top 93 dyin hen din hand. Dropped thuh axe. Tooked tuh stranglin. 93 dyin hen din hand with no heads let em loose tuh run down tuh towards home infront of me. Flipped thuh necks of thuh next 23 more odd. Slinged um over my shoulders. Hens of thuh neighbors now in my pots. Feathers of thuh hens of thuh neighbors stucked in our mattress. They told and told and told. On me. Huh. Awe on that. Hen? You got uhway. Knew you would.

BLACK MAN WITH WATERMELON: Who gived birth tuh me I wonder.

BLACK WOMAN WITH FRIED DRUMSTICK: They dont speak tuh us no more. They pass by our porch but they dont nod. You been comed back goin on 9 years not even heard from thuh neighbors uh congratulation. Uh alienationed dum. Uh guess. Huh. Hen? *WE AINT GOT NO FRIENDS,—* sweetheart.

BLACK MAN WITH WATERMELON: *SWEET-HEART.*

BLACK WOMAN WITH FRIED DRUMSTICK: Hen!!

BLACK MAN WITH WATERMELON: Aint hungry.

BLACK WOMAN WITH FRIED DRUMSTICK: Hen.

BLACK MAN WITH WATERMELON: Aint eaten in years.

BLACK WOMAN WITH FRIED DRUMSTICK: Hen?

BLACK MAN WITH WATERMELON: Last meal I had was my last-mans-meal.

BLACK WOMAN WITH FRIED DRUMSTICK: You got uhway. Knew you would.

BLACK MAN WITH WATERMELON: This thing dont look like me!

BLACK WOMAN WITH FRIED DRUMSTICK: It dont. Do it. Should it? Hen: eat it.

BLACK MAN WITH WATERMELON: I kin tell whats mines by whats gots my looks. Ssmymethod. Try it by testin it and it turns out true. Every time. Fool proofly. Look down at my foot and wonder if its mine. Foot mine? I kin ask it and foot answers back with uh "yes Sir"—not like you and me say "yes Sir" but uh "yes Sir" peculiar tuh thuh foot. Foot mine? I kin ask it and through uh look that looks like my looks thuh foot gives me back uh "yes Sir." Ssmymethod. Try by thuh test tuh pass for true. Move on tuh thuh uther foot. Foot mine? And uh nother "yes Sir" so feets mine is understood. Got uh forearm thats up for question check myself out teeth by tooth. Melon mine?—. Dont look like me.

BLACK WOMAN WITH FRIED DRUMSTICK: Hen mine? Gobble it up and it will be. You got uhway. Fixed uh good big hen dinner for you. Get yourself uh mouthful afore it rots.

BLACK MAN WITH WATERMELON: Was we green and stripe-dly when we first comed out?

BLACK WOMAN WITH FRIED DRUMSTICK: Uh huhn. Thuh features comes later. Later comes after now.

BLACK MAN WITH WATERMELON: Oh. Later comes now: melon mine?

BLACK WOMAN WITH FRIED DRUMSTICK: They comed for you

and tooked you. That was yesterday. Today you sit in your chair where you sat yesterday and thuh day afore yesterday afore they comed and tooked you. Things today is just as they are yesterday cept nothin is familiar cause it was such uh long time uhgoh.

BLACK MAN WITH WATERMELON: Later oughta be now by now huh?: melon mine?

BLACK WOMAN WITH FRIED DRUMSTICK: Thuh chair was portable. They take it from county tuh county. Only got one. Can only eliminate one at uh time. Woulda fried you right here on thuh front porch but we dont got enough electric. No onessgot enough electric. Not on our block. Dont believe in havin enough. Put thuh Chair in thuh middle of thuh City. Outdoors. In thuh square. Folks come tuh watch with picnic baskets.—Hen?

BLACK MAN WITH WATERMELON: Sweetheart?

BLACK WOMAN WITH FRIED DRUMSTICK: They juiced you some, huh?

BLACK MAN WITH WATERMELON: Just a squirt. Sweetheart.

BLACK WOMAN WITH FRIED DRUMSTICK: Humpty Dumpty.

BLACK MAN WITH WATERMELON: Melon mines?

BLACK WOMAN WITH FRIED DRUMSTICK: Humpty damn Dumpty actin like thuh Holy Ghost. You got uhway. Thuh lights dimmed but you got uhway. Knew you would.

BLACK MAN WITH WATERMELON: They juiced me some.

BLACK WOMAN WITH FRIED DRUMSTICK: Just a squirt.

BLACK MAN WITH WATERMELON: They had theirselves uh extender chord. Fry uh man in thuh town square needs uh extender tuh reach em thuh electric Hook up thuh chair tuh thuh power. Extender: 49 foot in length. Closer tuh thuh power I never been. Flip on up thuh go switch. Huh! Juice begins its course.

BLACK WOMAN WITH FRIED DRUMSTICK: Humpty damn Dumpty.

BLACK MAN WITH WATERMELON: Thuh straps they have on me are leathern. See thuh cord waggin full with uh jump-juice try me tuh wiggle from thuh waggin but belt leathern straps: width thickly. One round each forearm. Forearm mines? 2 cross thuh chest. Chest is mines: and it explodin. One for my left hand fingers left strapted too. Right was done thuh same. Jump-juice meets me-mine juices I do uh slow soft shoe like on water. Town crier cries uh moan. Felt my nappy head go frizzly. Town follows thuh crier in uh sorta sing-uhlong-song.

BLACK WOMAN WITH FRIED DRUMSTICK: Then you got uhway. Got uhway in comed back.

BLACK MAN WITH WATERMELON: Uh extender chord 49 foot in length. Turned on thuh up switch in I started runnin. First 49 foot I was runnin they was still juicin.

BLACK WOMAN WITH FRIED DRUMSTICK: And they chase-ted you.

BLACK MAN WITH WATERMELON: —Melon mines?

BLACK WOMAN WITH FRIED DRUMSTICK: When you broked tuh seek your freedom they followed after, huh?

BLACK MAN WITH WATERMELON: Later oughta be now by now, huh?

BLACK WOMAN WITH FRIED DRUMSTICK: You comed back.

BLACK MAN WITH WATERMELON: —Not exactly.

BLACK WOMAN WITH FRIED DRUMSTICK: They comed for you tuh take you. Tooked you uhway: that they done did. You got uhway. Thuh lights dimmed. Had us uh brownout. You got past that. You comed back.

BLACK MAN WITH WATERMELON: Turned on thuh juice on me in me in I started runnin. First just runnin then runnin towards home. Couldnt find us. Think I got lost. Saw us on up uhhead but I flew over thuh yard. Couldnt stop. Think I overshot.

BLACK WOMAN WITH FRIED DRUMSTICK: Killed every hen on thuh block. Made you uh—

BLACK MAN WITH WATERMELON: Make me uh space 6 feet by 6 feet by 6. Make it big and mark it so as I wont miss it. If you would please, sweetness, uh mass grave-site. Theres company comin soonish. I would like tuh get up and go. I would like tuh move my hands.

BLACK WOMAN WITH FRIED DRUMSTICK: You comed back.

BLACK MAN WITH WATERMELON: Overshot. Overshot. I would like tuh move my hands.

BLACK WOMAN WITH FRIED DRUMSTICK: Cold compress?

BLACK MAN WITH WATERMELON: Sweetheart.

BLACK WOMAN WITH FRIED DRUMSTICK: How uhbout uh hen leg?

BLACK MAN WITH WATERMELON: Nothanks. Justate.

BLACK WOMAN WITH FRIED DRUMSTICK: Just ate?

BLACK MAN WITH WATERMELON: Justate. Thatsright. 6 by 6 by 6. Thatsright.

BLACK WOMAN WITH FRIED DRUMSTICK: Oh. —. They eat their own yuh know.

BLACK MAN WITH WATERMELON: HooDoo.

BLACK WOMAN WITH FRIED DRUMSTICK: Hen do. Saw it on thuh Tee V.

BLACK MAN WITH WATERMELON: Aint that nice.

[*A bell sounds once.*]

PANEL II: FIRST CHORUS

BLACK MAN WITH WATERMELON: 6 by 6 by 6.

ALL: THATS RIGHT.

BLACK WOMAN WITH FRIED DRUMSTICK: Oh. They eat their own you know.

ALL: HOODOO.

BLACK WOMAN WITH FRIED DRUMSTICK: Hen do. Saw it on thuh Tee V.

ALL: Aint that nice.

AND BIGGER AND BIGGER AND BIGGER: WILL SOMEBODY TAKE THESE STRAPS OFF UH ME PLEASE? I WOULD LIKE TUH MOVE MY HANDS.

PRUNES AND PRISMS: Prunes and prisms will begin: prunes and prisms prunes and prisms prunes and prisms and prunes and prisms: 23.

VOICE ON THUH TEE V: Good evening. I'm Broad Caster. Headlining tonight: the news: is Gamble Major, the absolutely last living negro man in the whole entire known world—is dead. Major Gamble, born a slave, taught himself the rudiments of education to become a spearhead in the Civil Rights Movement. He was 38 years old. News of Major's death sparked controlled displays of jubilation in all corners of the world.

PRUNES AND PRISMS: Oh no no: world is roun.

AND BIGGER AND BIGGER AND BIGGER: WILL SOMEBODY TAKE THESE STRAPS OFF UH ME PLEASE? I WOULD LIKE TUH MOVE MY HANDS.

[*A bell sounds 4 times.*]

LOTS OF GREASE AND LOTS OF PORK: This is the death of the last black man in the whole entire world.

PRUNES AND PRISMS: Not yet—

VOICE ON THUH TEE V: Good evening. Broad Caster. Headline tonight: Gamble Major, the absolutely last living negro man in the whole known entire world is dead. Gamble Major born a slave rose to become a spearhead in the Civil Rights Movement. He was 38 years old. The Civil Rights Movement. He was 38 years old.

AND BIGGER AND BIGGER AND BIGGER: WILL SOMEBODY TAKE THESE STRAPS OFF UH ME PLEASE? I WOULD LIKE TUH MOVE MY HANDS.

LOTS OF GREASE AND LOTS OF PORK: This is the death of the last black man in the whole entire world.

[*A bell sounds 3 times.*]

PRUNES AND PRISMS: Prunes and prisms prunes and prisms prunes and prisms prunes and prisms.

QUEEN-THEN-PHARAOH HATSHEPSUT: Yesterday tuhday next summer tuhmorrow just uh moment uhgoh in 1317 dieded thuh last black man in thuh whole entire world. Uh! Oh. Dont be uhlarmed. Do not be afeared. It was painless. Uh painless passin. He falls 23 floors to his death.

PRUNES AND PRISMS: No.

QUEEN-THEN-PHARAOH HATSHEPSUT: 23 floors from uh passin ship from space tuh splat on thuh pavement.

PRUNES AND PRISMS: No.

QUEEN-THEN-PHARAOH HATSHEPSUT: He have uh head he been keepin under thuh Tee V. On his bottom pantry shelf.

PRUNES AND PRISMS: No.

QUEEN-THEN-PHARAOH HATSHEPSUT: He have uh head that hurts. Dont fit right. Put it on tuh go tuh thuh store in it pinched him when he walks his thoughts dont got room. Why dieded he huh?

PRUNES AND PRISMS: No.

QUEEN-THEN-PHARAOH HATSHEPSUT: Where he gonna go now that he done dieded?

PRUNES AND PRISMS: No.

BLACK WOMAN WITH FRIED DRUMSTICK: Where he gonna go tuh wash his hands?

CHORUS: You should write that down. You should write that down and you should hide it under uh rock.

VOICE ON THUH TEE V: Good evening. Broad Caster. Headlinin tonight: thuh news:

OLD MAN RIVER JORDAN: Tell you of uh news. Last news. Last news of thuh last man. Last man had last words say hearin it. He spoked uh speech spoked hisself uh chatter-tooth babble "ya-oh-may/chuh-naw" dribblin down his lips tuh puddle in his lap. Dribblin by droppletts. Drop by drop. Last news. News flashes then drops. Thuh last drop was uh all uhlone drop. Singular. Thuh last drop started it off it all. Started off with uh drop. Started off with uh jungle. Started sproutin in his spittle growin leaves off of his mines and thuh vines say drippin doin it. Last news leads tuh thuh first news. He is dead he crosses thuh river. He jumps in thuh puddle have his clothing: ON. On thuh other side thuh mountin yo he dripply wet with soppin. Do drop be dripted? I say "yes."

BLACK MAN WITH WATERMELON: Dont leave me hear. Dont leave me. Hear?

QUEEN-THEN-PHARAOH HATSHEPSUT: Where he gonna go tuh wash his dribblin hands?

PRUNES AND PRISMS: Where he gonna go tuh dry his dripplin clothes?

YES AND GREENS BLACK-EYED PEAS CORNBREAD: Did you write it down? On uh little slip uh paper stick thuh slip in thuh river afore you slip in that way you keep your clothes dry, man.

PRUNES AND PRISMS: Aintcha heard uh that trick?

BEFORE COLUMBUS: That tricks thuh method.

QUEEN-THEN-PHARAOH HATSHEPSUT: They used it on uhlong uhgoh still works every time.

OLD MAN RIVER JORDAN: He jumped in thuh water without uh word for partin come out drippley wet with soppin. Do drop be dripted? I say "do."

BLACK MAN WITH WATERMELON: In you all theres kin. You all kin. Kin gave thuh first permission kin be givin it now still. Some things is all thuh ways gonna be uh continuin sort of uh some thing. Some things go on and on till they dont stop. I am soppin wet. I left my scent behind in uh bundle of old clothing that was not thrown out. Left thuh scent in thuh clothin in thuh clothin on uh rooftop. Dogs surround my house and laugh. They are mockin thuh scent that I left behind. I jumped in thuh water without uh word. I jumped in thuh water without uh smell. I am in thuh river and in my skin is soppin wet. I would like tuh stay afloat now. I would like tuh move my hands.

AND BIGGER AND BIGGER AND BIGGER: Would somebody take these straps off uh me please? I would like tuh move my hands.

BLACK MAN WITH WATERMELON: Now kin kin I move my hands?

QUEEN-THEN-PHARAOH HATSHEPSUT: My black man my subject man my man uh all mens my my my no no not yes no not yes thuh hands. Let Queen-then-Pharaoh Hatshepsut tell you when. She is I am. An I am she passing by with her train. Pulling it behind her on uh plastic chain. Ooooh who! Oooooh who! Where you gonna go now, now that you done dieded?

CHORUS: Ha ha ha.

PRUNES AND PRISMS: Say "prunes and prisms" 40 times each day and youll cure your big lips. Prunes and prisms prunes and prisms prunes and prisms: 19.

QUEEN-THEN-PHARAOH HATSHEPSUT: An I am Sheba-like she be me am passin on by she with her train. Pullin it behind/he on uh plastic chain. Oooh who! Oooh who! Come uhlong. Come uhlong.

BLACK WOMAN WITH FRIED DRUMSTICK: Say he was waitin on thuh right time.

AND BIGGER AND BIGGER AND BIGGER: Say he was waitin in thuh wrong line.

BLACK MAN WITH WATERMELON: I jumped in thuh river without uh word. My kin are soppin wet.

QUEEN-THEN-PHARAOH HATSHEPSUT: Come uhlong. Come uhlong.

PRUNES AND PRISMS: Prunes and prisms prunes and prisms.

LOTS OF GREASE AND LOTS OF PORK: This is the death of the last black man in the whole entire world.

PRUNES AND PRISMS: Not yet.

LOTS OF GREASE AND LOTS OF PORK: Back tuh when thuh worl usta be roun.

QUEEN-THEN-PHARAOH HATSHEPSUT: Come uhlong come uhlong get on board come uhlong.

OLD MAN RIVER JORDAN: Back tuh that. Yes.

YES AND GREENS BLACK-EYED PEAS CORNBREAD: Back tuh then thuh worl usta be roun.

OLD MAN RIVER JORDAN: Uhcross thuh river in back tuh that. Yes. Do in diddly dip didded thuh drop. Out to thuh river uhlong to thuh sea. Long thuh long coast. Skirtin. Yes. Skirtin back tuh that. Come up back flip take uhway like thuh waves do. Far uhway. Uhway tuh where they dont speak thuh language and where they dont want tuh. Huh. Go on back tuh that.

YES AND GREENS BLACK-EYED PEAS CORNBREAD: Awe on uh interior before uh demarcation made it mapped. Awe on uh interior with out uh road-word called macadam. Awe onin uh interior that was uh whole was once. Awe on uh whole roun worl uh roun worl with uh river.

OLD MAN RIVER JORDAN: In thuh interior was uh river. Huh. Back tuh that.

CHORUS: Thuh river was roun as thuh worl was. Roun.

OLD MAN RIVER JORDAN: He hacks his way through thuh tall grass. Tall grass scratch. Width: thickly. Grasses thickly comin from all angles at im. He runs along thuh path worn out by uh 9 million paddin bare footed feet. Uh path overgrown cause it aint as all as happened as of yet. Tuh be extracted from thuh jungle first he gotta go in hide.

BLACK MAN WITH WATERMELON: Chase-ted me outa thuh trees now they tree me. Thuh dogs come out from their hidin spots under thuh porch and give me uhway. Thuh hidin spot was under thuh porch of uh house that werent there as of yet. Thuh dogs give me uhway by uh laugh aimed at my scent.

AND BIGGER AND BIGGER AND BIGGER: HA HA HA. Thats how thuh laugh sorta like be wentin.

PRUNES AND PRISMS: Where he gonna go now now that he done dieded?

QUEEN-THEN-PHARAOH HATSHEPSUT: Where he gonna go tuh move his hands?

BLACK MAN WITH WATERMELON: I. I. I would like tuh move my hands.

YES AND GREENS BLACK-EYED PEAS CORNBREAD: Back tuh when thuh worl usta be roun.

LOTS OF GREASE AND LOTS OF PORK: Uh roun. Thuh worl? Uh

roun worl? When was this?

OLD MAN RIVER JORDAN: Columbus. Before.

PRUNES AND PRISMS: Before Columbus?

AND BIGGER AND BIGGER AND BIGGER: Ha!

QUEEN-THEN-PHARAOH HATSHEPSUT: Before Columbus thuh worl usta be roun. They put uh /d/ on thuh end of roun makin roun*d*. Thusly they set in motion thuh enduh. Without that /d/ we could uh gone on spinnin forever. Thuh /d/ thing endiduh things endiduh.

BEFORE COLUMBUS: Before Columbus:

[*A bell sounds once.*]

Thuh popular thinkin kin of thuh day back then in them days was that thuh worl was flat. They thought thuh worl was flat. Back then kin in them days when they thought thuh worl was flat they were afeared and stayed at home. They wanted tuh go out back then when they thought thuh worl was flat but thuh water had in it dragons.

AND BIGGER AND BIGGER AND BIGGER: Not lurkin in thuh sea but lurkin in thuh street, see? Sir name Tom-us and Bigger be my christian name. Rise up out of uh made up story in grown Bigger and Bigger. Too big for my own name. Nostrils: flarin. Width: thickly. Breath: fire-laden and smellin badly.

BLACK WOMAN WITH FRIED DRUMSTICK: Huh. Whiffit.

BEFORE COLUMBUS: Dragons, of which meanin these dragons they were afeared back then. When they thought thuh worl was flat. They stayed at home. Them thinkin thuh worl was flat kept it roun. Them thinkin thuh sun revolved uhroun thuh earth kin kept them satellite-like. They figured out thuh truth and scurried out. Figurin out thuh truth kin put them in their place and they scurried out tuh put us in ours.

YES AND GREENS BLACK-EYED PEAS CORNBREAD: Mmmmm.

Yes. You should write that down. You should write that down and you should hide it under uh rock.

BEFORE COLUMBUS: Thuh earthsgettin level with thuh land land HO and thuh lands gettin level with thuh sea.

PRUNES AND PRISMS: Not yet—

QUEEN-THEN-PHARAOH HATSHEPSUT: An I am Sheba she be me. Youll mutter thuh words and part thuh waves and come uhlong come uhlong.

AND BIGGER AND BIGGER AND BIGGER: I would like tuh fit in back in thuh storybook from which I camed.

BLACK MAN WITH WATERMELON: My text was writ in water. I would like tuh drink it down.

QUEEN-THEN-PHARAOH HATSHEPSUT: Down tuh float drown tuh float down. My son erased his mothers mark.

AND BIGGER AND BIGGER AND BIGGER: I am grown too big for thuh word thats me.

PRUNES AND PRISMS: Prunes and prisms prunes and prisms prunes and prisms: 14.

QUEEN-THEN-PHARAOH HATSHEPSUT: An I am Sheba me am (She be doo be wah waaaah doo wah). Come uhlong come on uhlong on.

BEFORE COLUMBUS: Before Columbus directs thuh traffic: left right left right.

PRUNES AND PRISMS: Prunes and prisms prunes and prisms.

QUEEN-THEN-PHARAOH HATSHEPSUT: I left my mark on all I made. My son erase his mothers mark.

BLACK WOMAN WITH FRIED DRUMSTICK: Where you gonna go now now that you done dieded?

AND BIGGER AND BIGGER AND BIGGER: Would somebody take these straps offuh me please? Gaw*. I would like tuh drink in drown—

*A glottal stop and choking sound.

BEFORE COLUMBUS: There is uh tiny land mass just above my reach.

LOTS OF GREASE AND LOTS OF PORK: There is uh tiny land mass just outside of my vocabulary.

OLD MAN RIVER JORDAN: Do in dip diddly did-did thuh drop? Drop do it be dripted? Uh huh.

BEFORE COLUMBUS: Land:

AND BIGGER AND BIGGER AND BIGGER: HO!

QUEEN-THEN-PHARAOH HATSHEPSUT: I saw Columbus comin Before Columbus comin/goin over tuh meet you—

BEFORE COLUMBUS: Thuh first time I saw it. It was huge. Thuh green sea becomes uh hillside. Uh hillside populated with some peoples I will name. Thuh first time I saw it it was uh was-huge once one. Huh. It has been gettin smaller ever since.

QUEEN-THEN-PHARAOH HATSHEPSUT: Land:

BLACK MAN WITH WATERMELON: HO!

[*A bell sounds once.*]

PANEL III: THUH LONESOME 3SOME

BLACK MAN WITH WATERMELON: It must have rained. Gaw. Must-uh-rained-on-down-us-why. Aint that somethin. Must uh rained! Gaw. Our crops have prospered. Must uh rained why aint that somethin why aint that somethin-somethin gaw somethin: nice.

BLACK WOMAN WITH FRIED DRUMSTICK: Funny.

BLACK MAN WITH WATERMELON: Gaw. Callin on it spose we did: gaw—thuh uhrainin gaw huh? Gaw gaw. Lookie look-see gaw: where there were riv-lets now there are some. Gaw. Cement tuh mudment accomplished with uh gaw uh flick of my wrist gaw. Huh. Look here now there is uh gaw uh wormlett. Came out tuhday. In my stools gaw gaw gaw gaw they all out tuhday. Come out tuh breathe gaw dontcha? Sure ya dontcha sure gaw ya dontcha sure ya dontcha do yall gaw. Gaw. Our one melon has given intuh 3. Callin what it gived birth callin it gaw. 3 August hams out uh my hands now surroundin me an is all of um mines? GAW. Uh huhn. Gaw gaw. Cant breathe.

BLACK WOMAN WITH FRIED DRUMSTICK: Funny how they break when I dropped em. Though they was past that. Huh. 3 broke in uh row. Guess mmm on uh roll uh some sort, huh. Hell. Huh. Whiffit.

BLACK MAN WITH WATERMELON: Gaw. Gaw. Cant breathe.

BLACK WOMAN WITH FRIED DRUMSTICK: Some things still hold. Huh. Uh old layed eggull break after droppin most likely. Huh. 4 in uh row. Awe on that.

BLACK MAN WITH WATERMELON: Gaw. Cant breathe you.

BLACK WOMAN WITH FRIED DRUMSTICK: You dont need to. No need for breathin for you no more, huh? 5. 6. Mm makin uh history. 7-hhh 8-hhh mm makin uh mess. Huh. Whiffit.

BLACK MAN WITH WATERMELON: Gaw. Gaw loosen my collar. No air in here.

BLACK WOMAN WITH FRIED DRUMSTICK: 7ssgot uh red dot. Awe on that.

BLACK MAN WITH WATERMELON: Sweetheart—. SWEETHEART?!

BLACK WOMAN WITH FRIED DRUMSTICK: 9. Chuh. Funny. Funny. Somethin still holdin on. Let me loosen your collar for you you comed home after uh hard days work. Your suit: tied. Days work was runnin from them we know aint chaseted you. You comed back home after uh hard days work such uh hard days work that now you cant breathe you. Now.

BLACK MAN WITH WATERMELON: Dont take it off just loosen it. Dont move thuh tree branch let thuh tree branch be.

BLACK WOMAN WITH FRIED DRUMSTICK: Your days work aint like any others day work: you bring your tree branch home. Let me loosen thuh tie let me loosen thuh neck-lace let me loosen up thuh noose that stringed him up let me leave thuh tree branch be. Let me rub your wrists.

BLACK MAN WITH WATERMELON: Gaw. Gaw.

BLACK WOMAN WITH FRIED DRUMSTICK: Some things still hold. Wrung thuh necks of them hens and they still give eggs. Huh: Like you. Still sproutin feathers even after they fried. Huh: like you too. 10. Chuh. Eggs still break. Thuh mess makes uh stain. Thuh stain makes uh mark. Whiffit. Whiffit.

BLACK MAN WITH WATERMELON: Put me on uh platform tuh wait for uh train. Uh who who uh who who uh where ya gonna go now—. Platform hitched with horses/steeds. Steeds runned off in left me there swingin. It had begun tuh rain. Hands behind my back. This time tied. I had heard of uh word called scaffold and thought that perhaps they just might build me one of um but uh uhn naw just outa my vocabulary but uh uhn naw trees come cheaply.

BLACK WOMAN WITH FRIED DRUMSTICK: 8. 9. I aint hungry. 9. 10. You dont eat. Dont need to.

BLACK MAN WITH WATERMELON: Swingin from front tuh back uhgain. Back tuh—back tuh that was how I be wentin. Chin on my chest hangin down in restin eyes each on eyein my 2 feets. Left on thuh right one right one on thuh left. Crossed eyin. It was difficult tuh breathe. Toes uncrossin then crossin for luck. With my eyes. Gaw. It had begun tuh rain. Oh. Gaw. Ever so lightly. Blood came on up. You know: tough. Like riggamartins-stifly only—isolated. They some of em pointed they summoned uh laughed they some looked quick in an then they looked uhway. It had begun tuh rain. I hung on out tuh dry. They puttin uhway their picnic baskets. Ever so lightly gaw gaw it had begun tuh rain. They pullin out their umbrellas in hidedid up their eyes. Oh.

BLACK WOMAN WITH FRIED DRUMSTICK: I aint hungry you dont eat 12 13 and thuh floor will shine. Look: there we are. You in me. Reflectin. Hello! Dont move—.

BLACK MAN WITH WATERMELON: It had begun tuh rain. Now: huh. Sky flew open and thuh light went ZAP. Tree bowed over till thuh branch said BROKE. Uhround my necklace my neck uhround my neck my tree branch. In full bloom. It had begun tuh rain. Feet hit thuh ground in I started runnin. I was wet right through intuh through. I was uh wet that dont get dry. Draggin on my tree branch on back tuh home.

BLACK WOMAN WITH FRIED DRUMSTICK: On back tuh that.

BLACK MAN WITH WATERMELON: Gaw. What was that?

BLACK WOMAN WITH FRIED DRUMSTICK: "On back tuh that?" Huh. Somethin I figured. Huh. Chuh. Lord. Who! Whiffit.

BLACK MAN WITH WATERMELON: When I dieded they cut me down. Didnt have no need for me no more. They let me go.

BLACK WOMAN WITH FRIED DRUMSTICK: Thuh lights dimmed in thats what saved you. Lightnin comed down zappin trees from thuh sky. You got uhway.

BLACK MAN WITH WATERMELON: Not exactly.

BLACK WOMAN WITH FRIED DRUMSTICK: Oh. I see.

BLACK MAN WITH WATERMELON: They tired of me. Pulled me out of thuh trees then treed me then tired of me. Thats how it has gone. Thats how it be wentin.

BLACK WOMAN WITH FRIED DRUMSTICK: Oh. I see. Youve been dismissed. But-where-to? Must be somewhere else tuh go aside from just go gone. Huh. Whiffit: huh. You smell.

BLACK MAN WITH WATERMELON: Maybe I should bathe.

BLACK WOMAN WITH FRIED DRUMSTICK: I call those 3 thuh lonesome 3some. Maybe we should pray.

BLACK MAN WITH WATERMELON: Thuh lonesome 3some. Spose theyll do.

[*A bell sounds twice.*]

PANEL IV: SECOND CHORUS

OLD MAN RIVER JORDAN: Come in look tuh look-see.

VOICE ON THUH TEE V: Good evening this is thuh news. A small sliver of uh tree branch has been found in *The Death of the Last Black Man*. Upon careful examination thuh small sliver of thuh treed branch what was found has been found tuh be uh fosilized bone fragment. With this finding authorities claim they are hot on his tail.

PRUNES AND PRISMS: Uh small sliver of uh treed branch growed from-tuh uh bone.

AND BIGGER AND BIGGER AND BIGGER: WILL SOMEBODY WILL THIS ROPE FROM ROUND MY NECK GOD DAMN I WOULD LIKE TUH TAKE MY BREATH BY RIGHTS GAW GAW.

LOTS OF GREASE AND LOTS OF PORK: This is the death of the last black man in the whole entire world.

[*A bell sounds slowly twice.*]

BLACK MAN WITH WATERMELON: I had heard of uh word called scaffold and had hopes they just might maybe build me one by uh uh naw gaw—

HAM: There was uh tree with your name on it.

BLACK MAN WITH WATERMELON: Jumpin out of uh tree they chase me tree me back tuh thuh tree. Thats where I be came from. Thats where I be wentin.

YES AND GREENS BLACK-EYED PEAS CORNBREAD: Someone ought tuh. Write that down.

LOTS OF GREASE AND LOTS OF PORK: There is a page dog eared

at "Histree" hidin just outside my word hoard. Wheres he gonna come to now that he done gone from.

QUEEN-THEN-PHARAOH HATSHEPSUT: Wheres he gonna go come to now that he gonna go gone on?

OLD MAN RIVER JORDAN: For that you must ask Ham.

BLACK WOMAN WITH FRIED DRUMSTICK: Hen?

LOTS OF GREASE AND LOTS OF PORK: HAM.

QUEEN-THEN-PHARAOH HATSHEPSUT: Ham.

PRUNES AND PRISMS: Hmmmm.

[*A bell sounds twice.*]

HAM: Ham's Begotten Tree (catchin up to um *in medias res* that is we takin off from where we stopped up last time). Huh. NOW: She goned begotten One who in turn begotten Ours. Ours laughed one day uhloud in from thuh sound hittin thuh air smakity sprung up I, you, n He, She, It. They turned in engaged in simple multiplication thus tuh spawn of theirselves one We one You and one called They (They in certain conversation known as "Them" and in other certain conversation a.k.a. "Us"). Now very simply: Wassername she finally gave intuh It and tugether they broughted forth uh wildish one called simply Yo. Yo gone be wentin much too long without hisself uh comb in from thuh frizzly that resulted comed one called You (polite form). You (polite) birthed herself Mister, Miss, Maam and Sir who in his later years with That brought forth Yuh Fathuh. Thuh fact that That was uh mother tuh Yuh Fathuh didnt stop them 2 relations from havin relations. Those strange relations between That thuh mother and Yuh Fathuh thuh son brought forth uh odd lot: called: Yes Massuh, Yes Missy, Yes Maam n Yes Suh Mistuh Suh which goes tuh show that relations with your relations produces complications. Thuh children of That and Yuh Fathuh aside from being plain peculiar was all cross-eyed. This defect enhanced their multiplicative possibilities, for example. Yes Suh Mistuh Suh breeded with hisself n gived us Wassername (thuh 2nd), and Wassernickname (2 twins in birth joindid at thuh lip). Thuh 2 twins lived next door tuh one called Uhnother bringin forth Themuhns, She (thuh 2nd), Auntie, Cousin, and Bro who makeshifted continuous compensations for his loud and odiforous bodily emissions by all thuh time saying excuse me n through his graciousness brought forth They (polite) who had mixed feelins with She (thuh 2nd) thus bringin forth Ussin who then went on tuh have MeMines.

YES AND GREENS BLACK-EYED PEAS CORNBREAD: Thuh list goes on in on.

HAM: MeMines gived out 2 offspring one she called Mines after herself thuh uther she called Themuhns named after all them who comed before. Themuhns married outside thuh tribe joinin herself with uh man they called WhoDat. Themuhns n WhoDat brought forth only one child called WhoDatDere. Mines joined up with Wasshisname and from that union come AllYall.

BEFORE COLUMBUS: All us?

HAM: No. AllYall.

LOTS OF GREASE AND LOTS OF PORK: This list goes on in on.

HAM: Ah yes: Yo suddenly if by majic again became productive in after uh lapse of some great time came back intuh circulation to wiggled uhbout with Yes Missy (one of thuh crosseyed daughters of That and Yuh Fathuh). Yo in Yes Missy begottin ThissunRightHere, Us, ThatOne, She (thuh 3rd) and one called Uncle (who from birth was gifted with great singin and dancin capabilities which helped him make his way in life but tended tuh bring shame on his family).

BEFORE COLUMBUS/BLACK MAN WITH WATERMELON: Shame on

his family.

LOTS OF GREASE AND LOTS OF PORK/BLACK MAN WITH WATERMELON: Shame on his family.

AND BIGGER AND BIGGER AND BIGGER/BLACK MAN WITH WATERMELON: Shamed on his family gaw.

YES AND GREENS BLACK-EYED PEAS CORNBREAD: Write that down.

OLD MAN RIVER JORDAN: (Ham seed his daddy Noah neckked. From that seed, comed Allyall.)

[*A bell sounds twice.*]

AND BIGGER AND BIGGER AND BIGGER: (Will somebody please will this rope—)

VOICE ON THUH TEE V: Good evening. This is thuh news: Whose fault is it?

BLACK MAN WITH WATERMELON: Saint mines.

VOICE ON THUH TEE V: Whose fault iszit??!

CHORUS: Saint mines!

OLD MAN RIVER JORDAN: I cant re-member back that far. (Ham can—but uh uh naw gaw— Ham wuduhnt there, huh).

CHORUS: HAM BONE HAM BONE WHERE YOU BEEN ROUN THUH WORL N BACK A-GAIN.

QUEEN-THEN-PHARAOH HATSHEPSUT: Whatcha seen. Hambone girl?

BLACK WOMAN WITH FRIED DRUMSTICK: Didnt see you. I saw thuh worl.

HAM: I was there.

PRUNES AND PRISMS: Didnt see you.

HAM: I WAS THERE.

VOICE ON THUH TEE V: Didnt see you.

BLACK MAN WITH WATERMELON/AND BIGGER AND BIGGER AND BIGGER: THUH BLACK MAN. HE MOOOVE.

CHORUS: HAM BONE HAM BONE WHATCHA DO? GOT UH CHANCE N FAIRLY FLEW.

BLACK WOMAN WITH FRIED DRUMSTICK: Over thuh front yard.

BLACK MAN WITH WATERMELON: Overshot.

CHORUS: 6 BY 6 BY 6.

BLACK MAN WITH WATERMELON: Thats right.

AND BIGGER AND BIGGER AND BIGGER: WILL SOMEBODY WILL THIS ROPE—

CHORUS: Good evening. This is the news.

VOICE ON THUH TEE V: Whose fault is it?

ALL: Saint mines!

VOICE ON THUH TEE V: Whose fault iszit?!!

HAM: SAINT MINES!

[*A bell rings twice.*]

—Ham. Is. Not. Tuh. BLAME! WhoDatDere joinded with one called Sir 9th generation of thuh first Sir son or You (polite) thuh first daughter of You WhoDatDere with thuh 9th Sir begettin forth Him—

BLACK MAN WITH WATERMELON: Ham?!

ALL (*Except* HAM): HIM!

BLACK WOMAN WITH FRIED DRUMSTICK: Sold.

HAM: SOLD! allyall[9] not tuh be confused w/allus[12] joined w/allthem[3] in from that union comed forth wasshisname[21] SOLD wassername[19] still by thuh reputation uh thistree one uh thuh 2 twins loses her sight through fiddlin n falls w/ugly old yuhfathuh[4] given she[8] SOLD whodat[33] pairs w/you[23] (still polite.) of which nothinmuch comes nothinmuch now nothinmuch[6] pairs with yessuhmistuhsuh[17] tuh drop one called yo now yo[9-0] still who gone be wentin now w/elle gived us el SOLD let us not forget ye[1-2-5] w/thee[3] givin us thou[9-2] who w/thuh they who switches their designation in certain conversation yes they[10] broughted forth onemore[2] at thuh same time in thuh same row right next door we have datone[12] w/disone[14] droppin off duhutherone[2-2] SOLD let us not forget du and sie let us not forget yessuhmassuhsuh[38] w/thou[8] who gived up memines[3-0] SOLD we are now rollin through thuh long division gimmie uh gimmie uh gimmie uh squared off route round it off round it off n round it out w/sistuh[4-3] who lives with one called saintmines[9] givin forth one uh year how it got there callin it jessgrew callin it saintmines callin it whatdat whatdat whatdat SOLD

BLACK MAN WITH WATERMELON: Thuh list goes on and on. Dont it.

CHORUS: Ham Bone Ham Bone Ham Bone Ham Bone.

BEFORE COLUMBUS: Left right left right.

QUEEN-THEN-PHARAOH HATSHEPSUT: Left left left whose left...?

[*A bell sounds twice.*]

LOTS OF GREASE AND LOTS OF PORK: This is the death of the last black man in the whole entire world.

PANEL V: IN THUH GARDEN OF HOODOO IT

BLACK WOMAN WITH FRIED DRUMSTICK: Somethins turnin. Huh. Whatizit.—Mercy. Mercy. Huh. Chew on this. Ssuh feather. Sswhatchashud be eatin now ya no. Ssuhfeather: stuffin. Chew on it. Huh. Feathers sprouted from thuh fried hens—dont ask me how. Somethins out uh whack. Somethins out uh rights. Your arms still on your elbows. I'm still here. Whensit gonna end. Soon. Huh. Mercy. Thuh Tree.

Springtime. And harvest. Huh. Somethins turnin. So many melons. Huh. From one tuh 3 tuh many. Must be nature. Gnaw on this. Gnaw on this, huh? Gnaw on this awe on that.

BLACK MAN WITH WATERMELON: Aint eatable.

BLACK WOMAN WITH FRIED DRUMSTICK: I know.

BLACK MAN WITH WATERMELON: Aint eatable aint it. Nope. Nope.

BLACK WOMAN WITH FRIED DRUMSTICK: Somethins turnin. Huh. Whatizit.

BLACK MAN WITH WATERMELON: Aint eatable so I out in out ought not aint be eatin it aint that right. Yep. Nope. Yep. Uh huhn.

BLACK WOMAN WITH FRIED DRUMSTICK: Huh. Whatizit.

BLACK MAN WITH WATERMELON: I remember what I like. I remember what my likes tuh eat when I be in thuh eatin mode.

BLACK WOMAN WITH FRIED DRUMSTICK: Chew on this.

BLACK MAN WITH WATERMELON: When I be in thuh eatin mode.

BLACK WOMAN WITH FRIED DRUMSTICK: Swallow it down. I know. Gimmie your pit. Needs bathin.

BLACK MAN WITH WATERMELON: Choice between peas and corns—my feets—. Choice: peas. Choice between peas and greens choice: greens. Choice between greens and potatoes choice: potatoes. Yams. Boiled or mashed choice: mashed. Aaah. Mmm. My likenesses.

BLACK WOMAN WITH FRIED DRUMSTICK: Mercy. Turns—

BLACK MAN WITH WATERMELON: My likenesses! My feets! Aaah! SWEET-HEART. Aaah! SPRING-TIME!

BLACK WOMAN WITH FRIED DRUMSTICK: Spring-time.

BLACK MAN WITH WATERMELON: SPRING-TIME!

BLACK WOMAN WITH FRIED DRUMSTICK: Mercy. Turns—

BLACK MAN WITH WATERMELON: I remembers what I likes. I remembers what I likes tuh eat when I bein in had been in thuh eatin mode. Bein in had been: now in then. I be eatin hen. Hen.

BLACK WOMAN WITH FRIED DRUMSTICK: Huh?

BLACK MAN WITH WATERMELON: HEN!

BLACK WOMAN WITH FRIED DRUMSTICK: Hen?

BLACK MAN WITH WATERMELON: Hen. Huh. My meals. Aaaah: my meals. *BRACH*-A-LEE.

BLACK WOMAN WITH FRIED DRUMSTICK: Whatizit. Huh. — GNAW ON THIS! Good. Uhther pit?

BLACK MAN WITH WATERMELON: We sittin on this porch right now aint we. Uh huhn. Aaah. Yes. Sittin right here right now on it in it ainthuh first time either iduhnt it. Yep. Nope. Once we was here once wuhduhnt we. Yep. Yep. Once we being here. Uh huhn. Huh. There is uh Now and there is uh Then. Ssall there is. (I bein in uh Now: uh Now bein in uh Then: I bein, in Now in Then, in I will be. I was be too but thats uh Then thats past. That me that was be is uh me-has-been. Thuh Then that was be is uh has-been-Then too. Thuh me-has-been sits in thuh be-me: we sit on this porch. Same porch. Same me. Thuh Then thats been somehow sits in thuh Then that will be: same Thens. I swing from uh tree. You cut me down and bring me back. Home. Here. I fly over thuh yard. I fly over thuh yard in all over. Them thens stays fixed. Fixed Thens. Thuh Thems stays fixed too. Thuh Thems that come and take me and thuh Thems that greet me and then them Thems that send me back here. Home. Stays fixed, Them do.)

BLACK WOMAN WITH FRIED DRUMSTICK: Your feets.

BLACK MAN WITH WATERMELON: I: be. You: is. It: be. He, She:

thats us. (Thats it.) We: thats he in she: you aroun me: us be here. You: still is. They: be. Melon. Melon. Melon: mines. I remember all my lookuhlikes. You. You. Remember me.

BLACK WOMAN WITH FRIED DRUMSTICK: Gnaw on this then swallow it down. Youll have your fill then we'll put you in your suit coat.

BLACK MAN WITH WATERMELON: Thuh suit coat I picked out? Thuh stripely one? HA! Peas. Choice: *BRACH*-A-LEE.

BLACK WOMAN WITH FRIED DRUMSTICK: Chew and swallow please.

BLACK MAN WITH WATERMELON: Thuh stripely one with thuh fancy patch pockets!

BLACK WOMAN WITH FRIED DRUMSTICK: Sweetheart.

BLACK MAN WITH WATERMELON: SPRING-TIME.

BLACK WOMAN WITH FRIED DRUMSTICK: Sweetheart.

BLACK MAN WITH WATERMELON: SPRING-TIME.

BLACK WOMAN WITH FRIED DRUMSTICK: This could go on forever.

BLACK MAN WITH WATERMELON: Lets. Hope. Not.

BLACK WOMAN WITH FRIED DRUMSTICK: —Sweetheart.

BLACK MAN WITH WATERMELON: SPRING-TIME.

BLACK WOMAN WITH FRIED DRUMSTICK: Sweetheart.

BLACK MAN WITH WATERMELON: SPRING-TIME.

BLACK WOMAN WITH FRIED DRUMSTICK: This could go on forever.

BLACK MAN WITH WATERMELON: Lets. Hope. Not.

BLACK WOMAN WITH FRIED DRUMSTICK: Must be somewhere else tuh go aside from just go gone.

BLACK MAN WITH WATERMELON: 6 by 6 by 6.

BLACK WOMAN WITH FRIED DRUMSTICK: Thats right.

BLACK MAN WITH WATERMELON: Rock reads "HooDoo."

BLACK WOMAN WITH FRIED DRUMSTICK: Now you know. Know now dontcha. Somethins turnin—.

BLACK MAN WITH WATERMELON: Who do? Them do. Aint that nice. Huh. Miss me. Remember me. Missmemissme-whatsmyname.

BLACK WOMAN WITH FRIED DRUMSTICK: Aaaaah?

BLACK MAN WITH WATERMELON: Remember me. AAAH.

BLACK WOMAN WITH FRIED DRUMSTICK: Thats it. Open wide. Here it comes. Stuffin.

BLACK MAN WITH WATERMELON: Yeeeech.

BLACK WOMAN WITH FRIED DRUMSTICK: Eat uhnother. Hear. I eat one. You eat one more.

BLACK MAN WITH WATERMELON: Stuffed. Time tuh go.

BLACK WOMAN WITH FRIED DRUMSTICK: Not yet!

BLACK MAN WITH WATERMELON: I got uhway?

BLACK WOMAN WITH FRIED DRUMSTICK: Huh?

BLACK MAN WITH WATERMELON: I got uhway?

BLACK WOMAN WITH FRIED DRUMSTICK: Nope. Yep. Nope. Nope.

BLACK MAN WITH WATERMELON: Miss me.

BLACK WOMAN WITH FRIED DRUMSTICK: Miss me.

BLACK MAN WITH WATERMELON: Re-member me.

BLACK WOMAN WITH FRIED DRUMSTICK: Re-member me.

BLACK MAN WITH WATERMELON: My hands are on my wrists. Arms on elbows. Looks: old fashioned. Nothin fancy there. Toes curl up not down. My feets-now clean. Still got all my teeth. Re-member me.

BLACK WOMAN WITH FRIED DRUMSTICK: Re-member me.

BLACK MAN WITH WATERMELON: Call on me sometime.

BLACK WOMAN WITH FRIED DRUMSTICK: Call on me sometime. Hear? Hear? Thuh dirt itself turns itself. So many melons. From one tuh 3 tuh many. Look at um all. Ssuh garden. Awe on that. Winter pro-cessin back tuh back with spring-time. They roll on by us that way. Uh whole line gone roun. Chuh. Thuh worl be roun. Moves that way so they say. You comed back. Yep. Nope. Well. Well. Build uh well.

[*A bell sounds twice.*]

FINAL CHORUS

ALL: "Yes. Oh, me? Chuh, no—"

VOICE ON THUH TEE V: Good morning. This is thuh news:

BLACK WOMAN WITH FRIED DRUMSTICK: Somethins turnin. Thuh page.

[*A bell sounds twice.*]

LOTS OF GREASE AND LOTS OF PORK: This is the death of the last black man in the whole entire worl.

PRUNES AND PRISMS: 19.

OLD MAN RIVER JORDAN: Uh blank page turnin with thuh sound of it. Thuh sound of movin hands.

BLACK WOMAN WITH FRIED DRUMSTICK: Yesterday today next summer tomorrow just uh moment uhgoh in 1317 dieded thuh last black man in thuh whole entire world. Uh! Oh. Dont be uhlarmed. Do not be afeared. It was painless. Uh painless passin. He falls twenty-three floors to his death.

CHORUS: Yes.

BLACK WOMAN WITH FRIED DRUMSTICK: 23 floors from uh passin ship from space tuh splat on thuh pavement.

CHORUS: Yes.

BLACK WOMAN WITH FRIED DRUMSTICK: He have uh head he been keepin under thuh Tee V.

CHORUS: Yes.

BLACK WOMAN WITH FRIED DRUMSTICK: On his bottom pantry shelf.

CHORUS: Yes.

BLACK WOMAN WITH FRIED DRUMSTICK: He have uh head that hurts. Dont fit right. Put it on tuh go tuh thuh store in it pinched him when he walks his thoughts dont got room. He diediduh he did, huh.

CHORUS: Yes.

BLACK WOMAN WITH FRIED DRUMSTICK: Where he gonna go now now now now now that he done diediduh?

CHORUS: Yes.

BLACK WOMAN WITH FRIED DRUMSTICK: Where he gonna go tuh. WASH.

PRUNES AND PRISMS: Somethins turnin. Thuh page.

AND BIGGER AND BIGGER AND BIGGER: Somethins burnin. Thuh tongue.

BLACK MAN WITH WATERMELON: Thuh tongue itself burns.

OLD MAN RIVER JORDAN: He jumps in thuh river. These words for partin.

YES AND GREENS BLACK-EYED PEAS CORNBREAD: And you will write them down.

[*A bell sounds 3 times.*]

BEFORE COLUMBUS: All these boats passed by my coast.

PRUNES AND PRISMS: Somethins turnin. Thuh page.

QUEEN-THEN-PHARAOH HATSHEPSUT: I saw Columbus comin /I saw Columbus comin goin—

QUEEN-THEN-PHARAOH HATSHEPSUT/BEFORE COLUMBUS: Left left left whose left...?

AND BIGGER AND BIGGER AND BIGGER/BLACK MAN WITH WATERMELON: Somethins burnin. Thuh page.

BEFORE COLUMBUS: All those boats passed by me. My coast fell in-to-the-sea. All thuh boats. They stopped for me.

OLD MAN RIVER JORDAN: Land: HO!

QUEEN-THEN-PHARAOH HATSHEPSUT: I waved my hands in warnin. You waved back.

BLACK WOMAN WITH FRIED DRUMSTICK: Somethins burnin. Thuh page.

QUEEN-THEN-PHARAOH HATSHEPSUT: I have-not seen you since.

ALL: Oh!

LOTS OF GREASE AND LOTS OF PORK: This is the death of the last black man in the whole entire worl.

OLD MAN RIVER JORDAN: Do in diddley dip die-die thuh drop. Do drop be dripted? Why, of course.

AND BIGGER AND BIGGER AND BIGGER: Somethins burnin. Thuh tongue.

BLACK MAN WITH WATERMELON: Thuh tongue itself burns itself.

HAM: ... And from that seed comed All Us.

BLACK WOMAN WITH FRIED DRUMSTICK: Thuh page.

ALL: 6 BY 6 BY 6.

BLACK WOMAN WITH FRIED DRUMSTICK: Thats right.

[*A bell sounds twice.*]

BEFORE COLUMBUS: LAND: HO!

YES AND GREENS BLACK-EYED PEAS CORNBREAD: You will write it down because if you dont write it down then we will come along and tell the future that we did not exist. You will write it down and you will carve it out of a rock.

[*Pause.*]

You will write down thuh past and you will write down thuh present and in what in thuh future. You will write it down.

[*Pause.*]

It will be of us but you will mention them from time to time so that in the future when they come along theyll know how they exist.

[*Pause.*]

It will be for us but you will mention them from time to time so that in the future when they come along theyll know why they exist.

[*Pause.*]

You will carve it all out of a rock so that in the future when they come along we will know that the rock did yes exist.

BLACK WOMAN WITH FRIED DRUMSTICK: Down down down down down down down down—

LOTS OF GREASE AND LOTS OF PORK: This is the death of the last black man in the whole entire worl.

PRUNES AND PRISMS: Somethins turnin. Thuh page.

OLD MAN RIVER JORDAN: Thuh last news of thuh last man:

VOICE ON THUH TEE V: Good morning. This is thuh last news:

BLACK MAN WITH WATERMELON: Miss me.

BLACK WOMAN WITH FRIED DRUMSTICK: Miss me.

BLACK MAN WITH WATERMELON: Re-member me.

BLACK WOMAN WITH FRIED DRUMSTICK: Re-member me. Call on me sometime. Call on me sometime. Hear? Hear?

HAM: In thuh future when they came along I meeting them. On thuh coast. Uuuuhh! My coast! I—was—so—po-lite! But. In thuh rock. I wrote: ha ha ha.

ALL: Ha. Ha. Ha. Ha. Ha. Ha. Ha. Ha. Ha. Ha. Ha. Ha. Ha. Ha. HHHHHHHHHHHH. HA!

BLACK WOMAN WITH FRIED DRUMSTICK: Thuh black man he move. He move. He hans.

[*A bell sounds once.*]

ALL: Hold it. Hold it. Hold it. Hold it. Hold it. Hold it. Hold it.

Elizabeth Wong

LETTERS TO A STUDENT REVOLUTIONARY

CHARACTERS:

Bibi, *a Chinese-American woman in her 20s*

Karen, *a Chinese woman in her 20s*

A Chorus *of four (three men and one woman) in the following multiple roles:*

    Charlie/Lu Yan/Chorus One

    Brother/Father/I.N.S. Officer/Chorus Two

    Soldier/Boss/Cat/Jonathan/Chorus Three

    Mother/Mexican Lady/Chorus Four

Time: One decade, 1979–1989
Place: China and the United States

The play is stylistic and presentational, but also grounded in the art and act of letter writing. The audience is an important part of the play, and any address or appeal to them should be personal and direct.

The set is divided into two separate areas representing China and the United States. However, the center space must be a neutral territory wherein the rules of time and geography are broken. Minimal props suggest occupation and/or location.

The CHORUS *must remain on stage throughout. Their presence is necessary, even if the action does not involve them directly. Choral movements are militaristic—crisp and spit polish.*

At curtain rise, the CHORUS *stands impassively together upstage.* BIBI *is downstage.*

BIBI: Day 35. No peanut butter . No cheese. No toast. And I'm sick of jook. Jook is no joke. Jook for breakfast—yesterday, today, and tomorrow. What is jook, you ask?

CHORUS ONE: [*Offers a bowl.*] Rice porridge.

CHORUS: It's good for you.

BIBI: Boring. That's it. I've had it. [*To audience.*] I rebelled against breakfast. I pushed myself away from the table. The chair went flying like a hockey puck on ice. I struck a defiant Bette Davis pose. [*To* CHORUS ONE.] Get that slop away from me...you pig! [*To audience.*] My parents were appalled at my behavior. I was impossible. But I couldn't help it. The ghost of James Dean. [*Heavy sigh.*] So, for thirty-five days, wherein I wished I was sunning in the Bahamas instead, I was Kunta Kinte of the new roots generation—touring China with mom and dad.

[*Chinese opera music clangs.* BIBI *smiles a bit too broadly.*]

Loved the music. Also, loved the toasting of the honored guests...

CHORUS: Gom bei!

BIBI: [*To* CHORUS.] Gom bei! [*To audience.*] Oh sure, I loved the *endless* tours—the jade factory, brocade factory, carpet factory. But how could I appreciate it without some proper grub. John Wayne wouldn't stand for it, he'd shoot the cook, who was probably a Chinese anyway.

[CHORUS ONE *offers the bowl again.*]

Cheerios?

CHORUS ONE: Jook.

BIBI: What a nightmare!

[BIBI *abruptly* runs *upstage. She, not the* CHORUS, *sets the scene. (Note: the* CHORUS *should not be individuated, nor should they be illustrative of any particular attitude or action.)*]

[*To audience.*] I took to the streets of Beijing. Wandered into Tiananmen Square—a hungry look in my eyes, a vain hope in my heart. [*To* CHORUS FOUR.] You there, sweeper. Could you please tell me where I might locate a golden oasis of fast food? [*To* CHORUS TWO.] Hey there Mr. Chicken man, spare

an egg for a simple sunnyside up? [*Goes downstage to audience.*]
Someday, right next to that rosy-faced mug of Chairman
Mao, there'll be a golden arch and a neon sign flashing—
billions and billions served. No place is truly civilized
without Mickey D and a drive-up window. [*Runs back upstage,
to* CHORUS THREE.] 'Scuse me Mr. Soldier, can you possibly
direct me to the nearest greasy spoon?

[CHORUS THREE *slowly turns to look at* BIBI.]

CHORUS ONE: [*To audience.*] Summer, 1979. Tourism was still so
new in China.

[KAREN *enters, pushing an old coaster bicycle.*]

KAREN: [*To audience.*] I am on my way home from the factory.
End of the graveyard shift. Is this the correct phrase? Yes, I
think so. Graveyard shift. This morning, there is much mist.
But it is already hot like hell. Do I say that right? Yes, I think
so.

CHORUS FOUR: [*To audience.*] I sweep. I sweep. Everything must
be clean.

KAREN: The square is very crowded, very many people
everywhere. But I see a girl. She looks like me. But her hair is
curly like the tail of a pig. She wears pink, lavender, indigo.
She is a human rainbow.

[KAREN *steps towards* BIBI. *But the* CHORUS *intimidates her.*]

CHORUS FOUR: [*To* KAREN.] I sweep *you* if you become unclean.
Watch out for contamination! [*Whispered, to* CHORUS ONE.]
You, you there waiter!

CHORUS ONE: [*Overlapped whisper, to* CHORUS TWO.] Watch out!
You, you there butcher!

CHORUS TWO: [*Overlapped whisper, to* KAREN.] Watch out! You,
you there.

[KAREN *backs away from* BIBI.]

CHORUS FOUR: [*To audience.*] My duty to sweep all day. My duty to sweep all night. My back hurts. But I have duty to perform.

KAREN: What harm is there to practice a little English?

CHORUS THREE: [*To* KAREN.] I am watching her, and... [*To audience.*] I am watching you.

BIBI: [*To audience.*] Oh look. Grandmothers with ancient faces, pushing bamboo strollers like shopping carts. Let's peek. [*She does.*] Ahhhh, sweetest little babies with wispy, fuzzy, spiky hair.

KAREN: [*To audience.*] Look, there is a butcher I know. He carries chickens upside down, hurrying to market. He does not see me.

BIBI: [*To audience.*] Talk about ego. Check these pictures, bigger than billboards on Sunset Boulevard. And what's playing? That's the Mao matinee. That's Lenin. Stalin. Is that guy Marx? Yup. Give the girl a piece of pie.

KAREN: [*To audience.*] There, a big strong worker shoulders his load of bamboo for scaffolds. He helps to build a hospital. He is too busy to notice me.

BIBI: [*To audience.*] Bricklayers push a cartful of bricks. A man carries a pole balanced with two hanging baskets, filled with live fish. Great smell! I think I'm going to faint. Bicycles everywhere in the square.

CHORUS ONE: Yes, a busy morning in the square.

[*The* CHORUS, *one by one, build an impenetrable human wall between* KAREN *and* BIBI.]

CHORUS FOUR: [*To audience.*] I am not you and I am not me. I *am* a good citizen of the State.

CHORUS TWO: [*To audience.*] With so much going on, so many people, who pays attention to an inconsequential girl on a bicycle?

KAREN: I will go up to her and speak to her. We will make beautiful sentences together.

CHORUS FOUR: [*To audience.*] I am watching too. Watching everything. It is my duty as a good citizen of the State.

[KAREN *tries to penetrate the wall.*]

CHORUS THREE: [*To audience, overlapping.*] Anarchy will *not* be tolerated.

CHORUS TWO: [*Overlapping.*] Even a spark of spirit will be squashed.

CHORUS ONE: [*Overlapping.*] Wild behavior will not be permitted.

CHORUS THREE: [*Overlapping.*] Wild thinking will not be permitted.

CHORUS ONE: [*Overlapping.*] Any messes will be cleaned up.

CHORUS TWO: [*Overlapping.*] That is what a broom is for.

CHORUS FOUR: [*Overlapping.*] This is my sword. My broom.

CHORUS: [*To audience.*] We must have cleanliness. The state will insist.

KAREN: [*Softly.*] Hello.

BIBI: [*Ignoring her.*] Like in *Vertigo.* Jimmy Stewart climbing the steps, looking down from the tower. Or is it Orson Welles with the funhouse mirrors in *Lady From Shanghai?* Well, anyway, like *everything* going round and round in a woozy circle. [*She examines each member of the* CHORUS.] I see me and I see me and I see me. But not really, you know. I don't fit in, not at all.

[KAREN *breaks through the wall, crosses over to* BIBI.]

KAREN: [*Tentatively.*] Hello.

[BIBI *doesn't hear.* KAREN *steps closer. The* CHORUS *steps into a line and turns their backs to the audience.*]

Please excuse.

BIBI: Oh hello.

KAREN: Please. Not so loud. [*Beat.*] Are you?

BIBI: [*Whispers.*] I am. How can you tell?

KAREN: Ahh. [*Pause.*] Your hair.

BIBI: Completely unnatural, I know. It's called a permanent. Why something's called a permanent when you have to have it redone every six months I'll never know. More like a temporary, if you ask me. Go figure.

KAREN: Go to figure.

BIBI: Right. It's like every time I go to the salon, they want to give me the same old tired thing—the classic bob and bangs, *exactly* like yours. So I plead, "Please do something different." Understand? But every time, without fail, I end up with...you know...[*Indicates* KAREN's *hair.*] *that*—bland and boring, like breakfast.

KAREN: Like breakfast.

BIBI: Right. They tell me, "But oh no, you look so cute. A little China doll, that's what you are." Make me *puke.* So I say, "Aldo baby darling, perm it. Wave it. Frizz it. Spike it. Color it blue." So if you look in the light. See? Not black, but blue with red highlights, tinged with orange. It's unusual, don't you think?

KAREN: You want haircut like me? That easy. Very simple. I do it for you.

BIBI: Sorry. I know I talk too fast. I'm what is known as an energetic person. I have so much energy, I sometimes think I'll leap out of my clothes.

KAREN: No, I'm sorry. My comprehending is very bad. My English is too stupid. But I wish to practice. I would like to have hair curly like yours. Can you do that for me?

BIBI: Sure, you come to California. And I'll set you up with

Aldo. But I warn you, he'll poof and pull and snip, and you think you're going to be a new woman, but you get *banged* and bobbed every time.

[KAREN *starts to touch* BIBI*'s sleeve; then withdraws shyly.*]

KAREN: Here we have only a few colors. Grey and blue and green.

BIBI: Grey and blue and green are good colors.

KAREN: May I ask what is your name?

BIBI: Bibi. My name is Bibi.

[*They reach to shake hands, but before they touch,* BIBI *and* KAREN *freeze. The* CHORUS *speaks to the audience.*]

CHORUS THREE: It was nothing. Conversation lasted two, three minutes tops.

CHORUS FOUR: [*Overlapping.*] Anything can happen in two, three minutes. Did they touch?

CHORUS ONE: [*Overlapping.*] Was there a connection?

CHORUS TWO: [*Overlapping.*] Did they touch?

CHORUS ONE: [*Overlapping.*] Did she have a newspaper?

CHORUS THREE: [*Overlapping.*] A book?

CHORUS TWO: [*Overlapping.*] Was there an exchange?

CHORUS FOUR: [*Overlapping.*] Did they touch?

CHORUS THREE: [*Overlapping.*] Did they touch?

CHORUS TWO: [*Overlapping.*] Watch her very closely. Such encounters might be dangerous.

CHORUS FOUR: [*Whispered.*] Dangerous.

CHORUS ONE: [*Overlapping, whispered.*] Dangerous.

CHORUS TWO: [*Overlapping, whispered.*] Dangerous.

BIBI: [*To audience.*] Our conversation lasted about two, three minutes tops. It was a fleeting proverbial blink of the eye. We didn't have a pencil or even a scrap of paper.

[*The two women move away from each other.*]

[*Shouts.*] That's Los Angeles, California. U.S.A. 90026. Can you remember all of that?

[KAREN *nods vigorously.*]

KAREN: [*To self.*] Yes, I will remember. Yes. Yes, I remember it.

BIBI: [*To audience.*] She didn't even tell me her name.

[*The* CHORUS *all sound like television newscasters.*]

CHORUS THREE: The girl peddled away.

CHORUS TWO: Merged with the other bicycles merging together.

CHORUS ONE: Bibi couldn't distinguish one rider from the other.

BIBI: I went back to the hotel, hamburgerless.

CHORUS FOUR: Then Bibi and her parents boarded the train to Hong Kong.

CHORUS ONE: Where she ate a fish filet at the McDonald's on Nathan Road.

CHORUS TWO: Where she also found a Pizza Hut.

CHORUS ONE: She stopped in every store and she shopped from dawn till dusk.

BIBI: Now that's freedom. Shopping from dawn till dusk.

CHORUS:	**BIBI:**
[*Whispers.*]	[*To audience.*]
There is no you and there is no me.	But China is changing.
There is no you and there is no me.	**KAREN:**
There is no you. There is no me.	But China is changing.

CHORUS THREE: Nowhere is a hint of anarchy tolerated.

CHORUS: Not here, nor there. Not anywhere.

CHORUS TWO: Bibi went back home to California, U.S.A. And that was the beginning.

CHORUS THREE: [*To* CHORUS TWO.] The beginning of what?

CHORUS ONE: [*To audience.*] The beginning of a most *uncomfortable* correspondence.

[KAREN *in her bedroom.*]

KAREN: [*Writes.*] Summer, 1979. My dear American friend... [*Scratches out, starts again.*] My dear new friend...Greetings from Beijing. [*She sits back, stares into space.*]

[BIBI *on the beach.*]

BIBI: [*To audience.*] Summer, 1979. *This* is Venice Beach. I have my chair, hunkered down in the sand, positioned for maximum good tanning rays. The pier to my left. The muscle boys to my right. The surfers in their tight black wet suits. Life can't get better than someone muscular in a tight black wet suit.

[CHARLIE, *a virile young man, brings on a blaring radio playing "Good Vibrations" by The Beach Boys. He's a nice guy.*]

Speaking of which, my friend. A cross between Frankie Avalon and Louis Jourdan, which I guess makes me a cross between Annette Funicello and Leslie Caron.

CHARLIE: Limon? Ma cheri Gidget Gigi?

BIBI: [*To audience.*] Not bad. But temporary. I mean this guy thinks *Casablanca* is a fine wine. He does try though, and he brings me lemonade. So here we are, me and Casanova under an umbrella of blue sky, hoping for a beach blanket bingo state of mind. But I admit, I've been a bit preoccupied. [*She shows a letter to the audience.*]

CHARLIE: [*To* BIBI.] Preoccupied nothing. You've been downright morose. Whatsa matter punky pumpkin? You been bluesy woozy all day.

BIBI: Turn that thing off.

CHARLIE: Okay dokey, cupcake.

[*She resumes reading the letter.*]

My lady Cleopatra, Queen of the Nile, command me. I live to serve.

BIBI: Oh, put a lid on it. [*To audience.*] Like I said. He does try. [*To* CHARLIE.] Caesar, look on this.

[BIBI *shows him the letter. He takes it, examines it.*]

CHARLIE: Nice stamp. [*Reads.*] "Summer, 1979. Dear Bibi, greetings from China. Do you remember me? I am the girl with whom you have shared a conversation." [*To* BIBI.] Looks like you've got a pen pal. I think it's very sweet.

BIBI: Keep reading.

CHARLIE: Read. All right. "I met you in Tiananmen Square, I write to you from my little room..."

[*Lights up on* KAREN.]

KAREN: [*Overlapping.*] ...Tiananmen Square. I write to you from my little room. There is no window, but I have big picture of a map to show me wondrous sights of America. The Grandest Canyon and OkayDokey Swamp. I share my room with my brother who teaches English at the high school.

[*Her* BROTHER *steps from the* CHORUS.]

BROTHER: Hey ugly, turn out the light!

KAREN: I would like to get a new brother. Is that possible in America? I think anything is possible where you live.

[*A* CAT *steps from the* CHORUS, *sits at* KAREN'*s feet.*]

CAT: [*To audience.*] Meeooww.

BROTHER: [*To* KAREN.] And get that hairball out of the room. Or I'll make kitty stew!

KAREN: [*To* BROTHER.] You wouldn't!

BIBI: [*To* CHARLIE.] In China, cats are not kept as pets.

KAREN: [*To* BIBI.] She is not a pet. I do not own her. She is a free cat.

BROTHER: [*To audience.*] Cats are functional. They eat rats. [*To* KAREN.] Or they are *to be eaten.* Which is it?

KAREN: [*To audience.*] I put the cat outside. [*To* CAT.] I say, "I am sorry kitty cat. So very sorry little kitty. Go on now, go to work and catch some micey mousies." [*To audience.*] And then, she say in extreme irritableness...

CAT: Meeooow.

KAREN: [*To audience.*] I pretend to go to sleep. And when my brother starts to snore, I get up and write to you, my dear friend Bibi.

BIBI: Here it comes.

CHARLIE: Bibi, you may sound like a tough cookie, but only I know what a soft, mushy cupcake you are.

BIBI: Oh yeah? Well, read on, *cupcake.*

KAREN: [*To audience.*] It is a happy feeling I have...to have you for a secret friend, a special friend. I have much stupidity since I realized I never told you my name. How do you like my name? Do you think this is a good name?

BIBI: [*To* KAREN.] Karen? Yes. I think Karen is a good name.

KAREN: [*To* BIBI.] Good. I am so glad for this. [*To audience.*] I chose my new name in secret. This is my choice. Only my best friend knows about this secret. We call each other Debbie and Karen. Where you live, you can be open about such matters. But here we must do everything in secret.

CHARLIE: This is a very nice letter, Bibi. Hardly appropriate of you to be so provoked about it, cupcake.

[*Provoked by the belittling endearment,* BIBI *takes the letter from* CHARLIE.]

Hey!

BIBI: You aren't helping. And *don't* you cupcake me anymore...stud muffin. Stop patronizing me, categorizing me, labeling me like some damned jar of jelly.

CHARLIE: Why so miffed, love bun?

BIBI: There you go again.

CHARLIE: I just...

BIBI: You just what? A lot you know. *This*, for one, is not a nice letter. This just *sounds* like a nice letter.

CHARLIE: Cupcake, not everyone has ulterior motives. Not everyone is suspect. Have a little faith in human nature. Not everyone is out to use and abuse.

BIBI: You are not listening. This letter, stud muffin, is crafted on two predictable emotions—guilt and more guilt. I will NOT be made to feel responsible before my time.

CHARLIE: Are we not our brother's keeper?

BIBI: No, we are not. Look here, silver spoon. I have lived in every ghetto slum in Los Angeles. Mom and Dad slaved so I could squander their hard work on college. And on top of everything, they got annoying letters like this.

KAREN: Bibi, you have such freedom.

BIBI: [*Overlapping.*] Bibi, you have such freedom. [*To* CHARLIE.] Mom calls them "Ailment-of-the-month" letters. Dear Mr. and Mrs. Lee, my dear rich American relation, could you send us some money since life here is so bad, and you have it so good.

KAREN: I have no freedom. None whatsoever. Is it my misfortune to be born in my country and you were born in yours? I look at you and it is as if I look at myself in a glass.

CHARLIE: [*To* KAREN.] You mean mirror.

KAREN: Thank you for this correction. [*Beat.*] Yes, I look in mirror, yes. I think, "You are me." I was meant to be born in the United States, to live in freedom like you. Do you understand? [*Beat.*] Two days after I met you, my boss at the factory where I am in the accounting department, asked to speak to me.

[*The* CAT *gets up, and with an abrupt turn becomes the smiling* BOSS, *who approaches* KAREN.]

My boss has a kind voice, but a frown is in his heart. I am taken to a small room in the basement. This is *not* a good sign.

BOSS: Please sit down.

CHARLIE: [To KAREN.] Then what happened?

KAREN: I sat down.

BOSS: [*Kindly, as if to an errant child.*] You were seen talking to an American. An American student. Now, you mustn't be worried. Don't be afraid. You may talk to Westerners now.

CHARLIE: [*To* BIBI.] I read about this. China is relaxing some of its policies.

BOSS: We are more relaxed under the new policies. But you must not listen to what they say. You must not get any ideas. [*Pause, recites by rote.*] Good citizens have only ideas that also belong to the State. The *State is your mother*. The *State is your father*. The *State is more* than your mother or your father. Do you understand?

KAREN: I said, "Yes." But in my heart, I do not understand. I have never understood why I cannot speak my opinions. I only speak of my opinions to my friend, my only friend Debbie. Never to anyone else, not even my father, not even my brother. My boss talks to me as if I am but a child. I want to say, "I can think for myself. You are not my mother. You are not my father. I already have a mother. I already have a father. I do not need you." [*Resignedly.*] But this is China. [*Beat.*] I ride my bicycle home. But then...I see something...something very strange, a curious event is occurring. I must disembark my bicycle to see what occasion takes place.

[*The* CHORUS, *in a semi-circle, turn their backs to the audience. Slides of Democracy Wall.*]

Very many people assemble in the street. A big man stands in my way. I cannot see. What is there to see? Something, something...

CHARLIE: Extraordinary?

KAREN: No. Something...

BIBI: Momentous?

CHARLIE: Catastrophic?

KAREN: No...no. Something...

BIBI: Important.

KAREN: Yes, important. I try to see for myself. I want to be a part of history. So, when a man got in my view, I used my bicycle to scrape him a little on the leg. He moved aside. Look! Look, Bibi! Do you see? A man with wire-rimmed glasses put a piece of paper with big writing on the wall. A newspaper. A poster. Many words I am shocked to read.

BIBI: [*To* CHARLIE.] Democracy Wall.

CHARLIE: [*To* BIBI.] I know, I'm not uninformed.

KAREN: [*To audience.*] Very brave to write these words, very brave to read these words. These...these...

CHARLIE: [*To* KAREN.] Criticisms.

KAREN: Yes. I do not stay to read these criticisms, or else my boss would have some more to say to me. I was a little afraid. Do you understand? To be afraid of words in such a public place. I go home, thinking of freedom. How good freedom must be. What I see in the square makes me feel brave enough to write to you.

BIBI: [*To* KAREN.] Why me?

CHARLIE: [*To* BIBI.] Stop wiggling the paper. I'm trying to read the rest.

KAREN: [*To audience.*] I think, Bibi, I want to be having freedom like you. I think maybe I deserve a little of this freedom. So I find my pencil and a bit of paper. I try and try. I have my dictionary from a present my brother made me last year. But, I make many mistakes. Bibi, I think you must be helping me. You are my only friend.

CAT: [*Annoyed.*] Meeow!

CHARLIE: Now that's what the American spirit is made of. Bring me your tired, your poor...et cetera, et cetera, uh you know...yearning to breathe free.

BIBI: I'm so glad you are such a patriot. Because she's all yours.

CHARLIE: What?

KAREN: I am thinking to accept your invitation to come live with you in California.

CHARLIE: Ooops!

BIBI: Bingo!

KAREN: Perhaps you, Bibi, will pay $10,000 for my airplane ticket and my living in California. Once I get to live in California, I will work and work and work and pay you back. Does this make sense? What do you think of my idea? I know this letter is my first letter to you and I am asking you for bringing an improvement to my life. But I know Americans have a great opportunity...do I say this correctly...for making money and for helping other people. I look forward to your favorable response. Your friend, Karen. My friend Debbie say hello too.

BIBI: Well?

CHARLIE: O.K. Maybe I was wrong. No matter, 'cuz Bibi cupcake, I think you will make an adorable guardian angel.

BIBI: This isn't funny, Charlie.

CHARLIE: You're her sweet savior. Her fondest hope. Her nearest future.

BIBI: I mean it. She's nothing to me and I'm nothing to her. Have you known me to ever be political?

CHARLIE: No.

BIBI: Exactly. And I could care less. I'm not political. I've never been political. And I resent that she is trying to make me responsible for her freedom. I'm barely responsible for my own. [*Beat.*] This is not the Promised Land and I do not have the muscle to be Moses.

CHARLIE: You most certainly do not have his beard. Kiss me.

BIBI: [*Ducking him.*] Oh, that will solve everything.

CHARLIE: Forget the ten commandments. How about Burt Lancaster?

BIBI: What?

CHARLIE: Enough foreign policy. Let's forget about breathing free. How about a little heavy breathing. I mean, we have the beach. The waves are crashing. You are Deborah Kerr, or is that Donna Reed? I forget.

BIBI: What about my letter?

CHARLIE: So headstrong and optimistic and naive—the true blue American character. Stubborn in all the right places. Naive in all the cutest spots. Hopeful sexy neck. I'm sure you'll think of something diplomatic. Now will you kiss me?

[BIBI *pauses to consider, then tosses the letter aside. In other words, she pounces on him. Lights out.*]

[KAREN *at home.*]

KAREN: I have no one else to tell, so I might as well tell you, my furry friend. You are my best friend. Did you catch any mice today, Debbie? You better earn your keep, or else.

CAT: Meeeoow.

KAREN: In America, kitty cats are friends. But we are not in America, but you *are* my friend anyway, aren't you, Debbie?

My good friend Debbie. Look, a letter from the United States of America. Do you want to open it, or shall I? I will read it to you? Yes? Yes, I read it to you. Come sit near me. Now we begin. January, 1980. Dear Karen…

[BIBI *at home.*]

BIBI: [*Overlapping.*] January, 1980. Dear Karen, how are you? I am fine. How's the weather? [*To audience.*] Too conventional. [*Resumes.*] Dear Karen, Happy New Year. I went to a party last night to ring in the new year 1980.

KAREN: Imagine a party in America, Debbie.

[*The* CHORUS *goes to a party—a tableau of drunken revelry.*]

BIBI: I drank tequila shots, and someone ended up on the floor wiggling like a cockroach, and someone pulled up the rug and danced underneath it, the Mexican Hat Dance. Temporary Terry, the military guy from Camp Pendleton, ate the worm. [*To audience.*] Nope. Too decadent. Bad first impression. [BIBI *scratches out the paragraph. Writes anew.*] Dear Karen, I am so sorry it's taken me nearly six months to write you back. [*To audience, resolutely.*] Honest and direct.

KAREN: [*To* CAT.] We didn't think she would write us, did we, Debbie?

BIBI: I hope the new year will bring you much happiness. I would have answered you sooner, but I was unsure about how to respond to your letter. It really packed a wallop.

KAREN: What means wallop, Debbie? Do you know?

CAT: Meeoow.

KAREN: Oh.

BIBI: Karen. I don't know what possessed me. But two months ago, I did go to the office of the Immigration and Naturalization Service. Have you ever seen that movie, *Mr. Smith Goes to Washington?* Well, we have this problem in America. It's called bureaucracy.

KAREN: Don't I have a good eye for choosing friends, Debbie?

CAT: Meeow.

KAREN: Oh, don't be jealous.

[*The* CHORUS *queues up at the Office of Immigration and Naturalization. The* CAT *joins the chorus.*]

BIBI: There were a lot of people there. Long lines. I waited in one line and they sent me to another and another and then another. It's been like that all day. Lines at the checkout stand, lines at the bank, so of course, lines at the good ol' I.N.S. I got very frustrated.

KAREN: What did they say?

BIBI: A lady from Mexico in front of me. Bewildered, but sweetest face. She was holding up the line, you know. Her English was poor, and she didn't have the right forms.

KAREN: What did they say about me?

CHORUS THREE: Hey, what's holding up this line? I've been here for four hours.

CHORUS ONE: Hey, what's holding up this line?

BIBI: [*To* CHORUS ONE.] Shush…be nice.

I.N.S. OFFICER: You've got the wrong form. This is an L1 Intracompany transfer I-21-B. I doubt, lady, you are an intracompany transfer.

MEXICAN LADY: Pero eso es que lo me han dicho. El hombre alla…no se.*

I.N.S. OFFICER: Well, he gave you the wrong form. Look, you have to fill out another form. You want to file for permanent status? Si? To stay in this country? Right? No deportee to the border?

---

*But this is what they told me. The man over there…I don't know.

MEXICAN LADY: Huh? No, no, no. No es para mi. Es para mi hermana.*

I.N.S. OFFICER: For your sister? Why didn't you say so? I haven't eaten all day, lady. And my feet hurt.

MEXICAN LADY: Si, si. For my sister in Mexico. Mi hermana quiere vivir aqui.**

I.N.S. OFFICER: Yeah, right. Everybody wants to live in America. Look, just fill this out, Petition I-130, to start immediate relative status. Next!

MEXICAN LADY: Mande usted, como?***

I.N.S. OFFICER: Lady, look at this line. You are holding up all these people.

BIBI: Hey, why don't you just answer the lady's question?

I.N.S. OFFICER: Do you wanna be next or do you wanna see the back of the line?

BIBI: Senora, este tipo es un pendejo.

CHORUS THREE: What'd she say?

CHORUS ONE: She called him an asshole, asshole.

BIBI: Este es el formulario de la Peticion E-ciento trenta.

MEXICAN LADY: Oh, si.

BIBI: Lo tiene que llenar para reclamar a su hermana. To claim your sister, understand? Espere usted en esa fila. Then you stand in line over there, por favor.

MEXICAN LADY: Gracias, senorita. Muchas gracias.

BIBI: De nada. [*To* I.N.S. OFFICER.] Please and thank you. You should try adding them to your vocabulary.

---

*No. No. Not for me. For my sister.
**My sister wants to come live here.
***What did you say?

[*The* I.N.S. OFFICER *mimes closing the window.*]

CHORUS: The sign says "Closed for lunch."

[*The* CHORUS *groans with annoyance.* BIBI *mimes opening the window.*]

BIBI: Wait a minute, sir. We've been here in line for hours.

I.N.S. OFFICER: Hey, I'm entitled. What a day. My back is killing me. Go to the next window.

[I.N.S. OFFICER *closes the window.* BIBI *reopens it.*]

BIBI: Look, you. Some of these people can't speak up for themselves. But they deserve your respect, and if not your respect, then at least some courtesy. I want to see your supervisor.

[*The* I.N.S. OFFICER *closes the window.*]

KAREN: Bibi, did you talk about me?

BIBI: [*To* KAREN.] Can't you see I'm trying to prove a point here?

I.N.S. OFFICER: I thought you people were the quiet ones.

[I.N.S. OFFICER *exits.*]

BIBI: [*Shouts.*] Hey, you want quiet! I can be very, very quiet! I said, everybody deserves to be treated with respect.

CHORUS ONE: Look what you did. Now we all suffer.

CHORUS: Look what you did. Now we all suffer.

BIBI: [*To audience.*] You gotta stand up for yourself, or else your face is a doormat.

CHORUS: We're used to it.

BIBI: Well, I'm not.

CHORUS ONE: Well, get used to it, Chinita.

[*The line dissolves. The* CHORUS *moves upstage. The* CAT *returns to* KAREN.]

KAREN: Will you help me, Bibi? Will you help me?

BIBI: Karen, the government told me I was *not* a suitable sponsor. To be a sponsor, I have to prove I can support you as well as myself. Karen, I'm just starting out in life. I don't have much in the way of money, just my prospects like you.

KAREN: So when you are rich, you can sponsor me, yes?

BIBI: Karen, I really don't think I can do more. I mean, I don't even know you. I mean, we're not even related. I'm sorry. Sincerely, Bibi.

KAREN: [*To* CAT.] Then she must get to know me. Isn't that right, Debbie? She must get to know me, and when she will get rich in America, she will send for me, and I will go to live in California.

CAT: Meeow.

KAREN: I know she will help me, when she gets to know me. Then I will go, but you mustn't be sad or jealous, Debbie.

CAT: Meeow.

KAREN: No kitty cats on boats to America. But I will send you letters? Yes? Many, many letters.

CAT: Meeoow.

BIBI: Well, that's the end of that.

[*The* CHORUS *steps forward.*]

CHORUS: Wrong!

CHORUS TWO: Karen continued to write to Bibi.

CHORUS ONE: Long letters about her life in China.

CHORUS FOUR: Her longings for America.

KAREN: While Bibi wrote detailed accounts about her new job as a newspaper reporter. Going to sewer commission meetings, the planning board.

BIBI: Karen sent me letters once a month. I was developing quite a stamp collection.

CHORUS TWO: Karen would bring up the subject every now and then.

CAT: Karen is very "purrr"sistent.

CHORUS FOUR: Bibi tried to ignore the subject.

CHORUS THREE: But finally Bibi got fed up.

BIBI: Winter, 1980. Dear Karen, you may ask me if you wish. But please do not bring my parents into this. They are not rich. The streets here are not paved with gold. They are paved with concrete, sweat, hard work, and struggle. My mother and father struggle every day.

KAREN: [*Reads.*] Bibi says her mother works in a sewing factory in the downtown. Debbie, are you paying attention?

[*The* CAT *sleeps.* BIBI'*s* MOTHER *steps from the* CHORUS *and into the bedroom.*]

Bibi says her mother brings home a big canvas bag filled with pieces of a shirt. Collars for five cents each and sleeves for three cents American money.

BIBI: In my mother's bedroom, there is a big, worn-out sewing machine.

KAREN: [*Reading.*] Her mother is sewing, sewing, sewing. Bibi says this is the only time they have chance to talk to each other.

[BIBI *joins her* MOTHER.]

BIBI: [*To audience.*] My mother hands me a wooden chopstick. I use the chopstick to poke these collars, making a point in the tip, you see? Oh, I'm sorry, I made another hole. Damn.

MOTHER: If you are tired, go to bed. And watch your mouth.

BIBI: Mommy, no, you quit for the night. You look really tired.

MOTHER: I have few more to go, O.K.?

[*They work in silence. Then...*]

Bibi, why don't you quit newspaper? Get respectable job!

BIBI: Gosh, look at that pile. We'll be up all night. That Sam is a lecherous old dwarf, and he's a slave driver.

MOTHER: Always running around late at night. Ladies do not chase people, asking them why why why.

BIBI: That lovesick Sam still chasing you around, pinching you on your...you know what.

MOTHER: I do what I have to do. When you are a mother, then you will understand what mothers do for their children. [*Beat.*] Sam says he's going to finally put everybody on insurance. He better. [*Points to a collar.*] Do that one over. [*Beat.*] Plan for the future, Bibi. You are too wild. What if something happens? I'm not getting any younger. I might die tomorrow, then what do you do?

BIBI: I hate it when you talk like that. Nothing's gonna happen to you. You are still young. Forty is the prime of life. Why do you put up with that slimy toad? Just get another job where they have insurance.

MOTHER: Who will hire me? I'm too old. Who wants someone with no education.

BIBI: You could go to night school like you did before. Stop working all these jobs. Three jobs is for three people, not one.

MOTHER: I was much younger before.

BIBI: Mommy, you're still young. Look in the mirror.

[*Both look into audience, as if into a mirror.*]

You got old Sam running circles around you, the old lech. Mommy, you're still pretty. You still are.

[*A short pause.*]

MOTHER: Before I had my children, I had more choice. Now everything seems grey. No, my life all set. I live for you now.

That's why I live. For you. [*Beat.*] Watch what you are doing, you made another hole.

BIBI: [*Pause, thoughtfully.*] Before you had your children? Are we your regrets, Mommy? Would it have been better if...if I wasn't around? Would you have worked less? Lived more?

MOTHER: [*Disgustedly.*] Aiiii!

[MOTHER *and* CAT *rejoin* CHORUS.]

BIBI: Of course, my mother cares about me. She doesn't mean it. All that about her life being ruined...but when I think about all she's given up just because of me...I sometimes... sometimes, Karen, I wish...then maybe she'd be free. Got anything in the way of a razor blade?

KAREN: Bibi, you make abundant jokes, but I know you are feeling upset and sad. [*Beat.*] Bibi, we do not choose to be born. In China, as in America, this is not a choice we have.

BIBI: Sleeping pills in large quantities, however, is an equal opportunity. This is America.

KAREN: In China, we have only few freedoms. There is a saying. Do you know it? Zu yo sung ye tai sheng, Yo ching yu hǔng mao.* We may choose when to die, how to die, and for what we will die. Yes, I think there are times for such a choice. But this is not a good choice for you, especially if you are going to help me.

BIBI: [*Choral tone.*] Spring, 1981.

KAREN: You asked about my mother. My mother is dead.

BIBI: When did she die?

KAREN: When I was very young. Near my house, next to the pig pens, there is a rice field. Yes, a warm day in the rice field. Many mosquitoes. I am raw from the bites. [*Pause.*] My mother is in the field. She has long black hair, just like mine. I see her. I run to her. I wave to her. I'm running and so

---

*Death can be as heavy as the biggest mountain, or as light as a feather.

happy. The water from the field splashes up. The ground grabs, holds my feet as I run.

BIBI: [*To* KAREN, *softly.*] Watch out. The sheaves of rice are sharp.

KAREN: Yes. The rice cut my legs as I run. Blood trickling down my legs. But I don't care. I brought my mother her lunchbox. [*Waves.*] MaMa! Bao bao gay ni dai fan lai! (Your baby brings you your lunch.) [*Beat.*] Wait! Who is that? It is the commissaire! He is the man who reports everything.

BIBI: I see him. He's very tall.

KAREN: He is shaking my mother. He's shaking her. Why is he doing that? Where is he taking her? MaMa! MaMa! Where are you going? MaMa! MaMa! [*Pause.*] I fell in the rice, and I was wet from the water. I just watched my mother as they took her away.

[KAREN's BROTHER *steps from the* CHORUS.]

BROTHER: It was my duty.

KAREN: She was our mother.

BROTHER: I do not apologize. People must reform their thinking. I miss mother as much as you. But wrong thinking and wrong action must be made into right action and right thinking.

KAREN: My brother...the little red guard.

BROTHER: [*Overlapping.*] ...is a good citizen of the State. The individual is not important.

CHORUS: [*Whispers.*] When the dust settles, the wolf stands alone.

BROTHER: The People have spoken. The individual is dead.

KAREN: Yes, our mother is dead.

BIBI: I'm sorry.

[KAREN *and* BROTHER *speak dispassionately, devoid of any sentimentality.*]

KAREN: Why?

BIBI: Something bad happens and someone should apologize for it.

KAREN: The cat eats the mouse. He doesn't apologize for doing what is in his nature to do.

BROTHER: My mother took property that belonged to someone else. She was punished for stealing.

BIBI: But she stole food to feed you.

BROTHER: To steal from the People is wrong thinking.

BIBI: That was too severe a punishment. Punishment should fit the crime.

KAREN: She was punished. Not for stealing, but for resisting. If the mouse struggles, the cat grips tighter, first with one paw then with two. The only thing the mouse can do is escape, run away. As fast as you can. If you can.

BROTHER: And if you cannot, you'll be executed. Crimes against the State.

KAREN: A common occurrence. Public execution is part of our daily lives, part of our education process. It is the one activity my brother and I do together. [*Beat.*] Lu Yan, a friend who is a teacher from the high school where my brother works, often came with us.

[LU YAN *joins* KAREN *and the* BROTHER *centerstage. The following scene must be devoid of sentimentality.*]

BIBI: I covered an execution once. But from afar. I mean I made some phone calls to the parole board, part of a series of articles on capital punishment. And there was the time I did a piece on the Ku Klux Klan. [*Beat.*] You know, Karen, I keep thinking that if I write about this stuff, maybe something would change, get better...I don't know. I'm doing the best I can, right?

KAREN: In the street, there is a truck.

BIBI: We have the electric chair. The cyanide capsule...

LU YAN: Soviet made. Flatbed.

BIBI: We have death by hanging. No guillotine though, that's barbaric, right? And firing squads are definitely passé.

BROTHER: See him there. The enemy of the People.

KAREN: Which one?

LU YAN: He is the man wearing all white.

BROTHER: There, down his back. See it?

KAREN: Yes.

BIBI: What does it say?

LU YAN: Can't read it.

BROTHER: Nature of crime. Name. A marker to identify the body.

KAREN: What is he being executed for?

BROTHER: He is an enemy of the People.

BIBI: Karen, do something! How can you just sit there?

CHORUS: [*Whispers.*] This is what happens. This is what happens when wolves do not stay. In the group. In the pack. This is what happens.

KAREN: We all follow the truck to the stadium.

LU YAN: The man is taken out of the truck. He stands in the middle of the stadium. A loudspeaker announces his crime. Does he renounce his crime?

CHORUS: Do you renounce your crime?

[*A gunshot.*]

CHORUS ONE: Karen continued in the accounting firm at the import/export factory.

CHORUS FOUR: Bibi got a job at a newspaper in the desert, hated the desert. Then she got another newspaper job and moved to the beach. Got another job, moved to the East Coast.

[BIBI *at an airport.*]

BIBI: Summer, 1982. I'm writing this quick note at a press conference at an airport, actually the National Guard Armory in Windsor Locks, Connecticut. Look on your map under...[CHORUS *moos.*]...near a cow pasture.

[*The* CHORUS *in a tableau, as eager members of the media.*]

Air Force One is about to touch down and when it does the Vice President is going to get a whiff of what rural America smells like. The wind has definitely shifted to the right. My dress is going up over my head, no one notices, which depresses me greatly, as I'm doing a very good Marilyn Monroe impression.

[BIBI *freezes in a demure Monroe pose.*]

KAREN: Lu Yan, who is this Marilyn Monroe?

LU YAN: She was the looker with the great gams.

KAREN: Do I have great gams?

LU YAN: Maybe. Read to me the rest of the letter from Bibi.

KAREN: She says here her father received an illness recently, and that why...

LU YAN: [*Correcting.*] ...and that IS why...

KAREN: ...that IS why she has not...she did not write to me.

BIBI: My father owns a grocery store on Hope Street. I know that's corny, but it's true. It's called The Little Golden Star Market, corner of Hope and California Streets in a place called Huntington Park. It's too small to be on your map.

[BIBI's FATHER *steps from the* CHORUS *and joins* BIBI. *He sings a few bars from "The Yellow Rose of Texas."*]

FATHER: The yellow rose of Texas, ta da ta da ta da, ta ta da ta da da...she's the only girl for me... [*Tickles* BIBI.]

BIBI: I'm done with the price tags.

FATHER: Good. Did you...?

BIBI: I counted the register.

FATHER: Good. And the...?

BIBI: I swept front and back. Can I go now?

FATHER: You know, Bibi, I think you are gaining weight. Smart is one thing, but I want a pretty rose, not a balloon for a daughter, O.K.? [*Tickles* BIBI *again.*] Hey, no long face. Smile, smile.

BIBI: Daddy, please. I'm a big girl now.

FATHER: Yes. Too much ice cream. [*Tickles her again.*]

BIBI: Stop that. Karen, this is my father. He likes to sing.

KAREN: He's standing in the middle of his store. Look at all the shelves. Soy sauce, oyster sauce, spaghetti sauce. So much food. So many vegetables...

LU YAN: Cigarettes. American cigarettes. I would like to smoke those Marlborough cigarettes and wear a big hat from Texas.

FATHER: [*Stops singing.*] I feel funny. I feel a little woozy. Must have been your mother's bird nest soup. I think I'm going to sit down right here.

[FATHER *collapses.*]

BIBI: Dad, you don't look so good. Daddy?

KAREN: Bibi, what's happening?

BIBI: My father, Karen. [*Pause.*] My father is on the floor. Daddy, wake up. Stop playing around. Daddy? I put his head in my lap. What's this? What is this? Blood all over me.

KAREN: Yes, I know the blood.

BIBI: On my legs. On the floor.

KAREN: Yes, the blood on my legs. Yes, the blood turned the water warm.

BIBI: Wake up, Daddy. No fooling now. You see, Karen, my father doesn't mean to hurt me. He likes to joke around. He's forever making a joke. I'll lose weight, Daddy, really I will. Daddy? [*She gives her father a little shake.*]

KAREN: Is he all right?

BIBI: My daddy works all the time. He's always at work. I never really knew my father.

KAREN: Are you all right? Bibi?

[*Pause.*]

BIBI: He's always at work.

KAREN: Is everything all right?

BIBI: He likes to call me his little yellow rose. He worked all the time. I didn't really know my father. He liked to call me his little yellow rose. I'm my Daddy's little yellow rose.

[*Lights out on* BIBI. *A short pause. The* CHORUS *steps forward.*]

CHORUS ONE: Bibi and Karen continued their correspondence, but sporadically. About once or twice a year.

CHORUS FOUR: Bibi took her father's death very badly.

CHORUS THREE: In 1983, *Death of a Salesman* came to China.

CHORUS TWO: Biff. Happy. Linda. Willy Loman.

CHORUS ONE: Willy Loman didn't know who he was. He had all the wrong dreams.

CHORUS THREE: I have those same dreams.

CHORUS FOUR: I don't know who I am.

BIBI: I don't know who I am. I'm looking, though, real hard.

CAT: Meeoow.

CHORUS THREE: In late winter, 1984. Debbie died. She choked on a mouse.

CAT: Meeow. (Cough.)

BROTHER: Shhh. Cats from the grave know too much. Yes. It was me. I turned in my mother. I confess it, but I do not apologize. [*Beat.*] I didn't tell anyone about my sister or her letters. I don't know why. Things seem a little different now. More relaxed.

CHORUS FOUR: It is Spring, 1985.

CHORUS THREE: Yes, Spring, 1985. By now, economic reforms. Farmers sell their surplus in the markets and keep the profit. Unheard of.

CHORUS ONE: But the more China changes, the more discontented I become.

CHORUS TWO: The more western China becomes, the unhappier I feel.

KAREN: Summer, 1985. Thank you, Bibi, for the fashion magazines. Someday I hope to make such pretty dresses for sale.

BIBI: Fall, 1985. You're welcome.

MOTHER: Spring, 1986. Bibi, you not a grasshopper. Stick to your job.

BIBI: But mother, I don't like my job.

MOTHER: Who likes job? If you quit, naw mmn yein nay.*

KAREN: Summer, 1986. Dear Bibi, I took my first trip to the mountains. In China, you must get a permit for travel anywhere. Five years ago, I asked for permission, and now it has arrived. My brother and Lu Yan are coming with me.

[*The* BROTHER, LU YAN, *and* KAREN *are lying on a plateau on a mountainside.*]

Look at that sky. I see a dragon coiling ready to spring. I see a water buffalo. There's a big, fat, lumbering pig. That's you.

BROTHER: I feel restless. It's funny to feel so restless.

LU YAN: Ask Bibi to send us a copy of this Bill of Rights.

*I don't know you.

BROTHER: What is this "pursuit of happiness"? Even if I were to have it, I would not know how to go about this "pursuit of happiness."

LU YAN: I think to be on Lotus Mountain is what is meant by "Life, liberty, and the pursuit of happiness."

KAREN: [*To* BROTHER.] It means even YOU would count for something, you good-for-nothing.

BROTHER: Oh? Who is lazy and who is not? I have written a novel.

LU YAN: So why do you hide it?

BROTHER: Because I am a bad novelist.

KAREN: Well then, your book will be very popular.

LU YAN: I think I will be a teacher in a great university. I have already applied for a transfer.

BROTHER: Impossible.

LU YAN: Maybe.

KAREN: If only I could leave my job. I hate accounting.

LU YAN: You do?

BROTHER: I didn't know that.

KAREN: Bibi sends me many fashion magazines. Only Bibi knows how I wish to be a designer of great fashion for very great ladies.

BROTHER: Burlap sacks for old bags.

KAREN: Lace, all lace and chiffon.

LU YAN: You would look beautiful.

KAREN: [*Shyly.*] Not for me. For the people. I would be a dress designer and go to…

LU YAN: Paris?

BROTHER: London?

KAREN: New York City.

LU YAN: People would clap and say, "Ahhh, of course, a Karen original."

BROTHER: People will say, "How ugly. I will not wear this in a million years."

KAREN: I would have a name. Then once I became famous as a clothes designer, I will quit and I would do something else. Maybe be a forest ranger.

BROTHER: Or a fireman.

LU YAN: Or an astronaut.

BROTHER: Or a member of the central committee.

LU YAN: Hah! You must be very old to be a member of the central committee.

KAREN: Yes, a fossil. [*Beat.*] Is it possible to be a somebody?

BROTHER: Yes, I am a grain of sand!

KAREN: A piece of lint.

LU YAN: Those old men on the central committee. What do they know about us? Perhaps we should all take up our books and *stone* the committee with our new ideas.

BROTHER: Lu Yan thinks he can change the world. But I'm telling you if we are patient, all things will come.

KAREN: Oh, my brother is a philosopher. I think change must start from within. We need to have a personal revolution, as well as a political one.

BROTHER: Oh, Karen, these old fossils will never change. Only things that die allow new things to grow and flourish.

LU YAN: Yes, he is right. They will die off and leave us with a nation of students. No politicians. Just you and me and Karen.

KAREN: Three wolves on the mountainside, sitting in the sun.

BROTHER: Change is sure to come.

LU YAN: Only if we insist on it.

KAREN: Well, this is changing me. [*She waves a small pile of books.*]

LU YAN: [*Looks at the titles.*] Hemingway. Martin Luther King. Jean-Paul Sartre.

KAREN: Bibi sent them to me. And this.

[KAREN *turns on a tape recorder. The music is The Carpenter's "We've Only Just Begun." They listen.*]

BROTHER: Ugh, not this song again. That's it. I'm leaving. I will go for a walk now. [*He rejoins the* CHORUS.]

LU YAN: No good citizens of the State anywhere I can see.

KAREN: What?

LU YAN: Only clouds above and insects below to watch.

KAREN: Watch what?

LU YAN: This.

[LU YAN *leans in to kiss* KAREN—*it's a very short awkward peck on the cheek. Lights out.*]

[BIBI *at home.*]

BIBI: [*To audience.*] Fall, 1986. The anniversary of my father's death. Today, my mother made tay and we went to sit at his grave. We bowed three times. I don't even know what that means, bowing three times. But I do it because this is how my mother says we remember our ancestors. She says it's important to remember.

KAREN: That's funny. On the anniversary of my mother's death, I try to forget.

BIBI: Mmmm. [*Beat.*] You know what, Karen?

KAREN: Mmmm.

BIBI: Sometimes, I wish someone would tell me. This is what you are good at, Bibi, so go and do it. This is the man who is good for you, Bibi, marry him.

KAREN: You wouldn't listen anyway, and you know it.

BIBI: No, I probably wouldn't. [*To* KAREN.] How is...?

KAREN: Lu Yan?

BIBI: Yes, Lu Yan. Lu Yan sounds like a very nice guy.

KAREN: Lu Yan is the only guy I've ever...how you say?...

BIBI: Slept with?

KAREN: No...he is the first man I ever dated. Yes, that's the word, dated. Only one to ask, only one to go out with, understand? Not much choice here in China, even though we are very many millions of people.

BIBI: Choice! Talk about choice. Shall I regale you with tales from the darkside? Dates from hell? By my calculations, since I *was* a late bloomer, having lived at home throughout my college career, but making up for it like a fiend AFTER I moved out of the house, I would say I've met a total of, or had a disastrous dinner or ahem, et cetera et cetera, with at least 127 different men—and that's a *conservative* estimate. Indeed, 127 men of assorted shapes and sizes and denominations. And colors. Don't forget colors.

KAREN: I am getting married next year. During the Mid-Autumn Festival. Yes, I am getting married. I'm not sure I want to be married. I want to do and see so much, but my world is so small.

BIBI: Here in America, we are free, free to choose our lovers and make our own mistakes. The most wonderful thing about freedom, Karen, is you get plenty of rope in which to hang yourself. Wait! Backspace. Did I hear correctly? Did you say getting married? Getting married.

KAREN: Mmmmm.

BIBI: How wonderful. It is wonderful, right?

KAREN: Mmmmm.

BIBI: I think I'm feeling…wow, what a novel concept! I think I'm actually jealous.

CHORUS THREE: Lu Yan and Karen were married in the fall of 1986.

CHORUS FOUR: Lu Yan's family gave as a dowry to Karen's father and brother—two live chickens, eight kilos of pig's intestines, 500 steamed buns, a sea lion bicycle, 20 kilos of fish, and 10 cartons of American cigarettes.

CHORUS TWO: Karen moved in with Lu Yan's family. Lu Yan's father was a violinist with the city orchestra. There was always music in the house.

LU YAN: [*To audience.*] For our wedding, Bibi sent us a box filled with books and music tapes. It was like a time capsule from the west.

[*With quiet enjoyment,* LU YAN *and* KAREN *listen to a few bars from Louis Armstrong's version of "Ain't Misbehavin'."*]

I could eat them up. Every one, this Hemingway. This Truman Capote. This biography of Mahatma Gandhi. [*To* KAREN.] Look! Newspaper clippings about the new China, our new economic experiments.

KAREN: Our friends from the university come to our apartment. We sift through the box. [*To* LU YAN.] This is what Christmas must be like!

CHORUS FOUR: Tammy Wynette! Patsy Cline!

LU YAN: Mickey Spillane!

CHORUS THREE: *Jonathan Livingston Seagull.* James Michener!

CHORUS FOUR: *A Streetcar Named Desire!* The theory of relativity!

CHORUS THREE: Dr. Spock Baby Book!

KAREN: Dear Bibi, Lu Yan would like to thank you for the book,

I'm O.K., You're O.K.

CHORUS THREE: New ideas. New dissatisfactions.

LU YAN: The more she read, the more Karen grew depressed.

CHORUS FOUR: Even though the sun seemed to shine very bright in China.

CHORUS THREE: Politically speaking.

CHORUS ONE: Summer, 1987.

KAREN: Dear Bibi, I am a bird in a cage. A beautiful bird with yellow and green and red feathers. I have a great plumage, but no one can see it. I live in a place that is blind to such wonderful colors. There is only grey and blue and green.

[BIBI's MOTHER *steps from the* CHORUS, *is on the telelphone.*]

MOTHER: Bibi? Are you listening to me?

BIBI: Winter, 1987. Dear Karen, do you know why I live so far from home? So I don't have to face their disapproval. My sister, my mother. My family.

MOTHER: Come home. It's too cold in Connecticut. You do not miss your mother? I miss you. Don't you miss me?

BIBI: I like the seasons. I like long red coats and mufflers, ice-skating on a real lake. I like snow.

MOTHER: You're crazy. Come home. Are you losing weight? Are you drinking that diet tea I sent to you?

BIBI: It tastes terrible.

MOTHER: Sure it does. That's because it's good for you. Are you warm enough?

BIBI: Yes, I'm warm enough. I'm sitting by the fireplace at what's-his-name's apartment.

MOTHER: Come home, get rid of what's-his-name. I do not like him. He has a frog face.

BIBI: Oh, can we please drop that subject?

MOTHER: [*Disgustedly.*] Aiii.

BIBI: Mom. [*Beat.*] I'm thinking of quitting the newspaper and becoming an actress.

MOTHER: Actress! Aiii, nay gek say naw!*

[BIBI *is silent.*]

There's no money in it. How you live? How you pay rent? All those actresses, all they ever do is fool around and get divorced. You want to get divorced?

BIBI: Mom, I'm not even married yet.

MOTHER: See what I mean? If you quit job, I disown you. You are not special enough to be an actress.

BIBI: Gosh, my stomach hurts.

[*A short pause.* BIBI *composes a letter.*]

Dear Karen, what's so special about being special? Mother is absolutely right. I'm not special. And damned proud of it. Special is entirely overrated.

KAREN: You are joking, aren't you? [*A short pause.*] See? I'm getting good at knowing you.

BIBI: Nothing I do pleases my mother. Karen, I'm not overweight, but I'm too fat. I'm not stupid, but I'm not sensible. I've got a job, but I don't have a lady-like profession. I'm a disappointment and I don't know why I am. Maybe...maybe she doesn't...maybe she doesn't... Gosh, my chest hurts.

KAREN: Dear Bibi, your chest hurts because you are crying inside. Your mother doesn't mean what she says. She is just doing her duty. She's your mother. She wouldn't be a good mother if she didn't say those things. Threaten your children to the straight and narrow, this is written on the list for what it means to be a good mother.

BIBI: [*To* KAREN.] Ancient Chinese proverb?

*You are killing me!

KAREN: Fortune cookie.

BIBI: She means it all right. You watch. If I go to acting school, she'll tell everyone I'm in law school. Just wait and see if she doesn't.

KAREN: Bibi, I think you love your mother very much. But maybe you will love her better, if you listen less.

BIBI: Well, she can send me all the diet tea in China, I'm still going to drink Coke Classic. Mothers are overrated.

KAREN: I wish my mother were alive to lecture me.

CHORUS: New age, new wave, new roads.
New thinkers, new entrees, new hairdos.
New buildings, new careers, new lives.
Who am I? Where am I going? America, always on the move!
Many choices, many roads, many ways to go.
Who am I? Where am I? Which way?

KAREN: Winter, 1987. Dear Bibi, Lu Yan is always telling me what to do. Married life isn't what I thought. His mother tells me how to wash his shirts, how to make a dinner. She complains I do not concentrate, as my head is always spinning in the clouds. She asked me what mischief I am making. I tell her I feel much puzzlement, as I do not know who I am.

BIBI: Spring, 1988. Dear Karen, I have changed newspapers five times in the past three years. It's easier to move up by moving out, but I'm getting a little tired of moving around. West Coast, East Coast. No place feels like home. Home doesn't even feel like home. Everywhere I go, I ask myself the question, "Who am I?," "How do I fit in?" The answer changes as fast as my address.

KAREN: Summer, 1988. Dear Bibi, I am a flower that will never open, never to be kissed by a bee. I want to open. I want to feel the sting of freedom. More and more, I feel bitter towards my life and my uselessness. I go to work, I have ideas to improve my job, and no one listens to me. I am a nobody. And I want to be a somebody.

BIBI: [*To* KAREN.] Do you realize, Karen, we've been friends for almost ten years?

KAREN: And for ten years you have not listened to one word I have said.

BIBI: I've listened.

KAREN: No you haven't. You are not my friend.

BIBI: I see.

KAREN: No, you do not see. You are too far away. I could be a real friend and see you every day. You could be a real friend to me, but you refuse. My hand hurts from writing. My dictionary is all torn up.

BIBI: Karen, but you are a married woman now.

KAREN: I thought my marriage would make a solution, but it doesn't. It is not what I wanted for my life. Bibi, you know my heart. But you won't help me. I want to count for something. I can count for something in California.

BIBI: Here or there, your struggle is my struggle. No matter where we are, the struggle is the same. I'm trying not to run away from my problems. Why can't you be happy where you are?

KAREN: Why can't you?

BIBI: You are so naive.

KAREN: You are so naive.

BIBI: You're one to talk.

KAREN: You live in a democracy, the individual can vote. You can count for something.

BIBI: What elementary school book did you read that from? Oh sure, Karen, my vote counts. Wake up from your dream, Karen.

KAREN: You have the luxury to be selfish. To think of only yourself. You live in Paradise, and I live in Hell.

BIBI: Well Karen, it can be hell living in Paradise.

KAREN: I want Democracy. Democracy for me. Freedom of speech. Freedom to choose.

BIBI: Freedom to be confused. But if you like America so much, come join me in the national pastime.

KAREN: What? Baseball? I like baseball.

BIBI: No, I'm talking retail therapy. Let's go shopping.

KAREN: I think you must be making a bad joke. Democracy is not the same thing as capitalism.

BIBI: Oh, you have the old definition.

KAREN: Even then I think the new definition is better than what we have here in China. At least you have incentives to strive for a better life. But here, whether I work one hour or ten hours, it's all the same. You just don't know what it's like.

BIBI: I've read Marx, thank you very much. Can I help it if good ideals are polluted by extremists and dictators? Can I help it if the desire to be fair and equal is completely antithetical to human nature? Health care for everybody. Jobs for everybody. Everyone EQUAL under the law. Everyone working towards the greater good. And here's a novel concept—people actually caring about the well-being of other people. In America, we call that welfare, and anyone on it is seen as a slackard and a mooch. In China, and probably in the eyes of God, it's called social responsibility and Charity with a capital C.

KAREN: If you think China is so good, you should come and live here. Bibi, I think you must be a Communist at heart.

BIBI: I shudder to think what you would do with a credit card. [*Beat.*] I can see it now. You'd be mesmerized by our shopping malls. We've got mini malls, gigantic malls, also Rodeo Drive—all linked by a chain of freeways stretching into infinity.

KAREN: I don't want to shop.

BIBI: I can see you now Karen—at the altar of the Church of Our Lady of Retail kneeling beside me at the cash register as it rings up our sale. FIFTY PERCENT OFF—the most beautiful three words in the English language. Now, that's America.

KAREN: I do not want to shop.

BIBI: Now, that's downright un-American. Forget it, Karen, you'll never fit in.

KAREN: Somewhere I read that there is a difference between democracy and capitalism.

BIBI: And you think I'm naive. Well, in America, we like to THINK we're a democracy, but we're definitely a nation of shoppers. [*Pause.*] Ahhh, I know. You're a K-Mart girl.

[BIBI*'s new beau,* JONATHAN, *interrupts.*]

JONATHAN: Bibi, let's get going, we'll be late.

BIBI: Sorry, Karen, I've got to go. [*Pause.*] Karen, what do you think of him? Jonathan is very reserved. A damned Yankee blue blood. He says I'm the only person he can really talk to. A real solid person. My opposite in every way. [*Pause.*] He brings out the best in me and it feels right. I'll keep you posted. Love, Bibi.

KAREN: [*To audience.*] What's K-Mart?

CHORUS: Everything happens in the mall.
We meet in the mall. We see movies in the mall.
We buy presents in the mall. We eat lunch in the mall.
We are a nation of shoppers. Attention shoppers.

[BIBI *and* JONATHAN *are in the shopping mall. Slides from life in the galleria.*]

BIBI: You are joking, right? Jonathan?

JONATHAN: You yourself said I have a rare and seldom seen sense of humor.

BIBI: I guess you aren't joking. Let me get this straight. You think I'm too passionate, too adventurous, and too enthusiastic. You think I'm special, so special that you don't deserve someone as special as me. Jonathan, I assure you special is very overrated. Ask my mother.

JONATHAN: Let's not talk about it right now, O.K.? Let's just go to the movie.

BIBI: No, no. Permit me a small public scene. It's only our future we're talking here. No, Jonathan, you can't drop a bombshell and then go sit in the dark with a bag of popcorn.

JONATHAN: I told you I don't want to do this, make a scene here between the Sears and the JC Penny's.

BIBI: I won't cry or shout, if that's what you are afraid of. Besides, the mall is where all of America gets dumped. Latchkey kids graduate from television to the local galleria.

JONATHAN: Do you have to be cute all the time? Just stop it, O.K.? Look, don't get me wrong. I think you are terrific. But it's just...well, I don't require so much.

BIBI: I see.

JONATHAN: Since you asked.

BIBI: Go on. I know there's more.

JONATHAN: It's just too intense for me. You're like a pebble in my still pond. When I'm with you I feel like I'm riding a horse run wild, and I can't get my feet into the stirrups.

BIBI: The real issue here. The real issue, Jonathan, is that your mother likes me. You wanted to shock your family, and instead, they embraced me with open arms to your complete dismay. You are a rebel without a cause, and you're about to sacrifice your future for your infantile desire to horrify your mother. I can't change the fact your mother thinks I'm terrific. If I have to change to keep you, then…I'm not going to change.

JONATHAN: You couldn't even if you tried. You don't know how to be anything less than terrific.

BIBI: So essentially, you are dumping me because you prefer less than terrific.

JONATHAN: I'll probably regret it later.

[JONATHAN *rejoins the* CHORUS.]

BIBI: Not that it matters, but [*Mouths the words.*] I love you.

[KAREN *at home.*]

KAREN: Winter, 1988. Dear Bibi, my nephew asks if you would send him a baseball glove. Also, Lu Yan's mother would like the same perfume you sent to me. Oh, by the way, the Madonna tapes must be great, but the tape recorder is broken. Can you send us another one?

BIBI: Dear Karen, I just can't afford anything right now. I'm unemployed—again.

KAREN: How can you help me, if you don't become a stable, responsible citizen?

BIBI: Very funny.

KAREN: Did you get fired from your job?

BIBI: No, I quit. And I'm glad I did. I had names, addresses, phone numbers. And the paper still wouldn't print it. We're having an election here, Karen, and a black man, an African-American, is on the ballot. Quote: "I'd never put a black man in office." Quote: "No nigger is going to run this country." Next morning, I read the paper; the quotes are gone. So, I storm in the editor's office during a budget meeting. Everybody was there. I said, "Hey, what is this?"

CHORUS: Calm down, Bibi. What's your complaint?

BIBI: How dare you sanitize the news, making it all pretty and clean for public consumption. I strenuously object. [*Beat.*] And that's when they said:

CHORUS: Hey, it's a family paper.

BIBI: [*To* CHORUS] And while we're on the subject, what about that story about the Vietnamese girl who was harassed, spat on, with nasty racial epithets carved with a knife on her dormitory door. That was cut, and relegated to page three, inside. Nobody reads page three, inside.

CHORUS: Big news day, short of space.

BIBI: And what about the followup stories I did about racism on college campuses. You buried that story in the zone editions. That was a metro story, with national implications.

CHORUS ONE and **TWO:** Aren't you being just a little too sensitive?

CHORUS THREE and **FOUR:** Aren't you just being politically correct?

BIBI: Go to hell. My editors, they would rather put in a bloody photograph of a local car wreck than print the truth about racism in America. So, in short, Karen, I quit.

KAREN: How lucky you are.

BIBI: What do you mean lucky?

KAREN: You get to live your own life, your way.

BIBI: Sure I'm lucky. I get to fight my battles totally alone and unsupported, both at work and at home. I'm a lone wolf howling, and no one listens except my cat. No, I'm trading in my frustration for a new one. I am going to an acting school where they take all your money and teach you how to pursue all the wrong dreams.

KAREN: Dreams. I have them too. New ones.

BIBI: My mother doesn't support me. The only way to convince her is to make a clean break. Everyone disapproves. My sister is the worst. You...on the other hand...have a support system—the State, your brother, your husband. You even know who your enemies are and what you are fighting against.

KAREN: Perhaps you can swallow your pride. If the support system, the harmony of your family, is that important to you, then you should do as they tell you to do.

BIBI: Spoken like a true Chinese.

KAREN: I am Chinese.

BIBI: And I am American. And I will live my own life, my way. [*Beat.*] Even if it kills me.

KAREN: Bibi, I have been thinking about what you say about America, and I think you are right. I have been running away from myself, my marriage, and my country. [*Beat.*] I think the east wind has moved a little to the West, so I think voices of wolves perhaps now may be heard. You see, Bibi, my country is changing, and I have a new hope for a better life. And, I no longer wish to come to be an American like you. You are too confused. [*Beat.*] But I will always be your friend.

BIBI: Say, why don't you come and visit me?

KAREN: I don't know. There is much work to do here. I'm going to meetings for the first time. Many meetings.

BIBI: Look, why don't you come? You can meet my mother. I'm sure she'd be happy to lecture you too. Go to the consulate. Ask them for a visa.

CHORUS ONE: Karen went to the consulate.

KAREN: I have a friend in the United States who will vouch for me.

CHORUS THREE: Many people are exchanging, visiting from China to the world.

KAREN: I told them I wanted to be one of them.

CHORUS FOUR: Cultural exchanges. Ballet dancers, playwrights, artists, singers.

CHORUS TWO: Scientists, engineers, lawyers, architects, businessmen of all sorts.

CHORUS THREE: Bringing computers and cars and Coca-Cola and T-shirts.

CHORUS ONE: So many people and things and ideas flowing from west to east, east to west. Amazing!

KAREN: Since I am neither a student nor an important dignitary. I am only an accountant. A very ordinary speck of dust.

CHORUS ONE: Karen was refused a visa. No one would tell her why.

CHORUS TWO: But it all comes down to MONEY. She didn't have the…the dinero, [*Attempting to be hip.*] the bread, man.

CHORUS THREE: March, 1989.

LU YAN: Karen, when you write to Bibi, thank her for the Baudelaire. Tell her I love French poetry, and to send more of it.

KAREN: All right, I will. Lu Yan, should I tell her about…our news?

LU YAN: Huh? [*Pause.*] Ahhh, yes, yes, yes, yes. Maybe she can come up with a good American name for our boy.

KAREN: But what if it's a girl?

LU YAN: Then we will try again.

KAREN: But we can't do that. I told Aunt Wu, they are already making arrangements for me to have the operation after the baby is born. I too hope it will be a boy. But if it's a girl, I hope you will not be angry with me. [*Beat.*] If it's a girl, I think I will name her Bibi.

LU YAN: That's a good idea. But we will have a boy, I know it.

KAREN: The letter is finished. Come on, we better get going. The students are gathering at the university. And Hu Yaobang is speaking, we don't want to miss it. [*Beat.*] Is it considered to be counter-revolutionary to listen to a counter-revolutionary? Lu Yan, I made a joke. You never laugh at my jokes.

LU YAN: What if our baby is a girl? It's too distressing. Only one child per family. Karen, how can our life improve? I cannot teach at the university and you cannot quit your job to become a student. We cannot get permission for anything, so what's the point of trying to make improvements? What's the point of going to the meeting?

KAREN: You are so funny. Didn't you say yesterday we should be open to new ideas in order for our lives to improve? Wasn't it you who said we must always have hope.

LU YAN: You are right. [*Beat.*] Maybe we can talk to Hu Yaobang about this one child per family. I want to be a father of a great many children.

KAREN: [*Horrified.*] You do?

LU YAN: Come on, we'll be late.

[BIBI *in New York City, with her mother.*]

BIBI: Spring, 1989. Dear Karen, New York City is a place you should see. I've been living here for six months now and I LOVE IT. Recently, my mother came to visit me for the first time since I've been on the East Coast. She LOVED it!

MOTHER: It SMELL!

BIBI: She especially loved the efficient and clean public services.

MOTHER: It NOISY! [*Beat.*] Too many bums!

BIBI: She also thought my apartment was very cozy.

MOTHER: It so SMALL! How can you live like this! Like a mouse in a cage. Noisy all day, all night. How do you sleep?

BIBI: Happily, I took mother to see all the sights, including the Statue of Liberty.

MOTHER: Yes, I've always wanted to see it. Come on, let's go.

[MOTHER *and* BIBI *on the ferry, at the railing.*]

BIBI: It's a grey somber day. A bit choppy out. The ferry ride to Liberty Island doesn't take very long, it just SEEMS long when you'd rather be eating lunch at the Russian Tea Room. We get off at Liberty Island, magnificent view of the city. And we join the hundreds of people, from all over the world, as we jostle our way off the ferry and down the walkway.

[MOTHER *and* BIBI *at Liberty Island.*]

MOTHER: Look! She's so beautiful.

BIBI: Mother, are you all right? Hey, where are you going?

[BIBI's MOTHER *tries to read the inscription at the base of the statue.*]

MOTHER: [*Laboring over the words.*] Give me your tired, your poor...

BIBI: [*Overlapping.*] ...poor, your huddled masses, yearning to breathe free.
The wretched refuse of your teeming shore.
Send these, the homeless, tempest tossed to me.
I lift my lamp beside the golden door.

[*One by one, the* CHORUS *joins* BIBI.]

CHORUS ONE: [*Overlapping.*] The wretched refuse of your teeming shore.
Send these, the homeless, tempest tossed to me.

I lift my lamp beside the golden door.

CHORUS TWO: [*Overlapping.*] Send these, the homeless, tempest tossed to me.

I lift my lamp beside the golden door.

CHORUS THREE: [*Overlapping.*] I lift my lamp beside the golden door.

[*Lights out.*]

[KAREN *at Tiananmen Square.*]

KAREN: [*To audience.*] May, 1989. Dear Bibi, here I am—sitting in a tent on ChangAn Avenue in Tiananmen Square—do you know what this means—it means the Avenue of Eternal Peace. I cannot begin to describe—there is this change in the air—to be here, surrounded by my comrades—student activists and ordinary citizens—men and women, all patriots for a new China. I think this is what "pursuit of happiness" must be. Bibi, for the first time in my life, I believe I can be a somebody, I believe my contribution will make a difference. I believe freedom will not grow out of theory but out of ourselves. We are fighting for a system that will respect the individual. The individual is not dead. The government must listen to us. The government will listen to us. All we want is a dialogue. A conversation. We want an end to censorship. We want an end to corruption. We are the voices of tomorrow. And our voices will be heard. There is so much power to be here together—singing songs, holding hands, listening to the speeches of our student leaders.

CHORUS ONE: "The Power of the People will prevail."

KAREN: [*Overlapping.*] "…People will prevail."

CHORUS TWO: "To liberate society, we must first liberate ourselves."

KAREN: [*Overlapping.*] "…we must first liberate ourselves."

CHORUS THREE: "We must give our lives to the movement."

KAREN: Yes, I will give my life to the movement!

[KAREN *sings "Arise!," the national anthem of the People's Republic of China, in Chinese.*]

[BIBI *at home.*]

BIBI: May, 1989. Dear Karen, I've been watching the television reports. Everybody always asks me how I feel about what is happening in China. I'm so envious of your power—of how you have caused your government, caused the world to take notice. But I am also concerned about your naivete in striving towards a foreign ideal. I do believe change will come, but it must be at your own pace. I am not sure America is the proper model for the new China that you want. Perhaps you should look to make a Chinese democracy. Please understand that I feel a deep connection to you, but right now, I think that to be a somebody in China is suicide. I don't mean to dampen your spirits, but I am worried. Please, please be careful.

[*The* CHORUS *joins* KAREN *in singing China's anthem in English.*]

KAREN and CHORUS: [*Sing.*]

Arise for China and against slavery.
We'll give our flesh and blood for our country and our great wall.
The time has come, China! The most dangerous time.
Now each lion must stand firm and brave to the last roar.
Arise! Arise! Arise!
We 10,000 as one, fear no enemies' gunfire.
March on! March on ! March on!

CHORUS ONE: Students. The time is now for freedom. The time is now for democracy. For six weeks, we have felt a jubilation. A celebration of spontaneity.

CHORUS TWO: I think we should shave our heads in protest. We should shave our heads like prisoners because our government turned our country into a prison.

CHORUS ONE: The time for freedom is now. The time for democracy is now.

KAREN: We are lying on the floor. Students on a hunger strike. Most of us are women. We haven't eaten in days, and I will not until I have my freedom.

SOLDIER: This is foolishness. Resolutely oppose bourgeois liberalism.

CHORUS ONE: I'm sorry, but we disagree completely.

CHORUS FOUR: Yes, we disagree completely.

CHORUS ONE: The time is now for freedom.

KAREN: A clean division between what we want and what the government stands for. A clear break.

SOLDIER: Children should not defy their parents. Harmony must be preserved. Resolutely oppose bourgeois liberalism.

CHORUS FOUR: Mothers are here.

CHORUS TWO: Workers, laborers, doctors.

CHORUS ONE: Lawyers, bakers, bricklayers.

KAREN: Accountants, teachers, writers, students, children, babies.

CHORUS: We are all here. Will you hear the will of the wolf? Will you let the wolf roam free? We want to be free!

SOLDIER: The students gave me food, water. I did not want to hurt them.

CHORUS ONE: We heard speeches.

CHORUS FOUR: We heard songs.

CHORUS TWO: We are like a small plant, tender and young, trying to reach the sunshine.

CHORUS FOUR: From this movement, which is a movement across China, free thought will grow, and from free thought a new China will grow.

CHORUS TWO: The students erected a thirty-three-foot statue called the Goddess of Democracy.

CHORUS ONE: Seven weeks of freedom.

KAREN: So this is freedom. How good it is. Seven weeks of freedom.

CHORUS: Summer, 1989.

SOLDIER: Go home and save your life. This is China. This is not the West.

[*Gunfire. The* CHORUS *and* KAREN *link arms and march toward the audience. They move in military fashion, stepping up to replace others as they are mowed down by tanks.*]

KAREN: On June 4, 1989. Tanks, armored personnel carriers, and trucks full of troops marched into Tiananmen Square. Many of us linked arms and tried to stand in their way.

SOLDIER: Be a good Chinese and go home. Go home and save your life. This is China. This is not the West. Be a good Chinese and go home.

CHORUS ONE: I decided to stay. A man stood naked on the roof and shouted, "I am who I am. I am me."

KAREN: Tanks marched forward and crushed the first row. We marched forward.

SOLDIER: Go home and save your life.

CHORUS FOUR: Change is coming. March forward!

CHORUS TWO: Watch your head. Watch out behind you. March forward!

SOLDIER: This is not the West. Be good Chinese and go home.

CHORUS ONE: Run! Get out of the way. Get out of the way.

KAREN: Run! Get out of the way. Run!

CHORUS FOUR: This is the Avenue of Eternal Peace.

CHORUS TWO: The Goddess of Democracy is crushed.

KAREN: Lu Yan, watch out! Lu Yan!

SOLDIER: Troops pouring out of the gate.

CHORUS FOUR: The Gate of Heavenly Peace.

CHORUS ONE: Bullets riddle the crowd.

CHORUS FOUR: Beatings. Bayonets. Bricks. Rocks. Beatings. Bayonets. Bricks. Rocks.

KAREN: Lu Yan, where are you?!

CHORUS TWO: Blood.

KAREN: Blood everywhere.

CHORUS: Blood everywhere.

SOLDIER: Soldiers, forward. Students, comrades! Be good Chinese and go home. This is China. This is not the West.

CHORUS TWO: A black curtain.

CHORUS ONE: A black curtain.

CHORUS: A black curtain.

CHORUS FOUR: Over the entrance.

KAREN: A black curtain.

CHORUS FOUR: Blocking the view.

CHORUS ONE: Of blood and bodies.

CHORUS: A black curtain falls over China.

KAREN: Lu Yan? Where are you? Lu Yan.

SOLDIER: Be good Chinese and go home.

KAREN: The statue fell. Everyone was running.

CHORUS TWO: Everyone was falling.

CHORUS ONE: Everyone was pushing.

CHORUS FOUR: Blood everywhere. Screaming.

KAREN: [*Screams.*] You animals!

[*Lights out. Slides of the Tiananmen Square massacre flash in rapid-fire succession on a screen. The final image is the famous photograph of the lone man standing in front of a line of tanks. Black out.*]

[*A spotlight on* BIBI.]

BIBI: On that day, as I watched the news, as world events marched into my living room. For the first time in my life, I knew...I felt...Chinese. And as days past, I searched my TV set for reports that might answer my questions and ease my grief.

[*The* CHORUS *reports:*]

CHORUS ONE: And here is the news.

CHORUS TWO: According to newspaper and television reports...

CHORUS THREE: ...five days after the massacre in Tiananmen Square...

CHORUS FOUR: ...Deng Xiaoping congratulated his army troops on a job well done.

CHORUS ONE: He did not mention the killings.

CHORUS TWO: Leaders of the Democracy Movement were arrested, and many of their supporters were rounded up.

CHORUS THREE: Remarkably, some students were able to escape.

CHORUS FOUR: A Beijing army general who refused to attack the students was sentenced, eighteen years in prison. Lesser generals were summarily executed.

CHORUS ONE: The nineteen-year-old man who stood alone against a column of tanks is missing. The government claims he was never arrested.

CHORUS TWO: Statistics on the death toll have been confusing. The Chinese government says less than four hundred people were killed, and only twenty-three of them were students.

CHORUS THREE: But according to *unofficial* reports, at least five thousand died, and at least thirty thousand people were reportedly injured.

CHORUS FOUR: The world has turned its attention to other events of the world.

CHORUS ONE: Other struggles, other tragedies.

CHORUS TWO: And China has begun a policy of selective historical amnesia.

CHORUS THREE: And America has begun its habit of selective historical amnesia.

[BIBI *at her writing desk.*]

BIBI: Spring, 1990. Dear Karen, where are you? It's been several months since…I haven't heard…are you and Lu Yan all right? I know you will write to me when it is safe. [*Beat.*] I want you to know I haven't forgotten you. I want you to know I am thinking of you and Lu Yan. Somehow, let me know if you are all right. Love, your good friend, Bibi.

[*Lights out.*]

Joan M. Schenkar

THE UNIVERSAL WOLF
(A vicious new version of *LITTLE RED RIDING HOOD*)

CHARACTERS:
  Reader
  Little Red Riding Hood
  Monsieur Woolf
  Grandmother

A little proscenium stage with red velvet curtains. It sits on the larger stage like a telephone booth or a police box—and carries with it the same sense of isolation. Audience's stage right is a table and chair.

The READER *sits in the chair waiting to begin the play. PLAYWRIGHT'S NOTE: the* READER *will read all the stage directions that the actors can't, won't or don't do (indicated by indented material). The* READER *will also create the voices of the structuralists, the bird, the post-structuralists, the audience, the stagehands, and* LITTLE RED RIDING HOOD's *mother. The* READER *is very lightly miked.*

> **PART I.** LITTLE RED RIDING HOOD appears on the stage apron in a field of wild flowers, carrying a wicker basket. Since the play has not yet begun, her presence is a little insubstantial.

LITTLE RED: Oooooo. How pretty. How pretty.

> From offstage, an exclamation: "!!!!"

I'm coming, maman.

> Another exclamation: "!!!!!!"

I'm *coming*, maman. I have just to collect one last item for dear grandmother's little basket. (cheep cheep) Here birdie,

birdie. Come birdie birdie. How good you would look in a pâte brisé. (cheep cheep) Here birdie birdie. Come birdie birdie. Perhaps you would be more comfortable in a tarte tatin? That's right, birdie, perch yourself on my finger. (cheep) What a lovely little birdie. (cheep cheep cheep) [*to the audience*] Now watch this. This, too, will be lovely.

> LITTLE RED RIDING HOOD wrings the birdie's neck—"cheep cheep URK"—and exits, laughing an insupportably silvery little laugh.
>
> The house lights go down. A hairy paw parts the tiny velvet curtains. Voila! The head of a wolf emerges! Authentic teeth, authentic fur, authentic everything. Except the accent, which is the accent of Maurice Chevalier.

M. WOOLF: Bon soir, mesdames and messieurs. Bon soir. [*sings*]
I am ze Wolf   Aoow Aoww
I am ze Wolf   Aoow Aooow
I am ze 'orrible terrible
Creature zat lurks in your
Dreams when you scream
In your bed are you dead?
I am ze Wolf
Aowww Aowww
Bon soir. I am M. Woolf, a votre service. (snarrl yeowll, snap, snap, drool) Oh, excusez-moi, pardon, pardon. Forgive me, mesdames et messieurs. I 'ave a 'ard time to keep control when it comes to ze saying of my last name. Wiz your permission I will try it anozzer time. Woo...Wooo... Woooo...Woooolff! (snarrl, yowl, yeeowll) A thousand pardons again good people. [*a silk handkerchief dries the jaw*] It is such an inflammatory last name, non? So, 'ow do you say, provocatif? But it 'as a certaine ring, do you not agree? A résonnance of long white teeth and croque-messieurs made wiz ze fingers of five year old cheeldren. (snarrrl, arrrl, arrrl

snap!) Nom de dieu! I see I can keep nozzing from you tonight, good people. [*a toothy grin, a resettling of intentions*] Mesdames et messieurs. A small confession. I love to devour leetle cheeldren. (smack, smack, drool) Oui, monsieur, I assure you I speak only ze truth. Devouring leetle cheeldren is my mission in life. Mon destin. I do not choose it, it chooses me. For petit déjeuner, I like ze five year olds (smack, smack), for lunch ze nine to twelves, and for mon diner ze teenagers are always appropriate. And because, like all ze moderne French [*left paw on hip*], I am *structuraliste*, ze meaning of my obsession wiz cheeldren 'as no meaning for me. I eat cheeldren raw and I eat zem cooked. Ça y est.

> The image of Claude Lévi-Strauss appears behind M. WOOLF. It holds up an enormous carte de visite labelled MYTHS ABOUT THE ORIGINS OF COOKING, then gently fades away.

I can substitute one child for anozzer, I can change *zere* names, I can change *my* name. [*a graceful shrug of lupine shoulders*] It is all ze same to me, so long as I 'ave my leetle collation.

> The image of Roland Barthes appears in an armchair, deliberately crosses its legs and says: "An eminently structural object is created by two modest actions: *substitution* (one part replaces another as in a paradigm) and *nomination* (the name is in no way linked to the stability of the parts)." The image uncrosses its legs and is instantly replaced by the velvet curtain.

You see good people. It is merely a question of application. Ze right part for ze right part. Ze bon dieu gave me zees lovely teeth—ze better to eat leetle limbs wiz—and [*a hairy paw taps a canine*] Aowwww! Oh zat hurrts! Pardon!

Aooowww! Aooowwrrr! Zis tooth must be replaced! [*the silk handkerchief comes out and dries the jaw*] To continue, bon gens. You are 'ere tonight to witness the re-enactment of a leetle meet. Mit? Meeth? I *cannot* say zis word but you understand me, non? I come to you in a mytology. Zere are many people in zis room right now who think zey know how my small story will end. Eh? Am I right? Of course I am right. You see [*mouths the words, he's not going to lose control*] M. Woolf, you think fairy tale. And *zen* you think of ze Little Red Riding Hood wiz 'er cape and 'er basket and 'er benign grandmozzer in bed. Suddenly ze image of M. Woolf wis 'is teeth [*a coy display of dentition*] appears on ze screen of memory. Quel horreur! Eh? And *zen* you remember ze 'appy ending of your violent American childhoods. Ze brave Woodsman comes wiz 'is gleaming axe and commits an 'orrible vivisection upon ze suffering protagonist. Well *zat* was ze version of ze Brothers Grimm. Ze *German* version. Germans love to—'ow you say—compensate for zere national crimes and terrible cameras wiz 'eroic avoidances of ze *real*. But we French— anozzer style entirely. We French always—'ow do your American gangsters call it—face ze musique.

> The image of Alain Robbe-Grillet appears looking thru a pair of binoculars. It says: "Metaphor is never an innocent figure of speech," then drops its binoculars and vanishes.

And so tonight, good people, you will see ze French version of ze Little Red One. Tonight we will remove entirely ze concept of ze Woodsman from ze narratif and—'ow do your American landlords call it—*renovate* zis little story. For wizout ze Woodsman, wizout ze 'eroic male, zis simple tale returns to its sixteenth century spirit—bestiale, brutale, and trés, trés primitif. Tonight, mesdames et messieurs [*flourish of an imaginary cape*] M. Woolf (snarrrl, yowl, owl, howwwll) will be ze only male on ze stage!!

> The image of Julia Kristeva appears holding a glass of chartreuse. It sips and says: "Narrative is, in sum, the most elaborate attempts of the speaking subject to situate his or herself among his or her desires or taboos, that is at the interior of the Oedipal triangle...oooops!" The glass falls to the floor, the image disappears.
>
> The velvet curtains fold around M. WOOLF and, in the place where his teeth just were, the charming face of a charming LITTLE RED RIDING HOOD appears. Curls, big eyes, dimpled cheeks, cupid's mouth, cleft chin, the works. The face is framed by a red velvet hood and smiles insupportably.

LITTLE RED: Bon soir, tout le monde. I am Little Red Riding Hood, preparing to visit the house of my dear grandmother in the middle of the deep, dark, Bois de Boulogne. My grandmother [*a toss of the curls*] is the extraordinary person who gave me this little red hood which I wear everywhere and by which I am everywhere known. [*another insupportable smile*] You will notice that I speak American quite perfectly. But you must not feel badly about that. *I* have two languages and *you* have only one. This is life. This is also the result of the superior training all French children receive in their little lycées—where it is understood that Americans can speak no language but their own. For language, as everyone knows, is an ability limited to the happy few—most of whom dwell in my country. The happy few...the happy few. This is a phrase I once read and liked very much. The "happy few." It makes me think of my dear grandmother as well as myself, for my grandmother is *also* a very unusual person...[*an insupportable smile*].

From offstage, a question: "??"

Yes maman. I *do* have my little wicker basket.

Another question: "??"

No maman. Grandmère asked for fresh meat and *five* bottles of blackberry wine.

An exclamation: "!!!"

Grandmère does not have a *problem* with blackberry wine, maman. She *loves* blackberry wine.

Another exclamation: "!!!!"

Maman. Grandmère is a *professional* woman and would be *very* sorry to hear you speak about her in this way. Especially to me. [*to the audience*] My mother, unfortunately, is not a spiritually-inclined person. Quand même, she is my mother and for that I must respect her.

A statement: "."

No maman. You can be sure that I will not put my foot off the path to grandmother's house.

A question *and* an exclamation: "?!"

Yes maman. I *do* remember hearing stories of Big Bad M. Woolf.

> Snarrl, Owll, Howlll, Yeowl, Arff! is heard from behind the curtain. A stagehand screams: "Hold his *paws*, fa chrissake! Hold his jaws!! I never *seen* a stage wolf behave like that! *Grab* the sonofabitch, willya, *it's not his cue!!*" Aooooooowwww!

Believe me, maman. Though I have not the smallest idea of what M. Woolf looks like, his presence is so real to me that I imagine I can hear him howling outside our door at this very instant. Can *you* not hear him, maman? I am certain it is M. Woo...

> M. WOOLF bursts thru the curtains, his fur very disturbed. The heads of M. WOOLF and LITTLE RED RIDING HOOD appear

simultaneously for a nannosecond, there is a (dramatically) unrealized "incident," and the little head of LITTLE RED quickly withdraws.

M. WOOLF: Woolf! (arf arf snarrl) Woolf! (arll yeowl yargh) Oh pardonnez-moi, mesdames et messieurs. It is ze sound of my own name zat rouses ze beast in me. I meant, naturellement, only to complete ze charming child's sentence wiz ze word...(wurgh! worf! wlugh!) [M. WOOLF *stifles himself with a right paw.*] Please! Please! Charming Child! Come back I beg of you! Non? She is disconcerted for ze moment, ladies and gentlemen, but I assure you zere is more to 'er story. You 'ave not seen ze last of ze Little Red One, I promise you zat. What? What do you say, madame? You 'ave no sympathy wiz my little faux pas, madame? You cannot imagine yourself losing control, you think it is not in you to 'owl and yeowl like M. W...like me. Hah! It *is* in you, madame. Listen to ze sounds your own stomach makes ze next time you are 'ungry. Growl 'owl 'owl is what you will 'ear. Ze beast within, ze [*mouths the word*] wolf inside. Make no mistake, madame. Zere is a wolf in you and 'e wants to get out.

Howwl! Yeowl! Yeeowwll! M. WOOLF outdoes himself in the vocal department. A burly arm thrusts thru the curtains, hammerlocks M. WOOLF's neck, and drags him offstage. "Awright, awright, I got the sonuvabitch, but I don't know how long I can hold him."

The image of Jacques Lacan appears in academic garb, smoking a pipe. It assumes a speaking position, attempts to remove the pipe from its mouth, fails completely, and dissolves in embarrassment.]

LITTLE RED: Hello again, good people. Tout va bien. I am back and maman is resting. [*a slight, duplicitous smile*] To be accurate [*a bright smile*], maman is fainted. She insisted to believe that it was really the Big Bad Wolf who brushed past me in the doorway just now, and frightened herself into fits. In any case, she is now, as you phrase it in Hollywood, out of the picture—so I can share with you the *very* naughty thing I am about to do. [*a coy, coy, giggle*]

> In the audience we hear rude sounds in the gustatory mode—lip smacks, drools, a few low, appetitive whistles. LITTLE RED RIDING HOOD stamps her little red riding foot.

No no *no*! Not *that*! *Shame* on you. And *you*. And *you*, sir. And that man *there* in the raincoat who just made a crude gesture at me! Such a thing would *never ever* happen in my own country. *Never!*

> From the back of the hall: "Salope!" LITTLE RED resettles with effort.

What I was referring to as "naughty," good people, was my excursion thru the deep, dark, Bois de Boulogne, for the walk to the house of my grandmother is full of horrible dangers. There is a perpetual rotation of picknickers, venders, and unattached males watching for evil opportunities. Quand même, a walk once a week in the Bois fills me with fresh air and favorable feelings. And from time to time, I come upon the charming Woodsman of the Bois, leaning on his *remarkably* shaped axe—who always has a kind word for a little girl in a red hood bringing a basket of comfort to her dear grandmother.

> From the back of the hall: "Salope!" again. Also: "Dwarf! Dwarf! Lesbian dwarf!" LITTLE RED's embouchere tightens firmly. Someone in front shouts: "Where's the wolf?" Snarrrl! Yowl! Yyrrr! "My cue," says LITTLE RED and she hastens on her way as a

hairy snout once again thrusts itself thru the curtains. "My cue," says M. WOOLF. "Mon entrance, mesdames et messieurs." Snarrl! Owl! Urg! M. WOOLF is aggrieved.

M. WOOLF: *Forget* ze Woodsman, dear people, *and* 'is axe. Banish ze brawny 'ero from your mind. We 'ave dissolved 'is function by removing 'im from zis narrative. Zere is at present no one to rescue and no one to *be* rescued. Ze danger in zis leetle story is now a much more subtle matter. Am I right? Of *course* I am right. Ze narrator is *always* right. Now for ze worthless Woodsman we 'ave substituted zis wonderful chart.

> A hairy arm inserts a large white bristolboard thru the curtains. The board is fastened to a stick and appears to be completely blank.

We 'ave substituted zis chart for ze negligible Woodsman, good people, because we French do not ever remove something wizzout replacing it. And, in any case, wizzout ze false 'ero, Little Red Riding 'ood's little red story begins to resemble—may I say it good people—ze most mysterious encounter given to ze entire race of 'umans. [*a dramatic flourish of the paw towards the bristolboard*] Wizzout ze Woodsman, my friends, ze story of ze Little Red One come to approach zat terrible collision of 'umanity and 'opelessness known as Le Néant. Nozzingness. Absolute Existential Zero!!!

> And the bristolboard is rotated on its stick to reveal what is printed on its backside in big red letters punctured and dripping cocktail sauce: ZERO. Hideous shrieks from the audience.

Mon Dieu! Madame! Madame! Au succours! Au succours! Somebody must 'elp ze poor fainted lady in ze first row! And ze fainted ones in ze fifth, seventh, and ninth rows! And zere in the aisle a gentleman is 'aving a 'orrible serious 'eart attack! Sssshhhh! Ssssshhh! Good people. Shrieking is of no use in zis situation and merely interrupts my attempt to deconstruct ze narrative and penetrate its mysteries. Silence mesdames! Control yourselves messieurs! Think of your mothers!

> The image of Julia Kristeva appears with a glass of armagnac. The image grips the glass tightly and says: "By maternal I mean the ambivalent principle that derives on the one hand from the species and on the other from a catastrophe of identity." The image disappears, followed more slowly, by the armagnac.

Look again at zis sign, good people, and tell me what you see. A smooth [M. WOOLF *says* "*smooze.*"] white nacreous surface, eh? Not unlike ze concept of Existential Blank. And notice ze sharply cut edges of ze board—'ow it recalls ze serious side of an axe—eh? And ze wooden 'andle 'ere—a representation both of what ze removed Woodsman chops wiz *and* of what 'e chops. Zis sign, ladies and gentlemen, is not merely a sign. It is a SIGN and we must take it *very* seriously. [*the ears of* M. WOOLF *prick up*] Aha! My big ears 'ave just detected sounds of ze Little Red One picking forbidden flowers. Ssshh. Ssshh. If you are very quiet you can 'ear 'er too. [M. WOOLF *assumes his most factitiously welcoming smile*]

> Tum te tum. Offstage LITTLE RED is singing.

LITTLE RED:
> I pluck the flowers
> For grandmère
> I bottle the buds
> For her drink
> I gather berries

For grandmère
And crush them
And squeeze them
And dirty the sink
For my grandmère loves to see dying
Little ones struggling in pain
Puppies in ponds
Cats flat on the road
Bunnies in traps
A badly squashed toad
Are part of her fav-o-rite view
For ma chère
Grandmère.
[*And here* LITTLE RED *glares straight at the audience.*]
I'd even kill *you* and *you.*

M. WOOLF: Et voilà, mesdames. Regardez messieurs. Is it not as I said?

LITTLE RED: Oh my oh my. How very familiar you look, monsieur. And yet you are not the Woodsman with the remarkable axe. No no you are certainly *not* the Woodsman I know. But perhaps you are *another* Woodsman? A...[*she looks closely*] hairier, damper Woodsman?

> M. WOOLF makes a surreptitious attempt to smooth his arm fur, then whisks his handkerchief across his dripping lower jaw. He summons a reliable smile.

And if you *are* another Woodsman, monsieur, you will know the path to the house of my dear grandmother and you will direct me to it. [*and here* LITTLE RED *quavers just a bit*] For I seem, good M. Woodsman, to have...just a little...lost my way.

M. WOOLF: Lost, chère mlle? Lost? Oh do not say it. Though these woods are deep, dark, and threatened with meaninglessness, you are surely not lost. For, charming child [*an assessing glance*] in the eleven to fifteen year old category, you have found *me*. Me! Moi, M. Wooo [*the* WOLF *grabs his snout and censors himself just in time*] Woods. Ready, willing and able to shine ze bright light of my attentions on your leetle probleme.

> M. WOOLF broadens his smile and a little string of saliva appears at the stage right corner of his lower jaw. From the 7th row of the audience comes a warning: "Dwarf, dwarf, ya *dumb dwarf*. He's gonna *eat* you."

LITTLE RED: You are not, then, a Woodsman, kind sir. You are only M. Woods?

M. WOOLF: Ah, charming child. Your beautiful youth must be ze excuse for your ignorance. Zere is no longer a woodsman in your leetle story. Ze woodsman was a crude protuberance, an ugly thorn in ze primrose path of our leetle meet. Meeth. Myt. You know what I mean. A fiction with résonnance. No, zere ees no woodsman, charming child, zere ees only me, alone in all zis wooded space to guide you.

> The image of Gaston Bachelard appears with a postal sack on its back. It removes a card from the sack and reads in a whisper: "Space has always reduced me to silence," then disappears.

LITTLE RED: But I *insist* upon a woodsman! I *depend* upon a woodsman! *I must have a woodsman!*

M. WOOLF: Dear child—in an *exceptionally* succulent stage of development—not only is ze woodsman absent from zis recital but I shall personally see to it [*and here* M. WOOLF *smiles a smile of unimaginable wickedness and moisture from his salivary glands finally passes the point of control*] zat we do not 'ave even a sweet old grandmozzer to obstruct our wonderful duet. Your grandmozzer will be replaced wiz something *simpler*—something on ze order of zis placard. [*and* M. WOOLF *points to the dripping* ZERO]

LITTLE RED: That is *ridiculous*, M. Woods! There is *no question* of replacing my remarkable grandmère! Why in her youth grandmother dearest was a *serious professional*—the only female butcher in the Bois de Boulogne! [*proudly*] Most of the tiny mammals of the Bois have ended their lives on chère grandmère's butcher block. And now, *now* that she is *retired* you wish to *replace* her?! No, no, M. Woods, my dear grandmother will *never* be replaced!

M. WOOLF: [*a paw raised in placation*] I positively take your point, charming child. So, ze old relative 'as a good eye and a steady 'and, zen?

LITTLE RED: Better than that, M. Woods. Dear grandmother has a remarkably hard heart. It's a quality which replaces almost every other quality. But, M. Woods, dear *grandmother* will not be replaced *so just get over it!*

M. WOOLF: I take your point again, charming child. And by ze way, your command of the American vernacular is superbe. [*slyly*] I understand zis ability missed your poor mother entirely.

LITTLE RED: I *have* heard that, M. Woods. I *have* heard that maman lacks a certain…oh…[*shrugs*]…you know…

M. WOOLF: [*top of his form*] Ah, my dear child. Zere are things I could tell you about your poor mozzer, things only a man of my generation could know—but non, non I *must* not. I *will* not. I *shall* not.

> The image of Pierre Louys appears in a Paul Poiret evening gown. It drops a shoulder strap and says: "I will reveal something but not more than is permitted."—then shimmers away.

And now, charming child, let me encourage you to collect a

few more forbidden blooms for your noble grandmozzer. For I see zat ze bouquet you 'ave assembled for ze old paragon is a little scanty.

LITTLE RED: Scanty, monsieur? Is it possible?

M. WOOLF: It ees, darling dryad. As you say, everyone in zis deep, dark, forest knows ze reputation of your extraordinary grandmozzer and no one would begrudge 'er a full bouquet. So take zis leetle corsage from me [*and* M. WOOLF *hands her a blighted blossom*], pin it to your cape, and pick ze proscribed posies. Go on, go on! Enjoy yourself! And when you 'ave finished, *zat* is ze way to grandmozzer's 'ouse. [*and* M. WOOLF *turns to the audience with a villainous whisper*] In ze meantime, I shall snatch zis delectable morsel's leetle basket, arrive at grandmozzer's dwelling, and swallow ze old monster toute entière. Cap, spectacles, ze knitting and, if necessary, argh, ze needles.

LITTLE RED: Well, M. Woods. There is justice in what you say. I would not care to approach grandmother dearest with anything less than the best. But I must begin now—for I see that the shadows are getting longer.

> A large shadow suddenly extends itself across both M. WOOLF and LITTLE RED RIDING HOOD—and just as suddenly retreats.

[*to the audience*] And while this strange man, deluded by my clever story, imagines me picking flowers in a field, I shall run as rapidly as dignity permits to the house of my dear grandmother, using a short cut known only to me. For in this M. Woods I am smelling a rat. I do not like the way his mouth consistently drips moisture—though, to be sure, I am too polite to say so. [*to* M. WOOLF] Au revoir, M. Woods. I am on my merry way. Au revoir. [*and she forgets her basket as she backs out between the velvet curtains*]

M. WOOLF: [*wiping his mouth on his sleeve and surreptitiously* *slurping up the overflow*] Slurp slurp. Au revoir, charming child. And 'ow do zey say in American vacationlands, take your time my leetle one. Take your time. Ze forbidden flowers cry out for your attentions. [M. WOOLF *whirls 'round to the audience, a different wolf now, every one of his teeth available for viewing*] Aooow aaow aooooww! Ze leetle hors d'oeuvre 'as left 'er basket to assist me in my impersonation! M. Woolf 'as prevailed! Ha! HA! Grandmozzers beware! Leetle girls BEWARE! M. Woolf (Aooooow!) is on ze loose once again!!!!!!

> The same large shadow that fell across M. WOOLF and LITTLE RED falls again, this time accompanied by a piercing electronic chord. The lights darken ominously. End of Part I.

> **ENTRE-ACTE.** The curtains part once again. It is M. WOOLF—quiet, focused, pleasant, and quite dry. From offstage we hear the stagehands: "Jesus-god it took two towels to get that wolf's jaw cleaned off! The producer's gonna croak when she sees the laundry bills on this show!" "Are you kidding? I hadda stuff a washcloth under his tongue so he wouldn't drool all over the dresser!" "He's not human, he's just not human." M. WOOLF advances ingratiatingly.

M. WOOLF: I forgot! I forgot one leetle thing, good people. One tiny leetle thing to show you before ze Red One appears wiz yet anozzer side of 'er endless story. Ladies! Open your purses! Gentlemen! Search ze floor! I want ze entire audience to retrieve its programmes from wherever zey 'ave been concealed! I will now ask you to ...'ow do your American scholars call eet?...interact wiz ze texte! 'Ave we all found ze beautiful programmes? Bon. Turn to ze block of texte on page 5. You weel notice zat eet comes *after* ze inflated biography of ze playwright and *before* ze pitiful pleas for money by ze theatre. On zis page 5, you weel find ze structurally correct version of my story. My story in its primal state *before* ze 'orrible intrusion of ze stupide woodsman. Lights, M. le technicien! Lights eef you please! Of course ze lighting technicien might well be a woman, but in zis dim atmosphere eet is impossible to discern ze gender of *anything*.

> At this moment, the image of Teresa de Lauretis appears in full doctoral costume, holding a diploma and weeping. The image raises its right hand and says: "The female sex is invisible in psychology and in semiology it does not exist at all." The house lights come on and Dr. de Lauretis vanishes.

Raise your textes to ze light my dears, prepare your minds for a shock, and read. *Read.* To yourselves of course. But *read.**

> So the wolf took the path of the pins and arrived first at the house. He killed grandmother, poured her blood into a bottle, and sliced her flesh onto a platter. Then he got into her nightclothes and waited in bed.
> "Knock, knock."
> "Come in, my dear."
> "Hello, grandmother. I've brought you some bread and milk."
> "Have something yourself, my dear. There is meat and wine in the pantry."
> So the little girl ate what she was offered and as she did, a little cat said, "Slut! To eat the flesh and drink the

---

*At this point in the play, the actual audience in the actual theater finds this excerpt in its programs and reads the following text.

blood of your grandmother!"

Then the wolf said, "Undress and get into bed with me."

"Where shall I put my apron?"

"Throw it on the fire; you won't need it anymore."

For each garment—bodice, skirt, petticoat and stockings—the girl asked the same question; and each time the wolf answered, "Throw it on the fire; you won't need it anymore."

When the girl got in bed, she said, "Oh, grandmother! How hairy you are!"

"It's to keep me warmer, my dear."

"Oh grandmother! What big shoulders you have!"

"It's better for carrying firewood, my dear!"

"Oh grandmother! What long nails you have!"

"It's for scratching myself better, my dear."

"Oh grandmother! What big teeth you have!"

"It's for eating you better, my dear."

AND HE ATE HER.

M. WOOLF: [*looking around the house*] Is zere anyone who 'as not finished? Good. Is zere anyone who missed ze four beautiful words in ze last sentence? "And he ate her"? Good. You now 'ave all ze facts you need. Let ze carnage begin. [*and* M. WOOLF *makes a surprisingly dignified exit*]

End of Entre-Acte

PART II. The curtains open wider than they ever have on the same little stage. It is now GRANDMOTHER's house and the decor is that of a retired butcher who might at any time resume her career. We see chopping blocks, a full set of Sabatiers, and various small mammals hanging by their hindquarters in gruesome disarray. GRANDMOTHER sits in a rocking chair with cap, spectacles, two outsize needles (but no knitting), and a bottle of blackberry wine. She rocks and sips and sings her Grandmother song.

GRANDMOTHER:
They think that I'll knit by night
They hope I'll crochet by day
They want their socks mended
Their sad problems ended
Well it won't be by me
Hee hee
Hee hee
No it won't be by me
Not by me.

A loud knocking sound KNOCK KNOCK interrupts GRANDMOTHER's big aria. From offstage we hear: "Grandmother dearest grandmother! Open the door. Oh please please please please please open the door!!"

It's Little Red Riding Hood. For godssake Little Red Riding Hood! Are you blind? [*to the audience*] She must be blind. The door is open. Raise the latch. [*knocking continues*] For godssake Little Red Riding Hood. Are you deaf? [*to the audience*] She must be deaf. The latch! RAISE THE LATCH!

LITTLE RED: [*entering*] I raised the latch, Grandmère...

GRANDMOTHER: Smart girl. [*to the audience*] She's coming along.

LITTLE RED: ...and I ran all the way thru the Bois de Boulogne (pant pant) to advise you (pant pant) of the arrival of a very suspicious gentlemen with moisture around his mouth.

GRANDMOTHER: That will be the wolf, Little Red Riding Hood. I know this story very well.

LITTLE RED: [*marvelling*] The moist man with fur on his hands was M. *Woolf! That* was M. WOOLF!!

GRANDMOTHER: Sometimes I fear the girl has inherited more traits from her mother than from *me*.

LITTLE RED: Do not say it, grandmother dearest! I beg you.

GRANDMOTHER: We l l s i t d o w n a n d d r i n k w i t h m e, granddaughter, and we'll discuss why I forgot your visit and what to do about the possible new monsieur.

LITTLE RED: I am too young to drink, grandmère. Maman says it is drink that has dissolved your memory.

GRANDMOTHER: Drink is the proper partner for meat, Little Red Riding Hood, and it is meat that makes a memory. Or so we butchers always say. (gulp gulp) Now describe the strange monsieur for me. I must see him before I can deal with him.

LITTLE RED: [*carefully*] He was…hairy…damp…unctuous…and full of fine phrases.

GRANDMOTHER: It's the wolf, alright.

LITTLE RED: *Really*, grandmother dearest. That was *really* M. Woolf?!!

GRANDMOTHER: Oh for gods*sake* Little Red Riding Hood.

LITTLE RED: Well, then, grandmère. M. Woolf is coming to eat us both and with my little basket, too, which in my haste, I abandoned.

GRANDMOTHER: *My* little basket, you mean. [*avariciously*] What's in it? *Fresh meat?* Did you put *fresh meat* in my basket?

LITTLE RED: Six bottles of blackberry wine, some wilting flowers, and one deceased songbird at the bottom, dear grandmother.

GRANDMOTHER: Six bottles! Good for you, granddaughter! I detest cut flowers as you well know but the bird is a *wonderful* touch. I'll pop him in a pâte brisé. If I remember. Now in just a moment that *awful* wolf will be at the door trying to imitate *you*, Little Red Riding Hood.

LITTLE RED: Is he *that* stupid, grandmother dearest? Or does he think *you're* that stupid?

GRANDMOTHER: That is how the story goes, Little Red Riding Hood. At least I *think* that is how the story goes. My memory is as full of holes as a hairnet.

LITTLE RED: It's the wine, isn't it, grandmère?

GRANDMOTHER: [*taking a slurp*] It's the *meat*, Little Red. It's been days since I've had *fresh meat*. [*looks at the bottle*] Of course, every pleasure has its penalties. (glug glug glug)

LITTLE RED: Well, but dearest grandmère, what are we to *do*?

GRANDMOTHER: [*taking a slug*] I'm thinking, Little Red.

LITTLE RED: You're *drinking*, grandmère.

GRANDMOTHER: The one supports the other (glug glug). Or so we butchers always say.

LITTLE RED: Thank heaven, chère grandmère, that I do not have your responsibilities.

GRANDMOTHER: Ha HAH! I've *got* it. The *perfect solution*!

LITTLE RED: Oh grandmother. You are certainly the cleverest old person in the Bois de Boulogne! Tell me your solution!

GRANDMOTHER: [*raises her head to speak, but memory fails*] Woops, it's gone! The idea has flown my mind like a bird from a bough! [*to herself*] Must be a protein deficiency. [*to the audience*] Old age is a *miracle* of selective consciousness. A *miracle*.

LITTLE RED: We are lost! We are lost! Maman was right! You have drunk your mind away!

GRANDMOTHER: Stop that gibbering you brainless child. *No* one is lost. A *solution* is, that is all. And in one minute, I will have another. [*to the audience*] Old age is very resilient.

> GRANDMOTHER begins to think very hard while LITTLE RED advances in an irritating way, allowing her corsage to come in contact with GRANDMOTHER's allergenic zone. GRANDMOTHER sneezes explosively and we hear an offstage KNOCK KNOCK.

M. WOOLF: [*violently falsetto*] Grandmère oh grandmère. It is little red Riding Hood come to visit. Grandmère oh grandmère please let me in. Aooww.

GRANDMOTHER: [*Sneezing.*] An idea! I have an idea! Your corsage has sharpened the blades of my intelligence! Into the armoire, Little Red Riding Hood, and don't let me hear you breathe! You will find a well-honed axe on your right hand side. Achoo! Ha ha! Achoo! These sneezes will save our lives!

> LITTLE RED, hyperventilating, scrambles into the armoire just in time to avoid the entrance of M.WOOLF ("Grandmère oh grandmère"), heavily costumed in a cerise tablecloth and a cottonwool bib. In this disguise, M. WOOLF could fool no one.

Ah my darling little girl. My own daughter's child, laden with goodies for her short-sighted and arthritic relative. What's in the basket, kiddo, I'M HUNGRY.

M. WOOLF: Oooh dear grandmozzer. I was in such a hurry to arrive zat I forgot to look in ze basket. [*he flips quickly thru the top layer*] But you weel immediately find plaisir in zees lovely flowers which I labored to gather for you.

GRANDMOTHER: Have you dropped an oar in the water, Little Red Riding Hood? You *know* I'm violently allergic to *anything* that grows. ACHOO ACHOOO ACHOO. Why the moment I come into contact with chlorophyll [*and here she touches a leaf*] I break out in hideous pustules, boils filled with slime, wens, warts, carbuncles, and large purple spots!

Look! Look! And anyone who touches me suffers the very same affliction.

M. WOOLF: [*pulling back in horror*] Do you mean, dear grandmozzer, zat I cannot embrace you, encompass you, put my, uh, mouse, moufe, mout, I *can*not say zis word but you know what I mean—ze area below my nose—cannot kees your beautiful wizzered cheek? Your neck full of exquisite veins running in blood? [M. WOOLF's *bib fills with saliva*]

GRANDMOTHER: ACHOO Little Red Riding Hood ACHOO. Do you remember what happened the last time you approached me with a bouquet in hand?

M. WOOLF: Uh...I am a leetle vague on that subject, dear grandmozzer.

GRANDMOTHER: Why, we had to rush you right to the hospital, Little Red Riding Hood. Your lips swelled up like soccer balls, your eyes looked like fresh pamplemousse, even your ears were affected. [*peers*] Why Little Red Riding Hood, I believe your ears are *still* affected. How very large they look.

M. WOOLF: The better to hear you with, ancient relative.

GRANDMOTHER: And your mouth. Surely you had some serious dental work since your last visit? Your teeth seem twice as large as they once were.

M. WOOLF: No no, dear grandmozzer. I assure you my teeth are in a terrible condition. [*touches them*] Aooww.

GRANDMOTHER: And your nose, dear child. What happened to your nose?

M. WOOLF: Eet is ze way of adolescence, grandmozzer dearest. You know how quickly one feature can outstrip anozzer in ze process of growth. And now I can smell you so much better. Snif snif. Snif snif. I can smell you *and* something else. Are you certain we are quite alone, dear grandmozzer? Snif snif?

GRANDMOTHER: I was expecting no one but you, granddaughter

ACHOO ACHOO and now you have entirely forgotten my basket of presents which was so terribly important to me, living alone as I do so entirely and without consolation. SOB SOB.

> GRANDMOTHER's loud, false sobs touch M. WOOLF as real emotion never could.

M. WOOLF: [*to the audience*] Oh my goodness, I deed not calculate ze affects of my avidity on ze old woman. Zis touches me very much, very much indeed. [GRANDMOTHER *sobs louder*] I sink I must kill ze poor thing quickly to put 'er out of 'er extreme misery. [GRANDMOTHER *instantly cries more softly*] But 'ow can I kill 'er if I cannot *touch* 'er?

GRANDMOTHER: B o o H o o H o o . A l o n e ! F o r s a k e n ! Undernourished!

M. WOOLF: Eet ees clearly time to reveal myself and accomplish ze classical deed, but all zis emotion is, 'ow you say in American business circles, keeling my appetite for power.

GRANDMOTHER: Poor poor poor grandmother with nothing but a distant daughter, an ingrate grandchild, and a dull collection of carving knives! Boo! Hoo! Hoo!

M. WOOLF: Really, I cannot tolerate zis display of emotion. Grandmozzer dear grandmozzer! Cease your crying! Desist from your depression! See! See! [*he holds up the basket while rummaging thru it*] I have brought you 1, 2, 3, 4, 5, 6, *six* bottles of, of zis maroon liquid to drink. And beneath them...Argh! A dead hen of some sort.

GRANDMOTHER: I believe that's a songbird, Little Red Riding Hood.

M. WOOLF: Whatever it is, dear grandmozzer, I am certain it will make someone a very good meal. [M. WOOLF *begins to drip a little*] Now dry your dreadful tears and think about cooking.

GRANDMOTHER: I'd rather think about drinking, darling

granddaughter. Your foolish flowers have begun to raise welts on my skin. See here and here.

M. WOOLF: Mon dieu! Could ze old dragon be correct? Her forearm looks anyway like a bas-relief map of the Pyrenees. [*to* GRANDMOTHER] Grandmozzer dearest. Eet ees true, zen. You are poisonous to ze touch?

GRANDMOTHER: Lay a hand on me, Little Red, and that hand will never again be the same.

M. WOOLF: Heureusement, my appetite is momentarily suppressed by ze old lady's histrionics and, besides, I 'ave already confessed it, my serious preference is for prepubescent cheeldren. SLURP DROOL. Mon dieu! Mon bib! Uh, grandmozzer. Whatever can I do to offer you consolation for zis hideous condition?

GRANDMOTHER: Open a bottle for me, Little Red, and allow me to drown my misery in fermented blackberry juices.

M. WOOLF: Eet seems a small sing to ask, dear grandmozzer, 'ere you are. [*hands her a bottle*]

GRANDMOTHER: Salut salope. (glug glug glug) Ahhh. Much much better. But when thirst is satisfied, hunger begins to speak. Or so we butchers always say.

LITTLE RED sneezes in the armoire.

M. WOOLF: [*freezes in a predatory attitude*] Aha! Grandmozzer. Zere is someone in your armoire.

GRANDMOTHER: Is it possible?

M. WOOLF: Years of serious training 'ave allowed me to identify ze smallest sound of prospective prey. Eef only I could 'ear it again.

LITTLE RED: ACHOO ACHOO.

M. WOOLF: Merci.

GRANDMOTHER: [*to the audience*] The little fool is allergic to mothballs.

LITTLE RED: ACHOO ACHOO ACHOO

M. WOOLF: Oh merci merci. Now zat, eef I am not mistaken, is a female sneeze in ze 11 to 15 year old category. It is a blonde sneeze, moreover, and more zan likely ze sneeze 'as blue eyes. Am I warm, dear grandmozzer?

GRANDMOTHER: You're running a temperature, Little Red Riding Hood.

M. WOOLF: I can only conclude, dear grandmozzer, zat in your armoire is concealed a dreadful, female imposter, 'oping to supplant me in your abundant affections.

GRANDMOTHER: Could it be M. *Woolf*, Little Red? Could it actually be the *big, bad, wolf* and could that *wolf* be a *female*?!!

M. WOOLF: Aoww. Aowwww. Even my name uttered by anozzer person affects me 'orribly. Wooooolf! Wooooolf! Aoooww! Aoooww! Pardon, dearest grandmozzer. I am overly excited. I sink we might 'ave located ze terrible M. [*whispers*] Woolf in your armoire. I must enter and vanquish him. Or 'er, in zis case.

GRANDMOTHER: Go right ahead, darling granddaughter. I will sit here with my bottle and my needles and my knives at the ready.

M. WOOLF: At last! at last! My appetite will be satisfied! At last! Justice for ze Wolf! Aaaaooowwww!!!

> M. WOOLF enters the armoire and GRANDMOTHER shouts: "On the right, Little Red. Remember the axe is on the right and the blade is sharp." And then GRANDMOTHER locks the armoire. We hear LITTLE RED: "Where did you say that axe was, grandmère?!! On the left?" and horrible sounds of battle: "Take that! Beast!"

"Aooww aowww." Fur, blood, and tufts of blond hair drift, spurt, and blow out of the closet. Suddenly all is silent. GRANDMOTHER approaches the closet and opens the door. LITTLE RED RIDING HOOD steps out, bloody axe in hand, hood seriously askew.

LITTLE RED: I *did* it, grandmother dearest! I hacked the horrible M. Woolf into small, steak-like pieces and, what is more, I did it at close range in a closet with a *very* dull instrument.

GRANDMOTHER: I could have *sworn* I had that axe sharpened.

LITTLE RED: Alcohol, grandmère, has completely destroyed your mind. [*begins to boast and strut*] And not only, chère grandmère, did I accomplish this heroic deed under the very worst of conditions—to which you *heartlessly* exposed me—but I was even able to turn one of M. Woolf's own *signifiers* against him. To repeat, grandmère, I, Little Red Riding Hood, have *deconstructed* the Big, Bad Wolf.

GRANDMOTHER: [*sarcastically*] Oh brava brava, granddaughter. What a blow, what a blow. Now, give me the axe, take this kettle, and catch what remains of the wolf's blood—and we will have sausages as well as songbirds for our breakfast.

LITTLE RED: Ah, a boudin noir. I will do it with pleasure, dear grandmère. Your cooking has always been a lighthouse in the stormy seas of my childhood. Though to be frank, I think you use more wine in your sauces than is strictly necessary. [*she smiles her insupportable smile and reenters the closet*]

GRANDMOTHER: I don't know if I can support another decade of that smile.

LITTLE RED: [*from the armoire*] Tee hee.

GRANDMOTHER: I don't know why I should put up with another year of that voice.

LITTLE RED: [*from the armoire*] Ooooooo. Yuck.

GRANDMOTHER: I don't think I can *stand* another *second* of that *attitude*.

LITTLE RED: [*from the armoire*] Oh grandmère you would not *believe* the mess M. Woolf has made in your armoire. Really, it is *too awful*.

GRANDMOTHER: [*stroking her needles*] It wouldn't be infanticide. Not at her age. She's just at the point where I might even be *congratulated* for... [*a trickle of blood flows out from under the armoire door*] My my. Once the blood starts flowing, there's no telling what direction it will run in. Or so we butchers always say. Heh heh heh. Appetite comes with eating. *Another* thing we butchers always say. Heh heh heh. Come out! Come out, my dear! You've collected quite enough blood now. Come out and join your aged grandmother for a little nap before cooking. Or eating. Whichever applies. Heh heh heh.

> GRANDMOTHER's teeth seem to lengthen as LITTLE RED emerges with the kettle of blood.

LITTLE RED: Here is your full kettle, chère grandmère, but I fear there is as much saliva as blood in it. M. Woolf was *not* a very fastidious animal and in the closet the two fluids just seemed to run together.

GRANDMOTHER: Put it down here, Little Red Riding Hood, and take off your cloak. I feel overcome by an immense fatigue.

LITTLE RED: It's the wine, I'm afraid. And your very great age, grandmère.

GRANDMOTHER: [*to the audience*] Really, I marvel at the wolf's self-control. How could he not kill her immediately. Alright, Little Red, hop into bed, next to the wall where you will be warmed and protected.

LITTLE RED: [*to the audience*] Did I not tell you what a remarkable woman my grandmother was?

GRANDMOTHER: That's right little one. In you go. Hee hee hee.

> Suddenly the spirit of Djuna Barnes appears in the famous profile portrait by Berenice Abbott. The spirit points to the bed and says with an evil intention: "Children know something they can't tell. They like Little Red Riding Hood and the Wolf in bed."

Now let me sing you a little slumber song. Something I used to sing for you when you were a very *little* Little Red Riding Hood.

LITTLE RED: [*yawning visibly*] Oh, grandmother dearest. Maman says you never got thru a lullaby in your whole life. You were always too far gone in alcohol, Maman says. (yawn) My, there is nothing like murder to relax the limbs and senses.

GRANDMOTHER: *Now* you sound like my own real grand-daughter. At *last* you sound like a real Hood. It's quite late, of course, *too* late really, but it's very nice to hear.

LITTLE RED: And is Hood your surname as well, chère grandmère? I've never really known *what* name you choose to go by. (yawn)

GRANDMOTHER: Hood is really more of a condition than a name, Little Red. Now close your little eyes and Grandmother will sing you a lullaby to finish the day.

LITTLE RED: Yawn. Where is the blood, grandmère? Where is the blood I extracted from M. Woolf? Yawn.

GRANDMOTHER: It is just here in the kettle under the bed, Little Red. Waiting to be used for a court bouillon.

LITTLE RED: And the limbs of M. Woolf? And all that ugly fur?

GRANDMOTHER: All will be taken care of, I assure you my darling. I have a use for everything. Now close those little eyes and let Grandmother sing you to a final sleep.

LITTLE RED: Final, chère grandmère? What do you (yawn) mean by final?

GRANDMOTHER: Close your eyes, Little Red Riding Hood, and listen. [*sings*]

Life is grotesque
A terrible thing
Love is a joke
Choked by a ring
The wolf is alive
Under everyone's bed
And you would be better off DEAD
Little Red
You would be better off DEAD.

[LITTLE RED RIDING HOOD *is snoring gently by lullaby's end*]
Now let me see. Where was I? Ah yes, the blackberry wine. A perfect accompaniement to meat. *Certain* kinds of meat. Or so we butchers always say. Now where are my knives and my knitting needles?

> As the lights dim, GRANDMOTHER is backlit in murderous silhouette, plunging her sharpened needles over and over and over again into the increasingly lifeless form of LITTLE RED RIDING HOOD.
> Suddenly, the image of Roland Barthes appears, driving a laundry truck. It circles the set once, steps out of the cab, tries to make sense of the scene it sees, shudders, thinks, shudders again, shrugs its shoulders, remounts the truck and drives off. From offstage we hear the sounds of the stagehands killing each other in bloody battle over the meaning of what we've just seen. Cries of: "Structure! *I'll* give you structure! POW!" and "What do you mean, the wolf was the protagonist! BLAM!" echo

thru the set. GRANDMOTHER, back in her rocking chair, plies her yarnless needles as the battle sounds roll over her and blood from the bed stains the floor around her chair.

The set goes slowly and deliberately to black. *Finis*

ROSALYN DREXLER (*Occupational Hazard*). Plays: *Home Movies, The Investigation, The Line of Least Existence, Hot Buttered Roll, Softly and Consider the Distance, Vulgar Lives, Delicate Feelings, Transients Welcome, The Writer's Opera, The Flood,* and others. Among her awards and honors are four Rockefeller Grants in Playwriting, three Obie Awards, a Guggenheim Fellowship, an N.E.A. Grant, a New York Foundation for the Arts Playwriting Grant, and an Emmy Award. Ms. Drexler is a member of PEN, the Dramatists Guild, the Writer's Guild of America, and New Dramatists, and she is on the planning committee for the First International Women Playwrights Conference.

TINA HOWE (*Birth and After Birth*). Plays: *The Nest, Museum, The Art of Dining, Painting Churches, Coastal Disturbances, Approaching Zanzibar,* and *One Shoe Off.* Her awards and honors include an Obie for Distinguished Playwriting, an Outer Critics Circle Award, a Rockefeller Grant, an N.E.A. Fellowship, a Guggenheim Fellowship, and an Academy Award in Literature presented by the American Academy of Arts and Letters. Ms. Howe currently teaches at Hunter College and New York University, and she is a council member of the Dramatists Guild.

KAREN MALPEDE (*Us*). Plays: *A Lament for Three Women, Rebeccah, Making Peace: A Fantasy, The End of War, A Monster Has Stolen the Sun, Sappho & Aphrodite,* and *Going to Iraq.* Her most recent work is an adaptation for the stage of Christa Wolf's novel *Kassandra.* Her awards include a Ludwig Vogelstein Foundation Writer's Grant, CAPS Grant for Playwriting, and a PEN Writers Grant. She teaches at New York University's Tisch School of the Arts, and is a member of PEN American Center and the Dramatists Guild.

MARIA IRENE FORNES (*What of the Night?*). Plays: *Promenade, The Successful Life of 3, Fefu and Her Friends, Eyes on the Harem*, *The Conduct of Life*, *Abingdon Square*, and others. She is the recipient of seven Obie Awards, an N.E.A. Distinguished Artists Award, a Rockefeller Grant, a Guggenheim Fellowship, and a Lila Wallace-Readers Digest Literary Award. Ms. Fornes conducts playwriting workshops in theatres and universities throughout the United States and abroad, and has directed plays by Calderon, Ibsen, Chekhov, and several contemporary playwrights.

SUZAN-LORI PARKS (*The Death of the Last Black Man in the Whole Entire World*). Plays: *Betting on the Dust Commander*, *The Sinner's Place*, *Fishes*, *Imperceptible Mutabilities in the Third Kingdom*, *Devotees in the Garden of Love*, *The America Play*, and *Venus*. She has received an Obie Award for the "Best new American Play" (*Imperceptible Mutabilities*), two N.E.A. Playwriting Fellowships, a Rockefeller Foundation Grant, and a New York Foundation for the Arts Grant. Ms. Parks is an Associate Artist at the Yale School of Drama, a Member Playwright of New Dramatists, and a MacDowell Colony Fellow.

ELIZABETH WONG (*Letters to a Student Revolutionary*). Plays: *The Concubine Spy* and *Kimchee and Chitlins*. Her first play, *Letters to a Student Revolutionary* (1991), won a Playwright's Forum Award and the Margo Jones New Play Citation. Ms. Wong currently works as a Touchstone Television 1992-1993 Fellow, and is a member of the Circle Repertory Theater Playwright's Project, the Women's Project Lab, and the Dramatists Guild.

JOAN M. SCHENKAR (*The Universal Wolf*) . Plays: *Signs of Life*, *Cabin Fever*, *The Last of Hitler*, *The Lodger*, *Fulfilling Koch's Postulate*, *Bucks and Does*, *Fires in the Future*, *Hunting Down the Sexes*, and others. She is the recipient of more than thirty grants, fellowships and awards for playwriting, including seven N.E.A. grants. She has worked as playwright-in-residence with such experimental companies as Joseph Chaikin's Winter Project, the Polish Laboratory Theatre, and the Minnesota Opera new Music Theater Ensemble. Ms. Schenkar is an alumna of New Dramatists, and a current member of PEN, Societe des auteurs et compositeurs dramatiques, the Dramatists Guild, the League of Professional Theater Women, and The Women's Project.

ROSETTE C. LAMONT (*Editor*). Professor of Comparative Literature and French Literature at Queens College of CUNY and The Graduate School of CUNY, Ms. Lamont is the editor and author of three books on Eugene Ionesco, and has written numerous essays on Beckett, Jean Tardieu, Fernando Arrabal, Harold Pinter, Rosalyn Drexler, Hélène Cixous and others. Her latest book is *Ionesco's Imperatives: The Politics of Culture* (Ann Arbor, Michigan: The University of Michigan Press, 1993). She is European correspondent, reviewer and reporter for *TheaterWeek*, an editor for *Western European Stages*, and a staff writer for *Stages*.

PASSION AND PREJUDICE

A FAMILY MEMOIR

By Sallie Bingham

With a new introduction, "What Came After"

"Powerful, Mesmerizing...Writing with charm, poised and controlled fury, Bingham weaves a multi-generational saga."

—PUBLISHER'S WEEKLY

"A powerful, often riveting story of the sins and mountain-scalings of four generations of Southerners. All the markings of a Faulknerian landscape are here: the white Southern attitude towards blacks that went hand in hand with glorifying white women, the crippling power of inherited wealth, the fear-ridden mist that encompasses a household where secrets are never shared or demons exposed...An important [book] in chronicling the Bingham saga..."

—**Gail Caldwell**, THE BOSTON GLOBE

"*Passion and Prejudice* has the feel of a novel...the genre that most of her characters belong to is American gothic..."
—THE NEW YORKER

PAPER • ISBN: 1-55783-077-0

PLAYS BY AMERICAN WOMEN: 1900-1930

Edited by Judith E. Barlow

These important dramatists did more than write significant new plays; they introduced to the American stage a new and vital character—the modern American woman in her quest for a forceful role in a changing American scene. It will be hard to remember that these women playwrights were ever forgotten.

A MAN'S WORLD Rachel Crothers
TRIFLES Susan Glaspell
PLUMES Georgia Douglas Johnson
MACHINAL Sophie Treadwell
MISS LULU BETT Zona Gale

paper • ISBN: 1-55783-008-X

PLAYS BY AMERICAN WOMEN: 1930-1960

Edited by Judith E. Barlow

Sequel to the acclaimed *Plays by American Women: 1900-1930* (now in its fifth printing!), this new anthology reveals the depth and scope of women's dramatic voices during the middle years of this century. The extensive introduction traces the many contributions of women playwrights to our theatre from the beginning of the Depression to the dawn of the contemporary women's movement. Among the eight plays in the volume are smart comedies and poignant tragedies, political agitprop and surrealist fantasies, established classics and neglected treasures.

THE WOMEN Clare Boothe

THE LITTLE FOXES Lillian Hellman

IT'S MORNING Shirley Graham

THE MOTHER OF US ALL Gertrude Stein

GOODBYE, MY FANCY Fay Kanin

IN THE SUMMER HOUSE Jane Bowles

TROUBLE IN MIND Alice Childress

CAN YOU HEAR THEIR VOICES? Hallie Flanagan and Margaret Ellen Clifford

paper • ISBN: 1-55783-164-5

WOMENSWORK
Five new Plays from the Women's Project
Edited by Julia Miles

The voices of five major playwrights offering a vibrant range of styles and themes can be heard here as they resound from the stage of The Women's Project. The dramas which converge here from Maria Irene Fornes, Cassandra Medley, Marlane Meyer, Lavonne Mueller and Sally Nemeth emanate with international character and universal allure.

MA ROSE Cassandra Medley
FIVE IN THE KILLING ZONE Lavonne Mueller
ETTA JENKS Marlane Meyer
ABINGDON SQUARE Maria Irene Fornes
MILL FIRE Sally Nemeth

paper • ISBN: 1-55783-029-0

I AM A WOMAN

THE JOURNEY OF ONE WOMAN AND MANY WOMEN
A Dramatic Collage Conceived and Arranged by Viveca Lindfors & Paul Austin

"Lindfors delivered a revelation...her essential subject was not morality but love. It is precisely this sort of theatre that they ought to bring all people to these days."
—NEWSWEEK

"Miss Lindfors is excellent as she mercurially brings to life a cavalcade of 36 women, from Shaw, Ibsen, Colette, Shakespeare, Sylvia Plath, Brecht, a battery of women's liberation journalists and many other sources."
—THE NEW YORK TIMES

Among the excerpts:

Colette IN MY MOTHER'S HOUSE
Hellman PENTIMENTO
Frank DIARY OF ANNE FRANK
Lawrence CHATTERLY'S LOVER
Merriam A CONVERSATION AGAINST DEATH
Seaman THE LIBERATED ORGASM
Giraudoux THE MADWOMAN OF CHAILLOT

paper • ISBN 1-55783-048-7

WOMEN HEROES
Six Short Plays from the Women's Project
Edited by Julia Miles

The English Channel, the United States Government, Hitler, cancer—these are a few of the obstacles which these extraordinary women hurdle on their way to ticker tape parades, prison cells and anonymous fates.

COLETTE IN LOVE Lavonne Mueller
PERSONALITY Gina Wendkos & Ellen Ratner
MILLY Susan Kander
EMMA GOLDMAN Jessica Litwak
PARALLAX Denise Hamilton
HOW SHE PLAYED THE GAME Cynthia L. Cooper

paper • ISBN: 1-55783-029-0

THE SOCIAL SIGNIFICANCE OF MODERN DRAMA
by Emma Goldman

Introduction by Harry G. Carlson
Preface by Erika Munk

Out of print virtually since its completion in 1914, Emma Goldman's pioneer work bridges modern drama and political philosophy. Activist, feminist, philosopher, and anarchist, Emma Goldman was a passionate thinker about all things modern when the twentieth century was still raw and new. The emergence of her treatise on the theatre after years of obscurity is certain to arouse a new generation of artists and scholars with its timely and provocative vision.

paper • ISBN: 0-936839-61-9
cloth • ISBN: 0-936839-62-7

ANTIGONE
by Bertolt Brecht
A Play
With selections from Brecht's Model Book
Translated by Judith Malina

Sophocles, Hölderlin, Brecht, Malina—four major
figures in the world's theatre—they have all left their
imprint on this remarkable dramatic text. Friedrich
Hölderlin translated Sophocles into German, Brecht
adapted Hölderlin, and now Judith Malina has
rendered Brecht's version into a stunning English
incarnation.

Brecht's *Antigone* is destined to be performed, read
and discussed across the English-speaking world.

AVAILABLE FOR THE FIRST TIME IN ENGLISH

paper • ISBN: 0-936839-25-2

APPLAUSE

BLACK HEROES
Seven Plays
Edited with an introduction by
Errol Hill

Some of America's most outstanding playwrights of the last two centuries have catapulted the lives of legendary black men and women out of the history books and onto the stage. Errol Hill has collected the most resonant of these powerful examples in *Black Heroes* where we meet Nat Turner, Frederick Douglass, Harriet Tubman, Martin Luther King, Paul Robeson, Marcus Garvey and Jean Jacques Dessaline.

Here for the first time in one volume are plays—many of which have been unavailable for decades—which pronounce a Black American struggle for freedom, advancement and equality from the days of slavery to the era of civil rights. The full scope of their dramas becomes a *tableau vivante* of black history.

EMPEROR OF HAITI Langston Hughes
NAT TURNER Randolph Edmonds
HARRIET TUBMAN May Miller
IN SPLENDID ERROR William Branch
I, MARCUS GARVEY Edgar White
PAUL ROBESON Philip Hayes Dean
ROADS OF THE MOUNTAIN TOP Ron Milner

paper • ISBN: 1-55783-029-0

ONE ON ONE

BEST WOMEN'S MONOLOGUES FOR THE 90'S
Edited by Jack Temchin

You have finally met your match in Jack Temchin's new collection, **One on One**. Somewhere among the 81 monologues Temchin has recruited, a voice may beckon to you—strange and alluring—waiting for your own voice to give it presence on stage.

"The sad truth about most monologue books,"says Temchin. "is that they don't give actors enough credit. I've compiled my book for serious actors with a passionate appetite for the unknown."

Among the selections:
Wendy Wasserstein THE SISTERS ROSENSWEIG
Elizabeth Swados GROUNDHOG
Kathleen Tolan APPROXIMATING MOTHER
Jane Anderson DEFYING GRAVITY
Lavonne Mueller COFFEE AFTER THE STORM
Susan Miller NASTY RUMORS AND FINAL REMARKS
Theresa Rebeck LOOSE KNIT
Kate Shein "NON-BRIDLED PASSION"
Elizabeth Egloff THE SWAN

paper
WOMEN: ISBN: 1-55783152-1

APPLAUSE